FUNDAMENTALS OF NEGOTIATING

OTHER BOOKS BY GERARD I. NIERENBERG:

THE ART OF NEGOTIATING
CREATIVE BUSINESS NEGOTIATING
HOW TO READ A PERSON LIKE A BOOK
   (with Henry Calero)

FUNDAMENTALS
OF
NEGOTIATING

by GERARD I. NIERENBERG

W. CLEMENT STONE, PUBLISHER
HAWTHORN BOOKS, INC.
New York

FUNDAMENTALS OF NEGOTIATING

(Combining revised and expanded editions of THE ART OF NEGOTIATiNG and CRE-
ATIVE BUSINESS NEGOTIATING in one volume.

Library of Congress Catalog Card Number: 72-10985.

ISBN: hardbound edition, 0-8015-2868-2
    paperbound edition, 0-8015-2869-0

Design by Ellen E. Gal

7 8 9 10

To Richard A. Zeif, my law partner, in appreciation
of a long, successful negotiation

CONTENTS

PREFACE   xi

1. ON NEGOTIATING   3

What Is Negotiation? · A Real-Life Example · The Basic Ingredients · Sales Negotiations · Labor-Management Negotiations · Real Estate Negotiation · Applications

2. THE COOPERATIVE PROCESS   20

Not a Game · Newspapers Folded · "Cooperative Egotism" · Reaching a Life Balance · When Controls Become Uncontrollable · Applications

3. PEOPLE   31

Instinctive? Rational? · Predicting Behavior · Limited Consideration of the Why of People's Actions · Understanding What Is Happening · Applications

4. Preparing for Negotiation 47

Establishing Objectives · Individual vs. Team Negotiation · Issues and Positions · The Meeting Site · The Meeting: Preparation and Opening · Negotiating Agenda · Opening the Meeting · Revealing Position · Opposer's Maximum Position · Behavior and Objectives · Long-Range Training · Do Your Lessons · The Newer Methods · Applications

5. Assumptions 70

A Source of Misunderstandings · Categories of Hidden Assumptions · Applications

6. What Motivates Us? 82

Applications

7. The Need Theory of Negotiation 89

Three Levels of Negotiations · Varieties of Application · Sublimation · Need Fulfillment and Deprivation · Emotions and Negotiations · The Use of the Need Theory in Motivating Creative People · Applications

8. The Use of Questions 109

Affirmative Statements · How to Formulate Questions · Five Functions of Questions · Three or More Functions in a Question · Old Question Classifications as Compared to New Use of Question Function · Grammatical Questions and the Functions · Process of Question Construction · How Functional Questions Operate · The Importance of Functional Questions in Preparing for Negotiations · Statements as Questions · Self-Questioning · Levels of Questions · How to Answer (or Not) When Questioned · No Questions Asked · Applications

9. How to Recognize Needs 139

A Good Listener · Nonverbal Communication · Application

10. Negotiating Techniques 147

"When" Strategy · "How and Where" Strategy · An Operational Example of Creative Alternatives and Strategies and Tactics · Applications

11. CREATIVE-ALTERNATIVE ATTITUDES   182

Creative Alternatives Can Change Win/Lose Stands · Creative
Alternatives for Mutual Accommodation · Applications

12. PURCHASING AND SELLING   196

Components of Buying/Selling Negotiation · Price-Cost Negotiation
· Selling—The Reverse Side of the Coin · Applications

13. REAL ESTATE NEGOTIATIONS   208

Applications

14. DEALS AND NEGOTIATION   211

Getting Out of a Deal · Applications

15. CORPORATE NEGOTIATIONS   215

Don't Shoot the Works in an Acquisition · Setting Price · Success
Can Kill You · Blocking a Take-over · Applications

16. LABOR RELATIONS AND CREATIVE ALTERNATIVES   222

Creative Alternatives · Labor Relations and Communication · Shifting
Levels in Labor Relations · Evolving Stages in Labor Relations ·
Applications

17. LAW, LAWSUITS, AND EFFECTIVE NEGOTIATION   230

Remember: Meanings and Values Are Not Standard · Shifting
Levels · Investigation · Applications

18. SUCCESS   236

Applications

APPENDIX: LIFE ILLUSTRATIONS   238

I. Homeostatic Needs · II. Safety and Security Needs · III. Love
and Belonging Needs · IV. Esteem Needs · V. Needs for Self-

Actualization · VI. Needs to Know and Understand · VII. Esthetic
Needs · Application

BIBLIOGRAPHY   289

INDEX   293

PREFACE

Negotiating today is one of the least understood arts in human affairs.

Many people, due to their lack of awareness of any structured approach to the negotiating process, are forced to reuse self-taught methods that have merely appeared to work in the past—methods that were acquired, like diseases, from social contact. There is, however, an important and useful difference between merely knowing a few cunning homemade techniques and understanding the full cooperative human process of negotiation. In a successful negotiation everyone wins. Various skills and strategies are required to implement these negotiations on a moment-to-moment, day-to-day, and year-to-year basis, and when these are consistent with a basic philosophy, each adds to the overall strength of the other. The principle is similar to that of the laser beam. An ordinary light can illuminate, but its rays are scattered. In a laser the beams are lined up. They supplement each other. This accounts for the powerful effects of a laser beam. The same principle applies when strategies, tactics, and skills are directed by a philosophy. Each takes on an additional strength from the momentum and direction of the other.

The idea that everyone wins in a successful negotiation is not being presented here solely on ethical grounds. In actuality it is considered simply good business. It is a matter of securing long-range objectives instead of short-term advantages. Negotiated solutions are likely to be longer-lasting when each party has gained and has a stake in maintaining the conclusion. The negotiator who has acquired the skills and techniques presented here will be able to negotiate successful conclusions that will satisfy all parties—replacing the outdated win-lose attitude with genuinely creative negotiating.

At the end of each chapter of this book there will be presented certain applications designed to assist the individual in reexamining his negotiating process. What has been emphasized is the principle of learning by personal involvement. It is therefore hoped that you will follow some of the suggestions that are made in the applications and put them into immediate and active practice. The material presented is designed only to start you thinking of alternatives. It is up to you to test them by personal experience.

G.I.N.

FUNDAMENTALS OF NEGOTIATING

1

ON NEGOTIATING

Recently two of my sons were squabbling over some leftover apple pie, each insisting that he should have the larger slice. Neither would agree to an even split. So I suggested that one boy cut the pie any way he liked, and the other boy could choose the piece he wanted. This sounded fair to both of them, and they accepted it. Each felt that he had gotten a square deal.

This was an example of "perfect" negotiation.

A salesman is trying to close a large sale. Basically his proposition is acceptable to the prospective customer—but there are still a number of questions to be answered. How much discount can he give? Who will have to warehouse the bulk of the order—buyer or seller? Can delivery be sped up? Will the seller agree to give the buyer price protection on reorders for two years?

Buyer and seller *negotiate* the sale.

In a time when the computer has made many jobs obsolete, the role of the negotiator grows in importance. For we are all negotiators.

WHAT IS NEGOTIATION?

Nothing could be simpler in definition or broader in scope than negotiation. Every desire that demands satisfaction—and every need to be met—is at least potentially an occasion for people to initiate the negotiating process. Whenever people exchange ideas with the intention of changing relationships, whenever they confer for agreement, they are negotiating.

Negotiation depends on communication. It occurs between individuals acting either for themselves or as representatives of organized groups. Therefore negotiation can be considered an element of human behavior. Aspects of it have been dealt with by both the traditional and the new behavioral sciences, from history, jurisprudence, economics, sociology, and psychology to cybernetics, general semantics, game and decision-making theory, and general systems.

Yet the full scope of negotiation is too broad to be confined to one or even a group of the existing behavorial sciences.

Every day, *The New York Times* reports hundreds of negotiations. At the United Nations and in capitals around the world attempts are made to settle the "small" wars. Government agencies negotiate with the United States Congress for appropriations. A utility company confers with a regulatory agency on rates. A strike is settled. Two companies agree to merge but must obtain the consent of the Justice Department. A small but valuable piece of real estate changes hands. These are the types of negotiations that the *Times* might describe any day of the week. Occasionally there may be a spectacular agreement, such as the nuclear test ban treaty, to attract worldwide attention. But even more important, at least to the people that participated in them, are the countless negotiations that are not mentioned in the *Times* or in any other newspaper.

Even that age-old negotiating situation, subject matrimony, is but slightly influenced by the vaunted computer. The computer may take over the role of matchmaker—but it is merely predicting that two particular negotiators have the best chance of reaching a satisfactory agreement.

Up to the present time, no general theories were available to guide an individual in his day-to-day negotiating activities. All too frequently we have had to learn to negotiate the same way we learned such things as sex—by trial and error. The man who claimed to have thirty years' experience in negotiation might simply be making the same mistakes every year for thirty years.

Thus most of our knowledge about negotiation, unfortunately, has had to come from our limited personal experience. And most people impose further restrictions on the negotiation process. Here, for example, is an excerpt from a study by the Committee for the Judiciary of the U.S. Senate released a few years ago:

To an American, negotiation is the least troublesome method of settling disputes. Negotiation may be exploratory and serve to formulate viewpoints and delineate areas of agreement or contention. Or it may aim at working out practical arrangements. The success of negotiation depends upon whether (a) the issue is negotiable (that is, you can sell your car but not your child); (b) the negotiators interested not only in taking but also in giving are able to exchange value for value, and are willing to compromise; or (c) negotiating parties trust each other to some extent—if they didn't, a plethora of safety provisions would render the "agreement" unworkable.

The Committee's three requirements for successful negotiation drastically limit the area of possible action. Children are sold, even in America, as the occasional revelation of a black-market baby ring clearly indicates. And a parent whose child is kidnapped would not hesitate to negotiate for its release. *All* issues must be considered negotiable whenever there are human needs to be met.

As for the second requirement, it is impossible to foresee in any negotiation what the outcome is going to be. Therefore it is impossible to anticipate in advance that either party will be "willing to compromise." Compromise is usually arrived at during the normal course of bargaining. It develops naturally as a result of a thorough examination of the facts and the opposing and also the common interests of the negotiators involved. Although compromises may be worked out as a result of a negotiation, the parties should not enter into discussions with the sole intent of compromising. Even in a "simple" negotiation, a number of issues are involved. It would scarcely be to anyone's advantage to compromise on each of them. The old saying, "The wheels of diplomacy often turn on the grease of ambiguity," is applicable here. It is better to enter into a negotiation without self-imposed limitations, ready to seize any advantage that is offered.

The Committee's third stipulation is almost impossible to meet. Generally, the parties involved in a negotiation do not "trust" each other. Indeed, the handling of other people's mistrust is the skilled negotiator's stock in trade. To summarize, I doubt whether there would be negotiations if the Committee's three conditions were the prerequisites to success.

A REAL-LIFE EXAMPLE

Negotiation isn't always neat. And it is often not nice.

Commuters who park their cars at railroad stations have become aware in recent years that there are moves afoot that imperil their "rights" to park. They might be interested in an example of the kind of behind-the-scenes negotiation that can curtail those "rights."

Some time ago, the real estate department of a railroad approached a real estate firm. The problem: the railroad needed money. Was there some way they could utilize their vast excess property to make money?

The real estate firm was interested but there were certain facts that had to be faced. The first fact was a legal one—you cannot obtain clear title to railroad property. The railroads have not always purchased their land outright. They have received much of their land either by condemnation or by a deed in lieu of condemnation. Both of these methods vest a reversionary right in the original owner, the right to recover land if it is not used for railroad purposes.

After much digging and considerable thought, the real estate firm's legal advisers (my law office) came up with a solution. This involved not purchasing the land, but rather renting it for ninety-nine years.

And here is where the second factor began to crop up—the "human" factor. People who work for large organizations are not often inclined to stick their necks out. The railroad attorneys would take some convincing.

A title company was approached and finally persuaded to state that the plan was legal. The title company was even willing to back up the statement with a title insurance policy. When issuance of the policy was actually committed, the railroad attorneys had no alternative but to agree that the procedure was valid.

The next step involved getting the land released from the railroad mortgage. The law firm studied railroad mortgages in general, and this case in particular. Useful points emerged. Most of the railroads placed their mortgages in the 1930's and 1940's. After World War II, people lost confidence in the financial condition of the railroads, and there was little market for railroad bonds or mortgages. These mortgages also did not contain a clause that covered property acquired later.

The solution? Make a bookkeeping transaction. Take some land that the railroad had acquired *after* the mortgage—and exchange it with the mortgage trustee for the land covered by the mortgage.

This idea brought another party into the picture. The mortgage was controlled by a trustee. The real estate people approached the trustee with this appeal: anything that improves the financial condition of the railroad benefits all concerned. Furthermore, the trustee was shown the statements by the title company and the railroad lawyers asserting that the thing could be done. After some discussion, the trustee agreed to the land switch.

Now came a new phase of the negotiation. A railroad station was chosen. The excess property surrounding it was earmarked for development. Plans were submitted to the town for the construction of a shopping center.

The result was electrifying. The townspeople had been parking on this land for many years. They assumed that it was their *right* to do so. The prosperity of many of the town's businesses depended on the happiness and continued residence of the very people who parked on that land.

The town zoning board had never even bothered to zone the railroad property. Now, reacting adversely to the pressure from the citizens, they put the land in the category known as "Business B," one foot of parking for every foot of business space. This was not arbitrary, since the surrounding land was similarly zoned. But the citizens continued to apply pressure and within a week the land was rezoned "Business A," which required two feet of parking space for every one foot of business space. This was the first time that such a regulation had ever been applied in the town.

The real estate company might have had pretty good grounds on which to fight the regulation. Instead they went to the railroad, obtained more land along the right-of-way, and complied with the stricter zoning.

Having no further "out," the town granted a building permit. Permit in hand, the real estate firm approached a food chain, and a lease was negotiated and signed. The lease called for the chain's Florida architect to submit plans for the interior of the store within one month.

Meanwhile a full-scale political hurricane had blown up in the town. The "out" party made a major issue of the situation. The "in" party, seeing its mandate slipping away, arbitrarily revoked the permit. There was nothing for the real estate company to do but go to court. There was little question that they could win the case, if it were heard without bias.

In most negotiations of any importance there is an element of luck. Although the judges of the State Supreme Court in this county were predominantly Republican, one lone Democrat had gotten elected on a fluke. With luck (and a little maneuvering) the case came up before this lone Democrat—who was less hampered by party requirements and much more likely to provide an immediate and unbiased hearing.

The town, having elected all Republican officials, realized this too. The town attorney approached the real estate men and asked, "Can't this be disposed of?" "Certainly!" was the answer. "Grant us the building permit." Because of the political climate, the town representative explained, this couldn't be done. Instead, the town —knowing fully the title restrictions and so on—said they would like to buy the property.

For a price, all real estate is for sale. Furthermore, money was tight at the time, and the real estate people were having a little trouble with financing. The town offered attractive terms and the deal was consummated.

End of negotiation? No. The lease with the food chain was fairly explicit in stating that if municipal regulations prevented the building of the shopping area, then the lease was canceled. The chain was told that as soon as another convenient location could be found, their store would be built. But this promise was not enough for the food chain. They instituted a suit for breach of contract.

This kind of suit was the last thing the real estate company needed. They asked the chain, "Can't you see that this was not within our control?" The answer: "Well, we are a public corporation, and we owe a certain duty to our stockholders."

The real estate lawyers thought this one over. Yes, a public corporation has a duty to its stockholders. It also has the responsibility of reporting to the stockholders every major suit that is filed against them.

Could it be that the chain would find a suit embarrassing? Well, the real estate men thought, let's find out.

The original lease had called for submission of architects' plans within a month. The plans had arrived late. At the time no one had considered this a factor in the proceedings, but, technically, the chain was in default. So—claiming that proper submission of the plans might possibly have enabled building to start and avoided all the delay—the real estate firm instituted a large suit for damages.

Upon service of the summons, the food chain contacted the real estate organization. "Will you drop your suit? If so, we will drop ours." The answer was, "We like our lawsuit, and have no intention of dropping it." It was a stalemate. Neither side proceeded with its suit. This was the situation for about six months.

Then my law firm received an urgent phone call from their counterparts on the food chain side. Could they come over immediately? My firm answered, "We're tied up. We'll call you back."

Intuitively we felt something had changed. Intense research was instituted. We found that the chain was negotiating with a larger public corporation that wanted to take them over. Obviously the hanging lawsuit was an obstacle.

The chain people were called. The meeting was to take place at the offices of the real estate lawyers. Terms were dictated. The chain agreed to pay $25,000 in cash. Both parties were to drop their lawsuits.

This complex negotiation—or series of negotiations—contains good and bad examples of the elements that go into successful negotiation, the elements that this book will cover.

THE BASIC INGREDIENTS

Human beings in this case reacted on one another in all their fascinating and contradictory splendor. A *knowledge of human behavior* is essential to any negotiator.

The negotiators who *prepared*—who did their homework—were ahead of the game.

All parties to the negotiations made certain *assumptions.* Some of these assumptions held up, some did not. Successful negotiation can depend upon your own assumptions—and your anticipation of the other side's.

Techniques of negotiation—*strategy* and *tactics*—came into play. For example, the *reverse* strategy of the counterlawsuit is a technique we will discuss at greater length.

Each of the parties had *needs,* direct and indirect, which they wanted to satisfy. When the approach took into account the other side's needs, it was successful. When needs were ignored—when the negotiation was played as a game, with a total winner and a total loser—both sides came a cropper.

The anticipation and satisfaction of needs is central to the method that we are discussing. Let's look at a different kind of negotiation in which *needs* were all-important.

Party A to this negotiation was a broad-ranging investor and speculator, one of the "money men" who have achieved prominence in today's business climate. Let's call him Johnson.

Johnson has acquired several varied enterprises—hotels, laboratories, automobile laundries, movie theaters. For a number of good reasons he decided that he wanted entrée into the magazine publishing field.

A "finder" put Johnson in touch with a magazine publisher whom we shall call Robinson. For some years Robinson had been publishing and editing a good magazine in a specialized but growing field. The magazine had never actually "taken off"—but since Robinson did most of the work himself, costs were low and Robinson made a comfortable living. Robinson was good, probably the best in his particular area of publishing. Large publishers had made offers to acquire him and his magazine, but for one reason or another nothing had ever come of them.

Johnson decided that he wanted the magazine. More to the point, he wanted the services of Robinson, whom he saw as the nucleus of an expanding chain of specialized magazines. After a couple of luncheon get-togethers, the understanding was that they would get down to serious negotiation.

Through his own observation, and through investigation, Johnson had found out some things about Robinson. Robinson, with justification, held his own ability in extremely high regard. He had little use for the larger publishing houses—"factories," as he called them.

And Robinson mistrusted "outsiders"—those who were not part of his creative world. He particularly mistrusted "business types," especially those in the noncreative end of publishing.

However, Robinson now had a wife and a growing family. The high-risk joys of being an independent operator were beginning to pall on him. The late hours in the office—particularly those spent on noncreative tasks like bookkeeping—were no longer congenial.

When the time for negotiation came, Johnson opened by confessing his complete ignorance of magazine publishing. To him, one of the greatest values in their association would be that he would have a professional who would call all the shots.

Then Johnson placed on the table a check for $25,000. "Naturally we are talking about a lot more money," he said, "in stock and long-range benefits. But I feel, in any agreement like the one I hope to make with you, there should be immediate and tangible benefit."

Johnson introduced Robinson to a number of his associates, particularly his business manager, who would be at Robinson's disposal and who would relieve Robinson of any onerous chores that he wanted to get rid of.

As they proceeded to talk, Robinson held out for an immediate "clean" deal—cash—not stock in the parent company, which had strings attached. But Johnson emphasized long-term security, and showed how the parent stock had grown in value over the past few years and how a stock interest would tie them together. He further underscored his need for Robinson's full creative energies, undiminished by conflicts about another job, retirement, or whatever.

In the final analysis, Robinson turned over his magazine, and his own services, for a contracted period of five years. There was a $40,000 payment in cash. The rest was in stock, which could not be sold for five years.

Robinson came away with his major needs fulfilled. He would have help with the more "distasteful" parts of the business, while remaining assured of complete control in the creative area; he had backing for expansion; he had financial security; and his conflicts were resolved.

And Johnson had acquired a valuable property and the services of a uniquely valuable man for less than he might have been willing to pay.

What made this a successful negotiation? Knowledge of human nature, preparation, strategy—all combining to *satisfy needs.*

SALES NEGOTIATIONS

Today many businesses have begun to recognize the broad scope and importance of effective negotiating techniques. Some progressive sales organizations attempt to provide their salesmen with these techniques along with selling kits. The business of selling franchises, for example, has been very successful along these lines.

Almost every conceivable product and service is sold through franchise distributors. Prices for these franchises can run from hundreds to hundreds of thousands of dollars. Although the prospective franchise purchasers have usually had sufficient business experience to raise the funds necessary to go into the venture, they are rarely skilled negotiators. And their preconceptions about negotiating techniques often keep them from obtaining all the concessions they could get.

As an illustration, the prospective franchise purchaser shows up at the sales office, usually in response to a newspaper ad that had set forth the merits and potentials of the particular franchise. He walks in with a chip-on-the-shoulder attitude: "Okay, show me." The seller has been carefully trained in handling this type of person. Rather than oppose the purchaser's belligerent attitude, he redirects it and adopts a program called "qualifying the purchaser." He starts with a simple series of questions asking the purchaser his name, address, previous experience, and references, leading the potential purchaser into a position where he, the purchaser, feels he must show the franchise salesman that he is capable of handling the franchise and will be a valuable addition to their organization. Instead of being "sold," the purchaser has been negotiated into *selling himself*.

In another situation, a franchisor was selling a complex franchise. An involved sales presentation was necessary in order for it to be clearly understood and absorbed. The franchisor found that buyers—who were seemingly convinced as they left the office—subsequently lost interest.

It turned out that the difficulty arose when the buyer could not clearly explain the proposal to his wife, lawyer, or accountant. They raised troublesome doubts that could have been resolved only by a careful explanation of the proposal. Faced with the dilemma of going into a business he could not explain, the potential buyer lost his initial interest and enthusiasm.

The franchisor felt that the solution to this problem was neither to keep the buyer from discussing the proposal with whom he chose, nor to direct a salesman to present the same deal several times to satisfy all the doubters. Instead an attempt was made to guide the buyer to informed sources who thoroughly understood the proposal, and thus could answer his *need to know and understand*.

Thereafter, whenever the sales presentation was made, a great emphasis was placed on the point that the franchise was unique, and only a few people were capable of fully understanding it or giving any advice about it. The buyer, however, still needed to satisfy himself by outside verification. This need was answered by ending the presentation with the statement, "If you wish to purchase this franchise, you must do the following: first check it out with the Better Business Bureau; then speak to at least two actual owners of franchises on this list. After you have done that, call us for another meeting." No attempt was made to contact the prospect until he had invested the time and interest to check with these sources. It appears that when his *need to know and understand* is satisfied in this way, the buyer is fully convinced, and the final closing follows without complications.

LABOR-MANAGEMENT NEGOTIATIONS

Collective bargaining has evolved as a tool for settling labor-management disputes. Recognizing this technique as a subdivision of negotiation, both sides have initiated courses and studies in labor negotiation. As a result, highly trained negotiators have dominated both sides of the bargaining table.

In the words of Professor Leon M. Labes, "Few who have had first-hand experience in the field of labor-management relations will deny that decisions reached by collective bargaining are the only ones that are completely satisfactory. Everything that can be done to encourage and foster such negotiations must be done, and many new techniques have properly been developed." In the United States these industrial negotiations are carried on under at least two ominous threats, one from each side of the bargaining table: labor's power to strike, and management's power to close, relocate, or lock out. All labor-management negotiators are constantly aware that in the event of their failure to achieve a settlement, one or both of these threats will be implemented.

In spite of the tremendous strides labor has made as a result of collective bargaining, it has generally been content with limited methods of negotiating. On one occasion, an attempt to go beyond what were seen to be restrictive methods led to the firing of the innovator. The issue, however, was not his new negotiating techniques, but his neglect of public relations. David J. McDonald failed to win reelection as president of the United Steel Workers of America in 1965 after he had attempted to bring about settlement of minor incidents and disputes before they became points of disagreement.

McDonald worked closely with his brilliant general counsel, Arthur J. Goldberg, to put an end to the long and costly strikes that had plagued the industry since World War II. Their cooperation resulted in the establishment of a human relations committee.

The committee, composed of four top representatives of the industry and of the union, met throughout the year to discuss problems and make mutually beneficial suggestions, all of this without the necessity of working under contract deadlines. This would appear to be an ideal method, one that would lead to ideal solutions. In fact it worked so well that the steel industry began to be pointed to as a model of what could be accomplished with industrial relations.

Then something went wrong. McDonald lost the union presidency to I. W. Abel, who campaigned under the slogan "Give the union back to the membership." In devising a better collective bargaining system, McDonald, Goldberg's student, had neglected one essential aspect of negotiating, namely *communication*. He failed to keep the membership closely acquainted with exactly what was happening. Complete secrecy was permitted for the new human relations committee, in order to allow its members freedom to discuss problems without fear of the industry and membership reaction. Although the end was desirable, the means permitted an insurgent group to take advantage of McDonald's failure to inform and communicate with the membership.

The intellectual leaders of unions and management today utilize negotiation only to a limited degree. That limitation is termed collective bargaining. The larger scope of negotiation includes aspects of communication; it considers the effects upon a total community and also recognizes collective bargaining as an instrument for protecting the general public welfare. It is apparent that these and other higher considerations have been neglected to date.

The future will undoubtedly bring some type of change in the rules and climate of industrial collective bargaining. Strikes against the public interest will probably be forbidden or eliminated through some form of government participation.

How will such a change affect the techniques of negotiation? The answer is, not at all. The concepts of how to negotiate are basic in character and rise above the particular set of rules or regulations of collective bargaining that happen to be in vogue at any particular time.

REAL ESTATE NEGOTIATION

In the following negotiation, see if you can spot the elements of human behavior, preparation, assumptions, strategy and tactics, and need fulfillment.

A plain postcard is not usually the most interesting item in a stack of mail. However, a real estate associate and I discovered an exception one morning when we were reviewing offers of properties submitted by brokers. On a postal card was a broker's offer to sell an $800,000 property. If the broker had meant to attract our attention, he certainly succeeded. We had to know more about the property.

When we investigated, my associate Fred and I discovered a most interesting situation. The property was controlled by a trust company, and under ordinary circumstances the land itself would probably have been worth $800,000. But these were no ordinary circumstances. A fire had virtually destroyed the building on the property, leaving only a shell that was in danger of collapsing. The building department had already served the trust company officers with a summons demanding immediate action to make the property safe. Instead of the staid day-to-day routine of administering the property, the trust company was confronted with an unfamiliar and threatening situation, one it seemed unable to cope with. The only solution the officers could come up with was to sell immediately. Fred and I decided to relieve them of their dilemma, but of course on our terms.

We submitted our offer: $550,000 if they would take back part of the purchase price in a twenty-year mortgage, or, as an alternate proposal, $475,000 in cash. The property manager at the trust company refused even to entertain our written offer. Fred then called him and requested an appointment, which was reluctantly granted.

Fred came to the point at once. He told the property manager that the board of directors would have to make the ultimate decision whether to sell or not, that the manager was only their agent. Therefore, if the manager refused to act, Fred would by-pass him and submit the offer to the board himself. This threat—to his *security*—worked. Our offer was submitted to the board.

The board, being concerned with the dangerous condition of the property, had limited themselves to a single strategy: to accept the first firm offer they received. Our cash offer was accepted. Quite naturally the property manager was extremely unhappy when he notified us by phone. He said the contract would be ready at five o'clock Friday and we had better be there at five o'clock sharp. When Fred and I arrived, we were presented with a carefully worded thirty-page document.

The manager, still unhappy, scowled. "Here is the contract. Don't dot an 'i' or cross a 't.' Take it or leave it just as it is." After reading it, we decided to take it. Thirty minutes after arrival, we left the manager's office. We were now the contract owners of the property. Only the formality of the title closing remained before we became full legal owners.

As so often happens in negotiations, a "mere formality" became the springboard for still further discussion and adjustment of the agreement. Incredibly, a few hours after we signed the contract, a second fire swept the building, completely demolishing the damaged structure. The next morning I hurried to my office and spent the weekend deep in legal research. By Monday morning I had completed my "homework." Fred and I waited in my office for a phone call from the trust company. The telephone rang promptly at nine o'clock. We arranged a meeting that morning at the offices of a prominent Wall Street law firm.

The senior partner of the law firm was very cordial as he ushered us into his private office suite, and opened the discussion: "We are not here to discuss law, but merely to get rid of a very difficult situation." I nodded in agreement. He went on to explain what we already knew, that the streets around the property were closed because of the dangerous condition, and that the trust company was more anxious than ever to be rid of the property. The company and its lawyers insisted we take over the property immediately and eliminate the hazard.

I countered with the statement that Fred and I had not had a chance to discuss the matter thoroughly and that we would need a little time. A large conference room was put at our disposal, but before he left us alone the attorney took me aside. "Remember," he said, "in this contract your client waived all the statutory protection." The statute he referred to would have placed the fire loss on the seller. By waiving it, the loss would be ours.

"You're absolutely correct," I said carefully. "We waived all our statutory rights. But," I added, giving him the benefit of my weekend of research, "that means we have only the right that existed under common law before the statute was passed." The common law generally had placed a fire loss before title closing on the purchaser, but the courts had made many exceptions to this rule of law. I reminded the attorney of an exception applicable to our situation. In the event something specific, such as a building, was sold with the land, and the building was damaged by fire, the loss would be the seller's. The seller must deliver exactly what he contracts to sell or there must be an adjustment in price.

"Now," I continued, "that wonderful contract that you drew up made it extremely clear what we were purchasing. It made it so clear that not once but four times it stated we were buying a *partially* damaged building. Now it is completely demolished. We are entitled to a partially damaged building or an adjustment in price."

In the conference room, Fred and I put ourselves in the trust company's position. If the matter went into litigation, it would take at least two years to determine the equities involved. During that time the trust company would have to pay $25,000 a year in taxes on the property and would lose an equal amount in interest to be earned on our purchase price. According to our conservative estimate, the company would lose at least $100,000 even if it won the case.

We went back with our proposal: we would take over the property immediately instead of two or three weeks later if they reduced the purchase price by $100,000. A stunned silence was followed by an outburst from the property manager. But in a few minutes we agreed to a reduction of $50,000 and immediate possession of the property. Thereupon Fred and I became "fee title absolute owners" of a valuable piece of land and, of course, a *completely* demolished building—requiring far less expenditure for clearing the land.

The negotiation described above dealt with a fairly complex situation. Yet even to a person with no experience in real estate transactions, most of its elements are recognizable. This is because underlying every action and counterreaction was a desire to satisfy a basic human need. The *satisfaction of needs* is the goal common to all negotiations, and therefore it can provide us with a structural approach to the study of the negotiating process. This book will review the elements of the behavioral sciences applicable to the process, then define and develop the Need Theory of Negotiation, and finally present a variety of illustrations of the Need Theory in action. An understanding of this structure will permit you to operate in a negotiating situation with new power and depth of understanding. Negotiation will become the art of expanding possibilities.

CHAPTER 1 APPLICATIONS

1. Where did you learn to negotiate? What is your earliest recollection of a negotiating experience? Did you ever come into contact with a party from whom you acquired some negotiating techniques and skills?
2. Can you think of the various fields to which the process of negotiation is applicable?
3. Name seven fields in which you are personally involved in negotiating. Examples would be labor management, real estate, etc.
4. What skills, techniques, and strategies do you feel make for a good negotiator? An unsuccessful negotiator?
5. Can you think of examples of poor negotiating in your daily life, in your social life, in your business life, and in the national scene at this particular time?

2

THE COOPERATIVE PROCESS

In a successful negotiation *everybody wins*.

NOT A GAME

Negotiating has often been compared to a game. A game has definite rules and a known set of values. Each player is limited in the moves he can make, the things he can do and cannot do. True, some games have a greater element of chance than others, but in every game a set of rules governs the behavior of the players and enumerates their gains and losses. In games the rules show the risks and rewards. However, rules of this sort are not available in the unbounded life process of negotiation. In negotiating, *any* risks that are known have been learned from broad experience, not from a rule book. In a life situation the negotiator ordinarily has little or no control over the complex variables, the innumerable strategies, that the opposer may bring into the struggle. Even more difficult is to know the value structure upon which the opposer bases his strategy.

To look upon negotiation as a game to be played is to enter into the bargaining in a purely competitive spirit. With this attitude, the negotiator strives against other individuals for a goal which *he alone* hopes to attain. Even if he could persuade an opposer to "play" such a negotiating game, he would run the risk of being the absolute loser rather than the winner. In post-World War II Japan, some businessmen required that their employees study military strategy and tactics as a guide to successful business operations. How many of these employers realized that comparing business with war was only a metaphor? How many saw that the goal of a successful business deal is *not* a dead competitor?

The objective should be to achieve *agreement*, not total victory. Both parties must feel that they have gained something. Even if one side had had to give up a great deal, the overall picture is one of gain.

NEWSPAPERS FOLDED

Negotiation, then, is *not* a game—and it is not war. Its goal is *not* a dead competitor. A negotiator ignores this point at his own peril.

A classic example is the recent history of the newspaper business in New York City. Bertram Powers, head of the printers' union, became nationally known as a man who "drives a hard bargain." With the aid of a couple of paralyzing strikes, the printers in New York achieved what seemed to be remarkable contracts. Not only did they obtain higher wages, but the newspapers were forbidden to institute such money-saving practices as the automated setting of market tables.

The printers won their points at the negotiating table—because they held out to the end. But the newspapers were forced into an economic straitjacket. Three major newspapers merged and finally, after another long strike, folded, leaving New York with one evening and two morning papers—and leaving thousands of newspaper people with no place to work. The negotiation was "successful," but the patient died.

"COOPERATIVE EGOTISM"

Think of negotiation as a *cooperative enterprise*. If both parties enter the situation on a cooperative basis, there is a strong likelihood that they will be persuaded to strive for goals that can be shared equally. This does not mean that every goal will be of the same value to the participants. But it does mean that there is greater possibility for each participant to reach successful cooperative goals.

However, the competitive attitude need not be abandoned. It serves as an integrating process, a rivalry that coordinates the activities of individuals. A single side of a scissors by itself cannot cut. Competition that permits each man to measure his competence or means against the other's—and to be rewarded proportionally—is really a cooperative achievement.

A great impetus to reaching an accord is the search for common interest levels. Franklin D. Roosevelt stated: "It has always seemed to me that the best symbol of common sense was a bridge." However, let us add what Robert Benchley said: "It seems to me that the most difficult part of building a bridge would be the start."

Always be on the alert to convert divergent interests into channels of common desires. In exploring these channels, both parties to the negotiation may be stimulated by the idea of sharing common goals. These goals are reached by finding mutual interests and needs, by emphasizing the matters that can be agreed upon, and by not dwelling on points of difference. Queen Elizabeth II, during her tour of West Germany in 1965, urged this course of action when she said: "For fifty years we heard too much about the things which divided us. Let us now make a great effort to remember the things which unite us. With these links we can begin to forge a new and better understanding in the future."

What has been called the French definition of love, "cooperative egotism," can be applied to this approach to negotiation. An example occurred when I represented a trade association of radio and television servicemen in New York. At one meeting the order of business included seeking better ways of attracting members, and doing more for the existing members. The entire problem was reduced into one word, publicity. The question was how to get publicity.

It seemed perfectly logical to seek publicity on radio. After all, the servicemen were the radio stations' distant cousins. Thinking along these lines, the trade association presented an offer to each station. In return for free publicity on the air, the serviceman would advertise the name of the radio station, place program material in his store window, and—even more important to the radio station—make sure that the station was properly received on every set that he repaired. In addition, the repairman would make a survey of the entire area that he covered and report to the radio station any problem areas in which their transmission was not properly received. The first contract closed for this reciprocal arrangement amounted to $40,000 worth of free radio publicity for the servicemen's association.

There are many advantages to the cooperative approach. Results can be greater and the solution more lasting. Children are taught that one plus one is two and two minus one is one. Throughout their lives most people are inclined to apply arithmetical principles in their judgment of what is desirable or undesirable. It is not difficult, then, to understand the person who applies the "I win, you lose" (plus/minus) arithmetical concept to his negotiations. He is merely using simple equations in his judgment of human behavior.

However, these equations do not apply to *all* human efforts. Cooperative human efforts can be cumulative when ideas, rather than material goods, are exchanged. If you and I exchange ideas, where each of us had one idea we now each have two, and thus one plus one equals four. Certainly no one has lost by this transaction. You can give each one of your children all of the love you are capable of giving and no one loses. It is possible that in making other people wealthier, happier, and more secure you will have more of your own needs satisfied. This is, in fact, an ideal result of any negotiation.

Many negotiations conducted in a highly competitive manner have ended in what seemed to be a complete victory for one side. The alleged winner was in possession of everything he wanted and the loser had suffered a humiliating defeat. However, such a "settlement" will rarely stay settled. Unless the terms arrived at have been advantageous in some way to the "loser," he will soon seek means of changing the settlement. Unlike a game, there is no "end" to a life negotiation situation. Many times clients of mine are convinced that they have scored a complete victory over their opponents and have forced the losing side to accept absolute defeat. I attempt to explain that there are numerous continuing elements and side effects that may well affect the "final" consummation of the deal.

Even if my client has been able to overcome all objections from his opponent's attorney and accountant, the one-sided, forced settlement is not final, it will not stick. Often a wife, as final adviser, will upset the prior agreements. Husbands do have a habit of discussing their business affairs with their wives, and a wife will not hesitate to point out that he has agreed to a bad deal and that no preliminary agreement is sacred. In other cases, after quiet reconsideration, the dissatisfied party—or even a third party—may begin a lawsuit to set aside or reorganize the unfavorable settlement. An overwhelmingly one-sided settlement breeds trouble and in the end will only prove to be a great waste of time and effort. It contains the seed of its own destruction. Yet rigidly competitively oriented people often wonder why they can never seem to conclude anything. They say they work hard, but luck or life never seems to break for them. Something always goes wrong.

This should not be surprising. We could complete few tasks without the complete cooperation and assisting efforts of others. Who could drive an automobile if he could not rely on other people to comply with traffic regulations?

There are other advantages to the cooperative approach. Results can be greater, solutions more lasting.

A few years back a well-known professional athlete wanted more money in his yearly contract. For several seasons he had attempted to do his own negotiating but had failed to achieve what he considered a satisfactory settlement. Although the athlete was a man of considerable wealth and intelligence, he was shy and, by his own confession, no match for his hard-driving general manager. Furthermore, the general manager had an ace up his sleeve—the "reserve clause" that made it impossible for an athlete to move from one team to another.

The manager invariably forced the ball player to sign for less than he deserved. The athlete had become so demoralized that he conducted negotiations with this man solely by letter. He felt defeated before he even started to negotiate.

Then an agent approached the athlete. He suggested a solution. True, the "reserve clause" precluded any threat of playing for another team. However, there was nothing to keep the player from dropping out of sports.

Despite the athlete's shyness, he had a pleasant personality and was not bad-looking. People with far less in the way of presence have made it in show business. Negotiations were begun with an independent film producer. There was talk of a five-year contract.

Now, suddenly, the pressure was on the general manager. The fans would react adversely if the star left the team, and business would drop off. The athlete negotiated an enormous increase. The next season other members of the team used the same techniques. They pitilessly "held up" the manager for as much as the traffic would bear.

Had the manager been satisfied to negotiate, rather than dominate, he would have directed his efforts toward the cooperative goal of improving the club rather than toward resisting just demands. The lesson to be learned is, never press for the "best" deal and thereby corner your opponent. As Edna St. Vincent Millay observed, "Even the lowly rat in adversity has courage to turn and fight."

REACHING A LIFE BALANCE

Few negotiations proceed smoothly. I have participated in literally thousands of negotiations, and no two are ever alike. Sometimes a client managed to secure close to 100 percent of the pie —when he was bargaining from a position of strength. At other times I have been forced to negotiate with almost all the strength massed on the opposite side of the table. In such a case one has to be content with salvaging as much as possible from the situation.

In instances where I have been able to get my client only a small piece of the pie, I try to console him, and myself, with the story of Baron Z. Donneson. The baron, a white Russian, had established himself in Rio de Janeiro. I met him several years ago at a party given in honor of his eightieth birthday. His new bride was a beautiful Brazilian in her early twenties. All the men at the party were gathered around this charming creature, monopolizing her attention throughout the evening. I sat with the baron, chatting and drinking, and as the evening wore on we grew quite friendly. I finally mustered the courage to ask him why he had married such a young girl. He put his arm around my shoulder and replied quite simply that at his age it is better to have 10 percent of a good thing than 100 percent of nothing.

Negotiating is give-and-take. However, each side is watching the opposer for any clue to his prejudices that may provide a negotiating advantage.

Plutarch's metaphor is apt. He said, "As bees extract honey from thyme, the strongest and driest of herbs, so sensible men often get advantage and profit from the most awkward circumstances. We should learn how to do that and practice it, like the man who flung a stone at his dog but missed it and hit his stepmother, whereupon he exclaimed, 'Well, not so bad, after all.' "

It is fascinating to observe two master negotiators battling it out. As a rule they can arrive at a settlement very quickly. They go directly to the heart of the problem and waste no time on extraneous matters. Each side, after an initial period of probing and feeling out the other, promptly realizes that he is dealing with a master and that a quick solution is forthcoming. Many labor strikes could actually be settled at a first or second meeting, but for political or economic reasons the agreement is not verbalized until a later date. Negotiation, like a fruit, ripens in due time.

When the bargaining is conducted with all the coolness of professional gamblers at a poker game, this is merely a surface mannerism. In actuality, experts do not play a negotiating game. They are adept at the art of compromise and accommodation. They are fully aware of the necessity for finding a common ground of interest, and they avoid the pitfalls of a competitive I-must-win-the-game attitude. At the earliest possible moment in the negotiation, each side manages to convey to the other its maximum concessions and the minimum concessions expected in return. This is not done explicitly, but subtly, by innuendo and deliberate tip-offs. Such skills and techniques, arrived at through long experience and training, enable the master negotiators to reach a satisfactory settlement. Examples of this type of negotiation are seen daily in the United

Nations. However, remember that the final decisions are not within the control of these professionals. They act as agents for their individual governments and cannot effect satisfactory settlements to world problems by themselves.

WHEN CONTROLS BECOME UNCONTROLLABLE

Sometimes, when an opponent seems on the run, there is a temptation to push him as hard as possible. But that one extra push may be the straw that breaks the camel's back.

Simply stated, one of the first lessons the negotiator must learn is *when to stop*. Negotiation, like alcohol, does not conform to the simple mathematical principles we learned as children. It's that little extra "one for the road" that can kill you. There is a *critical point* in negotiation beyond which the reaction—like that of an atomic pile—can become uncontrolled and destructive. An example may be found in the extensive research that was conducted into the causes of unscheduled work stoppages—strikes, accidents, unavailability of supplies—occurring a few years ago in the coal mines around Manchester, England. It was found that when the group size in the individual work force *exceeded a critical number*, the stoppages occurred.

So the negotiator's aim should never be "just one more." He must sense when he is approaching the critical point—and stop short of it. *All parties to a negotiation should come out with some needs satisfied.*

This can't happen when one of the parties is demolished.

It's all too easy to lose sight of this principle. In the heat of negotiation, one can be carried away.

Once I was retained by a client who was the last tenant in an office building scheduled to be demolished. The new owner planned a skyscraper in place of this four-story building. All the other tenants had moved out. My function, in addition to protecting my client's rights, was to work out a solution acceptable to both parties.

The landlord recognized that, to get my client out of the building, he would have to pay money. His question was, "How little?" The landlord first approached me personally. (In my opinion, this was a mistake. Later we will take up the value, in certain situations, of bargaining through an agent who has only limited authority.)

"How much do you want?" the landlord asked. "I'm sorry," I replied. "You are the one who is buying. I am not selling." This placed the burden of opening the negotiations upon him. So far so good. We both recognized that my client was in a very strong position. He had two years to go on his lease, and the landlord needed to get started immediately.

The opening offer indicated the landlord's willingness to pay moving expenses and the differential in rent. I declined to get into anything other than the cash figure he was offering—"How much?" After some byplay he offered $25,000. I refused even to consider it. He left the office.

The landlord's next tactic was delay. But this worked against him, because my client was perfectly willing to stay put. When delay did not work, the next approach came through the landlord's attorney. I told the attorney that when he came up with a figure that was in the ball park, we would negotiate. "Fifty thousand," he said. "Not in the ball park," I replied.

Approaches continued, with the offer getting higher. I never named a figure until the final stages. But I did do some homework, figuring out what the landlord had paid for the building, what it would cost him to keep the building vacant, what it would cost him to hold the mortgage commitments until the end of my client's lease.

I came up with a figure of a quarter of a million dollars. Knowing that this was speculation, and not wanting to squeeze the last dollar, I cut this in half. The landlord's lawyer was forced to bid against his own figure and finally settle for $125,000. It seemed to me that this was a solution that satisfied everyone.

However, I was in for a surprise. When the landlord's lawyers delivered the check, a young attorney said to me, "Five dollars more and you might have had a crane hit the building." The crane was on the property, and it just might have struck the old building—"accidentally"—so that it would be declared a hazard that had to be torn down. In that case my client might have gotten nothing.

Now a few things may be noted about this. It was not the most intelligent thing in the world for the opposing lawyer to say. However, I realized that he meant what he said. (When a negotiation is over and the opponent is upset, his tendency is sometimes in the other direction—to make you feel bad by indicating that there was a lot more to be had if you had just held out for it.)

My client was vulnerable. If I had realized how close I was to the top figure, I would have settled at a lower price. The danger of going too far is not worth the risk.

Master negotiators are of course a rare commodity. Negotiation in itself is a useful tool of human behavior and as such can be mastered with study and practice. But to show how short we all fall of the ideal, here is a quotation from *How Nations Negotiate,* by Fred Charles Ikle: "The compleat negotiator, according to seventeenth- and eighteenth-century manuals on diplomacy, should have a quick mind but unlimited patience, know how to dissemble without being a liar, inspire trust without trusting others, be modest but assertive, charm others without succumbing to their charm, and possess plenty of money and a beautiful wife while remaining indifferent to all temptation of riches and women."

Successful negotiations are not sensational. No strikes, lawsuits, or wars occur. Both parties feel that they have gained *something*. Even if one side has to give up a great deal, the overall picture is one of mutual gain.

To sum up thus far: Negotiation is a cooperative enterprise; common interests must be sought; negotiation is a behavioral process, not a game; in a good negotiation, *everybody wins something*.

These are planks that make up the platform from which we will view some of the pleasures and complexities of successful negotiation.

CHAPTER 2 APPLICATIONS

1. The following are some negotiating philosophies:
   "Business is business."
   "In a successful negotiation everyone must be slightly bloodied."
   "Survival of the fittest."
   "Do unto others before they do it to you."
   "Do unto others and then beat it."

Can you think of other negotiating philosophies?

2. Give illustrations of different negotiating philosophies you have heard expounded by your opposers or associates. Group them into general areas. In what area would you place your own negotiating philosophy? In what way did you learn this negotiating philosophy? Was it adopted as the result of a conscious effort on your part?

3

PEOPLE

The cooperative approach to negotiation—the approach which postulates that all parties must come away having gained *something*—is based on a simple but important premise.

Negotiation takes place between human beings.

You cannot negotiate with a computer.

Therefore, to negotiate successfully, you must have a knowledge of people. Alexander Pope said, "The proper study of mankind is man." For the negotiator, the study of man is not only proper; it is essential.

The ways of learning about man are as diverse as man himself. We learn by reading, by listening, by observing, by finding out how people react—and have reacted—in certain situations. Every newspaper story, every casual conversation, every train or plane ride gives you a chance to build up your armory of information about human behavior.

In this chapter we consider and suggest some of the ways to find out all you can about the behavior of people—and how you can make that knowledge work for you in the negotiating situation.

INSTINCTIVE? RATIONAL?

According to Machiavelli, "Wise men say, and not without reason, that whoever wishes to foresee the future must consult the past; for human events ever resemble those of preceding times. This arises from the fact that they are produced by men who have been, and ever will be, animated by the same passions, and thus they must necessarily have the same results."

Negotiations involve the exchange of ideas between human beings directed toward changing a relationship. Gathered at the conference table will be a heterogeneous group of individuals with the most varied personalities, characters, and emotions. Viewed superficially, human behavior sometimes appears to be disorganized, haphazard, chaotic. The newspapers tend to confirm this impression. Senseless crimes, acts of aggression, often sparked by absurd trivialities, and eccentric conduct of all kinds account for many news items every day. With such evidence, it is hard to think of man as a reasonable being, and harder still to believe that his behavior follows a rational pattern.

How should we study behavior? What sorts of tests or experiments should we perform? What should be the nature of our approach? The answers to questions of this kind have undergone radical changes during the last fifty years. The various approaches can be classified as functional psychology, structural psychology, associationism, behaviorism, Gestalt psychology, psychoanalysis, hormic psychology, holistic psychology, phenomenology, existentialistic psychology, humanistic psychology, transactional psychology, biosocial psychology. In the first decade of this century, psychology was dominated by the behaviorist school under the leadership of John B. Watson. The behaviorists were inspired by the brilliant results in animal psychology achieved by Morgan and Thorndike. Man, Watson declared, should be studied like any other animal. Behavior should be observed like the phenomena of all other natural sciences, such as chemistry, physics, physiology, or biology. No behaviorist, Watson argued, has observed anything that he can call consciousness, sensation, perception, imagery, or will. Therefore all such terms should be dropped from descriptions of man's activity. Experiments should be confined to objective observations of the results of stimulus and response. A simple example of the type of experimentation pursued by the behaviorist school is the careful investigation of the act of eye blinking when the cornea is touched. Thousands of experiments of this kind were performed and a mass of useful data was accumulated.

The behaviorist school's approach, however, was subjected to critical attacks by the rising tide of the dynamic psychologists. They said man was not a mere machine. He cannot be explained purely in terms of stimulus and response. The how and why of behavior, a man's mental life, his emotions, cannot be banished from science. In Germany, the Gestalt psychologists revolutionized our ideas on how we perceive things and how we solve problems. The psychoanalytic school of Freud, Adler, Jung, and others developed theories of mental stresses and strains, of the influence of the unconscious, that have exerted a great influence on modern thought. The behaviorists of today do not limit their studies to trivial muscle twitches, but, with a modified definition of "behavior," they occupy a most useful area of applied psychology.

Other attempts to achieve a clearer understanding of human behavior have led to an analysis of its component elements. No suggested list of such components has met with unqualified approval, and there has been endless discussion of the definition of terms. For example, I suggest that it would be helpful if we considered behavior as made up of habits, instincts, and intelligence or learning; but it has proved quite difficult to define these traits or characteristics without realizing that they overlap and are not clear-cut. However, the concept that behavior is made up of these three elements is a useful one.

Habits are forms of behavior that have become permanent or settled by persistent repetition. Many of our peculiarities of speech and gesture are habit behavior. We think of drinking or smoking as habits. There is considerable agreement on the meaning of habits. But when we speak of man's instincts, we find great difference of opinion. What should be classed as instinct? Some authorities define instinct as a natural impulse or urge; they speak of the urge to preserve life, or the urge *toward* pleasure and *away* from pain, or the urge to secure happiness. Other authorities, observing the complex type of instinctive behavior in the lower forms of life, define the word as "a congenitally organized pattern of behavior." These opposing views correspond to the differences between the introspectionist and the behaviorist in the field of psychology.

When we come to decide what part of behavior is instinctive as opposed to learned, the relationship of the two areas is far from clear. Man's ancestor, we believe, adjusted to his environment primarily by the functioning of his instincts. Slowly but surely his intelligence began to challenge the dominance of his instincts. In this struggle between instinct and intelligence our present civilization had its genesis. As Roderick Seidenberg puts it, "History is seen as a specific process of continuous conflict and dynamic change arising out of the ever varying relation between instinct and intelligence in the structure of our world."

PREDICTING BEHAVIOR

In spite of its seeming complexity, human behavior *is* predictable and understandable. It has a discernible pattern of development and is governed by its own internal logic. To discover the predictable elements in behavior requires an intensive kind of analysis. We should begin by learning its latitudes and its balance of forces in "normal" circumstances. With these guides, we are in a position to predict a course of behavior under a given set of circumstances. We will give great emphasis to what people do rather than why they do it.

Under certain conditions, such predictions become simple if we consider the actions of individuals as members of a large group. Then we can apply the mathematical laws of probability. In any given number of tosses of a coin, the probability is that heads will come up 50 percent of the time and tails 50 percent. The greater the number of tosses made, the closer the results will agree with these percentages.

Shortly after World War II, an interesting case of mass behavior on the part of millions of inhabitants of New York City was the subject of intensive investigation by the city water department. For some reason the water pressure began dropping off in the evening hours exactly on the hour and the half hour. The drop in the pressure was so precipitous and so consistent that it caused great alarm. The department selected a random sample of the city's population large enough to give reliable results, and subjected these people to the investigations of psychologists, sociologists, mathematicians, and detectives. It was conclusively established that between the hours of seven and ten in the evening, precisely on the hour and the half hour, toilets were being flushed and a corresponding number of faucets turned on.

From the facts set forth here, you have probably already deduced the cause of the phenomenon. It was the advent of television. People left their sets for the kitchen and bathroom on the hour and the half hour, during the station breaks and commercials. Of course, it would be impossible to say with certainty that a particular person would visit the bathroom on the stroke of 7 P.M. But the mathematics of the situation makes it possible to guess that he might.

Even individual behavior can be predictable in certain cases— when the circumstances are known and understood. In Hong Kong there are certain individuals who, at certain times of the day, play Mah-Jongg for money. It can be predicted that they will win.

Why? Because it is traditional for health inspectors, after examining a restaurant, to drop into the back room for a fast turn with the Mah-Jongg tiles. In the entire history of the colony there has never been a case of an inspector losing.

Sometimes you will come upon an apparent suspension of the law of averages. Look for the facts behind it. There is a reason.

The predictability of mass behavior is a part of our daily life. For example, when we drive a car along the highway we stake our lives on the belief that we can predict the behavior of the drivers of the cars coming from the opposite direction. We wager our lives on the probability that not one of these drivers will suddenly decide to swerve in front of our car. Of course there exists the *possibility* that it could happen, but because of the probabilities of mass behavior, the event is not likely to occur very often. If this were not so, few of us would continue driving.

In the course of our life experience, we have formed many judgments on the basis of mass behavior and we apply them to many situations, without thinking. For instance, if you were traveling on a train and it came to a sudden stop, you would think with assurance that the train had stopped because of some mechanical trouble, not because the engineer had left his post to pick flowers along the tracks. In other words, you would realize that the mechanical behavior of the train is *less* predictable than the human behavior of the engineer. As Sherlock Holmes remarked to Dr. Watson, "While the individual man is an insoluble puzzle, in the aggregate, he becomes a mathematical certainty. You can never foretell what any one man will do, but you can always predict with precision what an average number of men will be up to. Individuals vary but percentages remain constant."

Many people involved in negotiation fail to utilize this type of working hypothesis as a convenient negotiating tool. I have sat down at the bargaining table with many lawyers, businessmen, and real estate operators. For the most part, they proved to be reasonably skillful, resourceful negotiators even though they may never have studied the elements of human behavior. They have had to rely upon their personal experiences, and from long years of practical bargaining they have acquired a remarkable comprehension of some of the skills and techniques involved in understanding others. These people say, "You can't argue with success."

However, I say that they are willing to settle for a poorer result than they are capable of obtaining. Learning by experience is a slow empirical process and can never lead to a broad knowledge of a subject. Individual experience may give you an adequate ability to negotiate, but it certainly can never give an insight into the wide range of possibilities that are available in a negotiating situation.

Some people recognize the inadequacy of their experience and attempt to broaden their outlook by studying the modes of behavior practiced by others while negotiating. Usually these other individuals they study are their adversaries in a bargaining situation. Benjamin Disraeli said, "There are exceptions to all rules, but it seldom answers to follow the advice of an opponent." I would change the word "advice" to "example." In such instances an accurate appraisal is very difficult because the methods these people study are the very ones being employed to counteract their own actions or techniques.

LIMITED CONSIDERATION OF THE WHY
OF PEOPLE'S ACTIONS

Here are some of the psychological labels given to a few problems involved in understanding our own behavior and that of individuals with whom we must negotiate.

Rationalization. When a person rationalizes, he is interpreting a situation in a manner that will place him in the most favorable light. A character in Gilbert and Sullivan's operetta *The Mikado* rationalizes a lie by calling it "merely corroborative detail, intended to give artistic verisimilitude to a bald and unconvincing narrative." To avoid unpleasant feelings and bring about greater conformity with their inner expectations, people often "reconstruct" past events into acts favorable to themselves. They rationalize to justify their decisions, to give vent to their feelings, or to make themselves acceptable to their peers.

At the conclusion of a negotiation, who doesn't try to rationalize the results? We are all familiar with the fable about the fox who, try as he might, could not reach a tempting bunch of grapes. He consoled himself by saying, "Oh well, they were probably sour and so I did not really want them." Now, as a matter of fact, he wanted the grapes very badly but when he realized that he could not get them, he consoled himself, covered up his sense of failure and frustration by saying that he did not want them after all. He was kidding himself, he was telling himself a lie. A psychologist would say he was rationalizing.

Another form that this type of rationalization can take might be called reverse sour grapes. When people are rejected by the in-group, they quite frequently seek emotional revenge by accepting the in-group's standard of values and attempting to excel them. A factory worker denied the need of belonging becomes a "rate buster," producing more than the in-group has set as the maximum of production. Many a successful man has been driven by the same compulsion to "show them" that he is superior.

Projection. When a person attributes his own motives to other people, he is projecting. Frequently this is done quite unconsciously. For example, recently I was authorized to negotiate the purchase of a motel chain from a Mr. Edwards. In the course of the transaction, I asked Mr. Edwards if he used any outstanding technique for negotiating. Not realizing the possible advantage that I might gain by what he was telling me, he confessed that his sole technique, applicable to every situation, was to take advantage of the desire of all people to make money. He was projecting. He was ascribing to other people his own overruling motivation to make money out of any negotiation. Edwards' method worked successfully in the majority of cases because it was based on basic human needs. However, in our negotiation it failed, and no agreement was reached. My client wanted the motel chain for its goodwill and the prestige of its name, and he valued his reputation and self-esteem more than the amount of money to be made.

Projection is one of the most common and most important ways human beings perceive and think about objects in the external environment. The process is usually (some say always) unconscious, in the sense that the individual does not know that he is coloring and perhaps distorting his perception of external objects and people by imbuing them with his own characteristics. Most accounts of projection emphasize the point that people typically tend to project their undesirable traits. A habitual cheater may console himself with the reflection that everyone cheats. Bernard Shaw is said to have remarked that the chief punishment of a liar is that he cannot believe others.

Displacement. People often give vent to their anger or take out their aggression on a person or object that is not the cause of their difficulty. They seek a scapegoat. Typical is the husband who comes home from the office after a good dressing down by his superior. Loaded with suppressed emotions, he relieves his injured feelings by kicking open the door to his home, spanking his children, and picking a fight with his unoffending wife. Throughout history men have been led by unscrupulous individuals who play on this weakness. Finding a scapegoat upon which to place the sins of a people has been a popular "sport" from ancient times right down to the present day. Unwarranted emotions in a negotiation may merely be the result of displacement.

Repression. The exclusion from conscious thought of feelings and wishes that are repugnant or painful to the individual is called repression. The convenient "forgetting" of an unpleasant past event or future duty is an example. Freud insisted that forgetting is motivated, *not* accidental. Certainly repression is at work when a person suddenly remembers a disagreeable appointment, but only after the time for keeping it is passed. A good negotiator, however, would know quite well that the other party did not want to attend.

Reaction Formation. People often repress strong, unacceptable drives, then think and act in ways that are exactly the opposite of these repressed drives. It should be borne in mind that the repression is entirely unconscious. In *Hamlet,* we have a famous example of reaction formation. The Player Queen, in a ludicrous, bombastic style, protests that she will never marry again if her husband should die. Hamlet's mother recognizes the truth in her much-quoted comment, "The lady doth protest too much, methinks."

Self-image. Every individual has an image of himself that he synthesizes from his aspirations, his experiences, and the evaluations of those who hold him dear. Many personal decisions are made either to protect the self-image or to enhance it. Therefore, if we can know how a man regards himself, we can make assumptions about his motivations and his reactions to future events. There is always the possibility, however, that he might not bring his entire self-image out in the open. Then we must arrive at a clearer picture of his self-image by studying his previous actions and experiences.

Role Playing. The kind of behavior shown in acting out a role is based to a great extent on previous experiences in life. A man who is called upon to act the role of a father and administer punishment to his young son will usually act the way his own father did, or even exactly the opposite. It largely depends on what his own boyhood conception of punishment was. Usually we have a fairly clear conception of what role we want to play, or perhaps we should say we *think* we have it. However, when in doubt, we work out a role that satisfies us by trial and error.

As if to make our task of understanding human behavior still more difficult, we are told by some psychologists that when two people, A and B, meet for a discussion, there are actually six different personality roles involved. For A has three separate personalities present: A1, the person that A *actually* is; A2, the person A *thinks* he is (his self-image); and finally A3, the person that A *appears* to be. The same threefold personalities of course apply to B, making six altogether. Whatever its overall validity, this concept is useful at the negotiating table. There every person plays a different role, depending upon his function in the situation. Very often he plays more than one role. If we understand the role-playing approach to behavior, we realize that we are apt to be dealing with a multiplicity of personalities even in the simplest negotiation.

Rational Behavior. Some types of behavior are often called irrational. However, behavior should not be referred to as irrational until the assumptions and premises upon which it is based are understood. Louis D. Brandeis once stated, "Nine-tenths of the serious controversies which arise in life result from misunderstanding, result from one man not knowing the facts which to the other man seem important, or otherwise failing to appreciate his point of view." Human beings act in accordance with their individual rationality. We tend to call an individual rational if he considers the possible consequences of each of the courses of action open to him; if he is aware of a certain preference order in the consequences; and if he chooses the course of action which, in his estimation, is likely to lead to the most preferred consequence. In other words, we understand the premises and the standards by which the individual acts. If we lack this understanding, then we might say his actions are irrational. But this is a misnomer. It is *our* understanding of his premises and preferences that we cannot rationalize. A party may "irrationally" fly into a rage, but below the surface this may be a rational strategy to make the other side believe his threats. "There's method in his madness."

The problem of defining rational behavior is further complicated because it depends to a large extent on the probable behavior of other individuals. In gambling, the rational individual is one who maximizes the utility expectation accruing to him. To achieve as much as possible of his expectation, he must take into account the efforts of all the other "rational" participants of the game, who are trying to do the same thing. All these factors show that rational behavior is not static but depends on many complex, changing elements—the individuals, their backgrounds, the behavior of the other people involved, the premises that each of the participants believes in, the whole structure of the situation. In the

Need Theory of Negotiation, dealt with in subsequent chapters, we will see that certain "irrational" behavior makes good sense when its relation to the overall structure of the negotiation can be understood and taken into consideration.

These thoughts of irrational behavior bring to mind the story of a man whose automobile tire went flat just outside an insane asylum. When he got out to change it, one of the inmates stood inside the fence watching him. He removed the wheel lugs and carefully placed each one in the hub cap, which he put on the side of the road. While he went to get the spare tire, a car sped past, hit the hub cap, and scattered the lugs all over the road. Search as he might, he was unable to find a single lug. He stood there bewildered, not knowing what to do. At this point, the inmate who had watched the entire occurrence called him over to the fence. When he approached, the inmate said, "I would suggest that you take one lug off each of the other wheels and put them on the fourth wheel, drive to the nearest service station, and buy some additional lugs to continue on your trip." The man naturally thought that this was a wonderful solution to his predicament. Then he was suddenly quite embarrassed. The inmate asked, "What seems to be the trouble?" The man answered, "I'm very upset—here you are on the inside, telling me, on the outside, what to do." Whereupon the inmate replied, "Well I may be crazy but I'm not stupid."

In this instance the behavior of the inmate of the asylum would be considered quite rational. Obviously the driver could not think that all of the inmate's thinking was irrational.

Failing to understand people's premises and calling their actions irrational is but one of the barriers people set up. All of us go through life setting up barriers of one kind or another. We erect obstacles to attaining objectives that could have great value for us, and we cling to these imaginary barriers—perhaps for a lifetime. The following story illustrates this point. A farmer put up an electrified fence around his pasture land. After the fence had been up about a year, the neighboring farmer complimented him on his wonderful fence, saying that he had noticed that throughout the entire year, the cows did not go anywhere near the fence. He went on to say that it was not practical for him because he could never afford the electric bill that such a fence must entail. The other farmer laughed at this. "Don't let that worry you," he said, "I turned the electricity off after the second day. Those cows never realized the difference."

Ask a group of kindergarten children how many of them can paint and they will all say that they can. Try a classroom group in their thirties and probably all will say that they haven't the talent or the skill to paint. These are merely barriers that they themselves have built. If they could free themselves from these barriers, they would act creatively. Negotiation calls for the handling of situations with as few self-constructed barriers as possible. This facilitates open-mindedness, which leads to creative applications. People who open themselves to more experiences will become more creative. To date there is no overall formula for behaving creatively, but there are some things that prevent creative activity. A person under great stress will rarely attempt creative work. He prefers to engage in purely routine matters. In the face of stress, or danger, or the strange and unknown, people tend to retreat to the familiar and to noncreative behavior. A person in a completely dark room often closes his eyes. The darkness that he feels when his eyes are closed is more familiar than the strange darkness he experiences when his eyes are open.

When a man commits himself in advance to a solution by saying, "This is the best way," or, "This is the only way," the door to a creative solution is locked. A better way may become evident— but the man with prefabricated notions will either be blind to it or, worse, will have worked himself into a position from which he cannot emerge.

When we consider all the tricks of the mind that research in psychology has unveiled to us, we begin to realize the difficulties involved in studying the art of negotiation from our own experiences or those of other people in relation to our own.

In former times, human behavior did not appear so complicated. Not long ago, reason was deemed capable of solving all problems. People were conditioned to believe that logic expressed truth and that actions were either logical or illogical. They believed, with Aristotle, that reason held sway over a hierarchy of human capacities, that reason was at odds with man's emotions.

Now the dynamic psychologists have changed all that. They have shown that human behavior is not a contest between the two forces of reason and emotion, the head against the heart, but a result of the combination of the two, plus many other factors—such things as environment (physical and cultural), cumulative experiences, and chemical balances.

However, as we have seen, this complexity need not create yet another barrier to the understanding of what people do.

It is essential to deal with elements that are common to all people, momentarily disregarding basic individual differences. By dealing only with similarities, we can also achieve a clearer understanding of human needs, the key to successful negotiations.

People *rationalize;* they *project;* they *displace;* they *play parts.* Sometimes they *repress* things or *react,* conform to *self-images,* and engage in *"rational" behavior.*

Today's experienced negotiator tries to look at a man across the table and make a pretty good guess not about why he is acting but about what he is doing.

Learn to listen to and recognize what Professor A. H. Maslow calls "the impulse voice" or "inner signals." With an awareness of their existence, you can recognize your likes and dislikes, make selections of what pleases you, when to eat, drink, and rest. This is a more reliable guide than other people's rules, programs, and schedules, or merely a clock and season. Oliver Wendell Holmes stated, "A moment's insight is sometimes worth a life's experience." This approach may permit us to see that what was formerly considered an impulse now becomes deep reasoning. We cannot but remember that any decision, reason, or guide can occasionally be wrong. Empirical verifying against external realities is always in order. Therefore, to amplify, use every mistake as experience to gain wisdom with the further use of your private conscience.

Maslow also says, "Psychology should study the human being not as a passive clay, helpless and acted upon by outside forces and determined by them alone. It should also study the ways in which he is (or should be) an active, autonomous self-governing mover, chooser, and censor of his own life." We forget that life is an ever-changing process. Still we look for the same results from our same actions. If we achieve inconsistent results from relatively the same behavior, we become frustrated.

UNDERSTANDING WHAT IS HAPPENING

When we try to break away from cause-and-effect linear thinking —what comes after this, what happens next, what happened before —as self-reflexive creatures we still ask ourselves, Can we control what happens? Are we responsible for the outcome? For it is difficult, if not impossible, to determine cause and effect.

The principle of causality is expressed by the assertion that whatever has begun to be must have had an antecedent or cause which accounts for it. If you went into a clock store and one clock began to chime first and then all of the others went into motion, could you say that the first clock was the cause for all of the other clocks to strike?

In *Inductive Reasoning* David Hume attacked causal connection. He started out with the belief that scientific method yields the truth, but ended with the conviction that even this belief is never rational, since we know nothing. Hume states, "All our reasonings concerning causes and effects are derived from nothing but custom; and that belief is more properly an act of the sensitive than a cognitive part of our nature." The simple fact that something has happened time after time causes animals and men to expect that it will occur again. It is important for us to remember that past uniformities cause expectations as to the future, and this is different from the question of whether there are reasonable grounds for giving any weight to such expectations.

Although we can make generalizations, predictions hold only a high degree of certainty. People can never be sure what they will do when the next instance comes along.

Social causality, of which negotiation is a part, is of a highly intricate nature. Social sciences, in attempting to create order out of these events, have turned to statistical control and explained any differences as "probable error." We deal with the probable. None of our knowledge is certain, and the degree or strength of our belief as to any given proposition is its probability. This is the classic view. Probability is also a state of mind with respect to an assertion, a coming event, or any other matter on which absolute knowledge does not exist. As John Maynard Keynes stated, "The probable is the hypothesis on which it is rational for us to act." Herodotus said, "There is nothing more profitable for a man than to take good counsel with himself; for even if the event turns out contrary to one's hopes, still one's decision was right, even though fortune made it of no effect: whereas if a man acts contrary to good counsel, only by luck he gets what he had no right to expect, his decision was not any the less foolish."

The importance of probability can only be derived from the judgment that it is rational to be guided by it in action; and a practical dependence on it can only be justified by a judgment that in action we *ought* to act to take some account of it. Henri Poincaré stated, "We choose rules for ordering our experience not because they are true but because they are most convenient." These are the views of many of today's negotiators.

Negotiation requires that we understand our own actions and work with the reactions of others. Methods to arrive at a solution do not come solely from within us, as the psychological approaches contend, nor from outside of us, as most people in negotiation have contended. They are a combination of at least the two.

This concept of a pattern, a form, or whole, is dealt with in Gestalt psychology. We must not let ourselves be enmeshed in elemental details but must try to grasp and comprehend the whole. Gestalt psychologists have proved by carefully controlled experiments that we apprehend an object or a situation as a whole or definite pattern in relation to its context or background; we do not respond as strongly to isolated elements in the environment as we do to the entire situation. This is a psychological approach which studies the learning process in terms of wholes in contrast to an atomistic concept dealing with separate elements. This principle was utilized during World War II to train personnel in aircraft recognition. The entire plane, rather than component parts, such as tail and wing shapes, was projected for identification.

As applied to a study of negotiation, Gestalt psychology asserts that the whole pattern of an experience is more important than its individual parts in determining its meaning. In negotiation no single move of one participant has the quality of meaning in itself; only the complete process as a whole can be assessed rationally. Even the complete strategy of one participant cannot be judged on assumptions or information about the strategies employed by the other participants. No matter what choice you make, everyone's strategy is dependent on everyone else's strategy.

We are moving into the area of negotiation proper. On the basis of our acceptance of the cooperative approach—and fortified by our knowledge of human behavior—we next come to the stage of *preparation.*

CHAPTER 3 APPLICATIONS

1. Can you think of examples from your own life where you have rationalized, projected, displaced, repressed, or had a reaction formation?

2. What is the self-image that you have of yourself? Might it affect your negotiating ability?

3. Consider people and their motivations. Reexamine your prior analysis of people and their motivations. Was such analysis concerned with why people were so motivated or what they did in being so motivated? Can you recognize a distinction between your "why" reasonings and what they did? Which do you believe is more dependable for you? Which do you think is more reliable in a negotiation?

4

PREPARING FOR NEGOTIATION

Preparing for a negotiation is a year-round function, as is negotiating. Negotiating does not stop or start when a contract expires. Every piece of information relevant to your negotiating position should be retained and its future use considered. General Motors attempts to analyze issues prior to negotiation by computerizing the number and type of previous grievances of union members, and how they were acted on, in order to be prepared to handle recurring problems.

If you know that within one month you will find yourself across the table from your negotiating opponents, how do you prepare for this face-to-face encounter? How can you foresee the strategy of the opposite side, and how can you prepare to cope with it? The answer is not a simple one. It may be summed up, however, in a phrase reminiscent of school days: *do your homework*. There are any number of life situations for which preparation is necessary. Negotiation is one of these. For successful results it requires the most intensive type of short- and long-range preparation and training.

ESTABLISHING OBJECTIVES

In different spheres of negotiation the objectives are different. They might be summed up generally, however, as meeting one or more needs of the participants involved. Working with what will be explained as the Need Theory of Negotiation can be useful in analyzing your opposer's position and strengths. Making the objective of a negotiation rigid might very well cause the negotiation to break down. An alternative method of formulating objectives might very well be to keep them fluid, in a process state, so that the expectations can change with the circumstances of the negotiation. Consider learning to deal with the objectives of negotiation as you would with the conditions of the wind. The strongest tree often has to compromise with the wind. When kites use the force of the wind, they go higher. Pilots who first flew supersonic planes found that when a plane broke the sound barrier the controls reversed, and everything had to be done in an opposite manner. Tremendous force used on the opposition may have an opposite effect, Vietnam being the operational example.

INDIVIDUAL VS. TEAM NEGOTIATION

The depth of preparation and the number and kinds of people that may or may not compose a negotiation team depend on the importance of the negotiation, the difficulty involved, and the time available. In most instances, a negotiation will be a team negotiation because the single negotiator will need help. Whether it should be an individual negotiator or a team negotiator depends on one important factor: What are the skills or functions that are needed in the coming negotiation? If you do use a team, use one whose members can carry out the plans and objectives. Carefully explain to them the statement by Ralph Waldo Emerson: "No member of a crew is praised for the rugged individuality of his rowing."

There are also functions of the entire team, those instances where a number of people are needed on the team for political or public relations effects. If, for instance, management has twenty members for public relations effect, the union may need twenty or more members on its team. There are at least two schools of thought about having members on a team who serve no function other than to produce a political or public relations effect. One school says that it does entail certain difficulties which the other side can take advantage of. Your opposer may be able to create disagreement between members by merely giving each team member an opportunity to talk about the issues as they arise. If a member of a team cannot serve a purpose and cannot help, it is astonishing how often he disturbs the pattern of the negotiation by trying to help. The other approach is that when your opposer brings in a large negotiation team, it must be balanced man for man. Still, if a member of your negotiating team does not have a function, there is a strong possibility that he will speak out of turn and that he will take the floor merely to give vent to his own emotional needs. Therefore it may be dangerous to have a nonfunctioning team member. Create a function for each member of your team. One such function can be similar to man-for-man defense in basketball. Let each member of your negotiating team observe and listen carefully and report during caucuses exactly what his opposite number is doing. He should report on the other's nonverbal communications, his relative strength or weakness in comparison with the other team members, his possible vulnerability to suggestions. In this way all your members will become functioning members.

The advantages of a single negotiator might be (1) to prevent the opposer from aiming questions at the weaker members of the team or creating disagreement among team members, (2) to place complete responsibility on one man, (3) to prevent the weakening of stated positions through differences of opinion between team members, (4) to make on-the-spot decisions and to make or gain necessary concessions. On the other hand, a team might be best because (1) it would use a number of people with different technical backgrounds who can correct misstatements of fact; (2) it enables a pooling of judgments, of planning in advance; (3) it presents the other side with a large opposition. An able team leader can use the various members of his team as excuses for gaining concessions or not having to make concessions: the "good and bad guy" tactic or the "I have to check with my partner" approach.

Determining whether to use a team or a single negotiator should be considered separately in each and every negotiation. The environment, the conditions, the methods—all these factors should determine the choice. They should also be used to determine who should be the chief negotiator. In all instances the team or the individual negotiator must be assured of full support and must be given the full support of his organization. High management's responsibility for an imminent negotiation, by either a team or an individual, includes guidance in setting the goals and the giving of information as to what the goals are and the assistance the negotiators can expect. Management must constantly be motivating their performance and making suggestions for corrective action. This does not mean that management should stay on top of the negotiator or team. Quite the contrary. It should set up the organizational structure to allow for feedback to occur. An entire negotiation might pass without consultation with a higher authority, but knowing that the authority is there and that it is responsible and will give assistance if necessary can give the negotiator a great deal of confidence in what he is doing.

The chief negotiator should be able to use the specialization of each member to its maximum advantage. He must have sufficient factual information to supply even the specialist and must know where to use a specialist. He must manage the fact-finding and the handling of men. Instances where a team negotiation can be used effectively are somewhat similiar to the use of offensive and defensive teams in football. The team may be composed of groups of specialists, and each specialist can negotiate the area of his competence; then the next team will come into play. For example, the first team might negotiate costs and the next company policy. Before going into the negotiation it is essential that team members understand more than just what is being said at the moment, that they have a method of signaling arranged among them beforehand: when to stop talking, when not to talk on a particular subject, when a team member is talking too much. An observer on a team would be in a much better position to know when this is happening than the person who is involved in the actual talking. A simple sign of the observer offering around a piece of candy or gum might mean to stop talking.

ISSUES AND POSITIONS

Any information upon which there is disagreement can be organized into the negotiation issues. The issues then are the things on which one side takes an affirmative position and the other a negative position. Issues should be pragmatic, for it is difficult to make a definite judgment about unrealistic issues. Instead of discussing them, people have a tendency to make accusations, which then become issues. But accusations are judgments of a situation, and a judgment, say, that the seller's price is too high may or may not be correct and is quite difficult to resolve. More realistic issues can be raised by dividing the fact of the cost into elements of cost and then determining whether any of the elements can be verified as not actual and therefore able to be cut.

Questions based on emotional reactions are also nonrealistic and should be used only for the emotional effect they may produce —e.g., "Don't you think you have a nerve asking that amount?" Such questions should not be considered issues on which decisions are made.

It is important to remember that we should try to negotiate problems rather than our demands. Our demands are only a one-solution approach to the problems. There may be other solutions. If the problems are discussed, we may see that our demands are not the only solution to these problems. In the course of our negotiation, we may want to change position. Excuses for changing position can be as follows: a mediator entering the case, a change in the other side's position, intentional misinterpretation of the other side's position as a change, or a change in available facts.

When the other side makes a commitment or, let us say, sets a limit, one way of handling it would be to ignore it or not comprehend it. Another might be to make casual conversation or a joke so that the seriousness of it may be lost. Humor can serve a vital function in negotiations. In one negotiation, after the union officials and management had concluded what they felt was an acceptable contract, the job of the union officials was to have the members accept the contract. As he left the room, one union official said that he was going to have them accept it or die in the attempt. The next day, when he returned to the negotiating session, he came with bandages wrapped around his head and his arm covered with tomato ketchup. Needless to say, everyone understood the message that he was trying to convey. If he had not entered the room in that comic manner, it is doubtful that the negotiation could have been concluded without a severe strike, but as the matter turned out, the parties laughed, the negotiations continued, concessions were made, and a contract was entered into.

It is said that your bargaining position should conceal as well as reveal, and it is somewhat basic theory that as negotiations continue, concessions alternate from each side. A motivating factor to cause such reactions is citing principles and precedents for the other side to work with.

Each position is the sum of all the issues involved. Some negotiations have many issues; some issues are broader than others. With the resolution of the broader, more important issues, some of the minor ones seem to disappear or be resolved. As new facts are developed in fact-finding and negotiation, the posture that one takes on an issue may change, and so will the position change. A skillful negotiator is ever alert to this particular chain of events: assumptions → facts → issues → positions → decisions. If you would like to change your opposer's decisions, first try to alter his assumptions. This will be more fully discussed in Chapter 5, on assumptions.

THE MEETING SITE

Should you meet in your office, your home territory, or should you go to your opposer's home ground? There are advantages to each. Every new negotiation requires fresh consideration. If the meeting is held in your own ball park, you have the following advantages: (1) it enables you to get the approval that may be necessary on problems that you did not anticipate; (2) it prevents the other side from concluding the negotiation prematurely and leaving, which he might do if he is in his own office; (3) you can take care of other matters and have your own facilities available while you are handling the negotiation; (4) it gives you the psychological advantage of having the other side come to you; and (5) it saves you money and traveling time.

Going to your opposer's home territory also has advantages: (1) you can devote your full time to the negotiation without the distractions and interruptions that your office may produce; (2) you can withhold information, stating that it is not immediately available; (3) you might have the option of going over your opposer's head to someone in his higher management; and (4) the burden of preparation is on the opposer and he is not free from other duties.

If neither of these alternatives seems satisfactory, you can meet your opposer in neutral territory.

THE MEETING: PREPARATION AND OPENING

Your regard for the opposer is evidenced by what happens after you first invite him to a meeting in your home territory. Have you assisted him in his travel plans? Booked reservations for him? The climate of settlement is established even before the meeting opens. With the opening of the meeting, have you made adequate arrangements at the meeting place? Is the environment conducive to a comfortable atmosphere? The importance of the meeting should be evidenced by the physical arrangements made. Ample time should be allowed and distractions should be avoided completely.

The physical arrangement of the room, such as the lighting, the color, and the seating, have a potential effect on the negotiation. Some people still consider the head of the table the father seat. They will listen more intently to what any person says while he occupies that seat. Once I was invited to a union-management negotiation, representing management. After I was introduced, the union representatives asked me to sit on the side of the table opposite them. When I sat down on "their" side, the union team looked at me rather strangely. Shortly after the negotiation had started, however, the union forgot that I represented management and the members were listening to my suggestions from their side of the table as carefully as they were to those of their own team. The attention they showed me was most helpful in bringing the negotiation to a satisfactory conclusion.

Other physical requirements for the conference room are a telephone for outside communications; a room large enough to hold all the facilities; adequate air conditioning; smoke exhaust; chairs that are comfortable, but not so comfortable as to make the negotiators drowsy or so uncomfortable that they want to leave earlier than necessary; appropriate visual aids available for you or your opposer to use in explaining details; and refreshments of various types ready to be brought in at any time. Sometimes it is important to have another area or adjoining conference room for caucusing.

Caution: When you are in your opposer's home territory and

check into a hotel, do not underestimate his ability to find out how long you have registered for, so that he may anticipate how long you think the negotiation might take.

Further consideration of the negotiating objectives can be divided into: (a) where and how to begin (agenda); (b) major and minor issues; (c) revealing your minimum and maximum position; (d) the opposer's maximum position; (e) behavior and objectives. Recognizing the relative strengths of each side has a great influence on your expectations and the setting of the objectives. Your negotiation objectives must be based on a thorough understanding of as many characteristics of the general conditions as you can recognize, and they should be tailored to the specific situation and to your particular operation or company. Do not have as your only strength mere opposition.

NEGOTIATING AGENDA

An agenda may be presented by one side or prepared by both sides, or each side may prepare two agendas: a general agenda and a detailed agenda. The general agenda is presented to the other side, and the detailed agenda is for one's own use. In a student-administration confrontation it might be possible for the agenda to consist of nonnegotiable demands. In turmoil situations the agenda is composed of items neither side would care to discuss.

Having the other side accept your agenda has its advantages. It can put the other side on the defensive. Your agenda contains the definitions of your terms in your own way. Therefore, it contains your assumptions. You should remember, however, that your agenda reveals your positions in advance and it may permit the other side to prepare a reaction to the areas that you wish to discuss. You also are not in a position to hear out the other side before presenting your agenda positions. This too is a disadvantage, for the order of procedure, or agenda, has to depend on the strategies chosen beforehand, before you know the actual posture of the opposer. The agenda might very well be considered one of the tactics used in negotiation.

Try not to permit your agenda to be bound to an arbitrary, uncontrolled arrangement. Many a negotiation has been circumscribed by an agenda based on a printed form, a contract, a lease, a union contract, or merely a chronological listing of issues. This should not be done. Attention should instead be given to the various issues to be discussed so that strategies can be developed. The issues might be listed so that the major ones are discussed first. This will prevent time from being wasted on minor issues, leaving sufficient time to discuss the major ones. As an alternative, minor issues might be listed first so that you can begin the negotiation by making concessions, expecting that as the issues become more important you will get concessions in return. Of course, the fact that you have made concessions may be regarded by your opposer as a precedent and he may expect them to continue. However, minor issues are sometimes easier to resolve, and their resolution creates an atmosphere of goodwill. If you disclose your major issue first, the other side may attempt to suspend the discussion of the major issues temporarily by embroiling the meeting in minor issues so that they can consider what they may or may not do, or they may introduce factors to balance your major issue.

Other people arrange it differently. Rather than classification on the basis of minor and major issues, they first set up a group of conditions or issues that they feel they can agree on. Having agreed, they then ask for concessions on the issues on which they are seeking agreement. Others break the issues into those involving dollars and those not involving money and attempt to resolve the nonmonetary matters first. Remember the maxim, "It's a bad plan that can't be changed."

OPENING THE MEETING

There are no strict rules on opening or conducting a meeting, but several different approaches have been suggested. Some experienced negotiators advise that a completely irrelevant topic start off the meeting. Others suggest that a humorous story can lighten the tensions. Still others propose that the introductory remarks set forth some of the general principles of negotiation: the need for each party to gain something, what your objective attitude might be, and how you will listen and evaluate all alternatives and suggestions. Also you can set forth the advantages to be gained for the opposer by dealing with you.

REVEALING POSITION

When do you reveal your minimum position? This may very well depend on your opposer. It is easier to deal with an experienced negotiator than with an inexperienced one. If you are confronted with an inexperienced negotiator and expose your minimum position immediately, he is unable to appreciate it. You must educate him to enable him to see the possibilities and yet, once shown them, he may lack the experience necessary to believe you. You do not reveal a minimum position early if your opposer needs publicity on how hard and well he has negotiated or if he must show his boss how diligent he is. If you reveal your position too quickly, it can be interpreted by the other side as excessive eagerness. It would be a better strategy to let the other side feel that it has worked very hard to move you into your position. No union or management team would chance the consequence of immediately accepting the other's first offer. There are rare situations where you may have an eager, intelligent, reasonable, well-informed, experienced opposer who does not have to report to anyone. It is possible under these circumstances that you can reveal your minimum terms at the start of the negotiation. Even in that event, however, state your objective in the negotiation indirectly. An outstanding negotiator on the other side will then work to assist you in achieving what you need as a minimum in the negotiation, and you at the same time will work with him to try to achieve the minimum that he needs.

OPPOSER'S MAXIMUM POSITION

Sometimes you will encounter an opposer who states a position that is so unreasonable that you would be wise not to reveal any position in the hope that as the negotiation continues he will change to a more favorable position because he cannot justify his first demand. At times it may be advisable, if you feel your opposer's position is completely unreasonable, to make counterproposals merely to balance his demands. State that these counterproposals are on the table as long as the demands that you consider arbitrary and unreasonable are there. For example: If the union wants a four-day workweek, a counterdemand might be that all paid holidays be eliminated.

BEHAVIOR AND OBJECTIVES

Before we consider the traits of your opposer, let us consider the traits involved in your own negotiating team. Does the leader of the team take the attitude that when things go right he makes the decisions and when things go wrong he starts to look for partners? Do the members of the team, even though they are of the same organization, refuse to work together? Do they discourage creative suggestions as team disloyalty? Do they subscribe to Murphy's Law —that is, if I didn't think of it, it's no damn good—or the not-invented-here syndrome—if it can go wrong it will? These can be standard operating traits when there has been a failure of communication within an organization. Whether you direct a big organization or a small organization, you want agreement to culminate in action. Some people have said that in a small organization you cannot get agreement but can get action; in a large organization you can get agreement but no action.

Negotiations must not rely merely on efficiency. One of its essential elements is interaction and reaction with people and their feelings. Try not to make a distinction between intellect and emotion. Think of them as one and the same process. Possibly the emotions are the intellect working at a deeper level. Many a businessman convinces himself that he is completely logical in his behavior, when in fact one could say it is really his emotional bias pitted against the emotional bias of his opposer that determines the negotiation. It is better not to consider the opposer's logic but rather the attitude created by his intelligence and emotions. Behavior that is designed to escalate emotional responses should rarely be used in a negotiation. This usually ends up being self-defeating. You can be unreasonable, but not to the point where your opposer feels it is impossible to deal with you.

If your opposer irrationally and unreasonably insists on talking about one particular issue first, it is possible to divert him without elevating the emotional response. For example, you can introduce new elements into the negotiation which your opposer would want to talk about even before discussing what he considers the first and primary issue. Choose an issue that he is vitally interested in, one where you can make a concession without cost, one that you know is desired by his boss, the union membership, or a higher company officer. You can thus force the opposer to relinquish his unreasonable position on what should be discussed first. This might be referred to as a red-herring concession.

In our relations with others during a negotiation we should also encourage the development of respect. A respectful atmosphere facilitates competition and is most conductive to negotiated resolutions.

While teaching college in Hawaii, Gregory Bateson interviewed a young Japanese girl about various forms of politeness and degrees of respect that the Japanese show to one another. For about an hour he wrote down the ways in which a daughter shows respect for her father—holding the door open for him, the different aspects of serving him, and so forth. After going through all of this at some length, the girl stopped and said, "But we don't respect the father in Japan." Bateson was taken aback. He couldn't understand why all these rituals were performed if there was no respect, so he asked why the Japanese behave with such deference toward the father. "Oh," the girl said, "we are practicing in case we have to show respect for someone."

A person who is able to create a supportive relationship with all the relevant people that he deals with has an important negotiating talent. It is vital to bring to the negotiation all the resources that are at your disposal.

LONG-RANGE TRAINING

Long-range training for negotiation calls for the exercise of a variety of skills. You must have the patience and accuracy of a scientist in searching the literature of past experiments. You must combine the scientific attitude with the cunning of a detective in digging up facts and figures about your opposition. You should be able to apply the current teachings of psychology to predict what the other fellow will try to do. To solve a problem it sometimes becomes necessary and important to learn many new long-range skills, an important one being the art of listening.

My father learned the art of listening at a rather early age. When he was fourteen and thought he knew everything, an old relative took him aside and said, "George, if you want to have the same knowledge at twenty-one that you have now at fourteen, then continue to talk rather than listen, because if you continue to talk, you won't know any more at twenty-one than you know now." La Rochefoucauld stated this another way: "One of the reasons that we find so few persons rational and agreeable in conversation is that there is hardly a person who does not think more of what he wants to say than of his answer to what is said." The skill of listening, concentrating on what is being said as well as what is not being said, can prove to be enormously helpful in negotiations.

After you have completed your research, you must keep an open mind and always be ready to make changes in your appraisal of the situation. It is possible that some of the facts may require modification or that your approach must be changed. Lapse of time alone often tends to call for a change in strategy. Therefore it is important to be constantly on the alert for new developments.

It has been said that one never loses until one gives up. Consider the following example. In 1935 the "Nuremberg decrees" went into effect. By 1936 all borders of Germany were sealed to the Jews. Yet sitting next to me at a closing in 1955 was a real estate investor who had managed the almost impossible feat, not only of escaping with his life, but also of taking his life's savings out of Germany. The passage of time did not dim his satisfaction and pride in telling the story of this feat. The essential elements were ingenuity and guts.

It was necessary for him to trade all of his holdings at a huge discount for United States-registered corporate bonds. Ingenuity enabled him to contact an agent in Switzerland, who, he hoped, would register the bonds in the United States in the name of the new Jewish purchaser. He had committed his fortune to the oral promises of others. All of this accomplished, he had to take the next step. After memorizing the precious serial numbers, with "guts" he lit a match and made a small "bond fire." Paying the necessary bribery fee, he was permitted to cross the German border "penniless." When he arrived in the United States, he went straight to the office of the register agent for the corporation that had issued the bonds. He reported the destruction of the bonds and their serial numbers, and received replacements shortly thereafter.

DO YOUR LESSONS

An important phase of short-range preparation for negotiation is research. Research should be objective—objective not in the quality of the evidence you gather but in your attitude toward such evidence. There is a positive reason for amassing information. It amasses a wealth of material in your mind so that you may take advantage of any new development in the negotiation.

You should be prepared with every possible kind of information about the people with whom you are going to negotiate. When President Kennedy was preparing to go to Vienna for his first meeting with Khrushchev, he made it a point to study all of Khrushchev's speeches and public statements. He also studied all the other material available relating to the Premier, even including his breakfast food and his taste in music. It is doubtful if such intensive research would be required in most negotiating situations, but the extreme importance of President Kennedy's conference warranted this meticulous search for every detail concerning his protagonist.

An increasing need for facts in all areas today is causing a growing furor about such ideas as a "National Data Center"—a giant computerized "dossier bank" that could pull together all the scattered statistics about any American and make them available to those who needed them.

It is a distasteful idea to many, and yet the negotiator must sometimes subordinate his personal feelings about snooping to the exigencies of the negotiation process.

To utilize the information you obtain from research, you must rely upon your general fund of knowledge and experience. It is essential to examine the opponent's past history, inquire into previous transactions he was connected with, and look into every business venture or deal he has consummated. Also investigate any deals he has failed to conclude successfully. Frequently you will learn as much, or more, about people from their failures as from their successes. If you carefully analyze the reasons that a certain deal fell through or a negotiation failed, you will probably get a good understanding of how the opponent thinks, his method of operating, his psychological approach. All this will give you clues to his needs and prepare you to negotiate with him more advantageously. Consider what proposals he made, what counterproposals he rejected and why, how flexible he was in the bargaining, how emotional was his approach.

You can obtain clues about the positions that business firms will take by studying some of their past transactions.

Sources like the following can prove helpful:

Budgets and financial plans.
Publications and reports.
Press releases.
Instructional and educational material.
Institutional advertising.
Reports of government agencies like the Securities and Exchange Commission.
Officers' speeches and public statements.
Company biographies in Moody's and Standard & Poor's.

Suppose you are studying an opponent's previous deal that involves the purchase or sale of real estate. The value of the tax stamps that were affixed to the recorded deed will tell the price at which the property was sold. Bear in mind, however, that there have been instances where an excess amount in tax stamps has purposely been used to attempt to hide the actual price of the property. Do not rely on one source. There are other agencies that will assist you in getting a fairly close idea of how much the property was sold for. Try to use more than one source for verification.

Merely by investigating a previous real estate sale, you can get an idea of what kind of man you are going to deal with. You can find out how long he held the property before he decided to sell it and how much profit he was satisfied to take. All these factors are useful in sizing up a prospective opponent. You can never know too much about the person with whom you will negotiate. In the words of Francis Bacon, in his essay *Of Negociating:*

If you would work any man, you must either know his nature and fashions, and so lead him; or his ends, and so persuade him; or his weakness and disadvantages, and so awe him; or those that have interest in him, and so govern him. In dealing with cunning persons, we must ever consider their ends, to interpret their speeches; and it is good to say little to them, and that which they least look for. In all negociations of difficulty, a man may not look to sow and reap at once; but must prepare business, and so ripen it by degrees.

A trial lawyer's cross-examination of his adversary's expert witness should be more than a spur-of-the-moment inspiration. It must be prepared effectively. In New York State negligence cases, lawyers are required to submit the plaintiff to an examination by the defendant's doctor. No experienced attorney would let the client attend such an examination without him. When the attorney is in the doctor's office, he may have a chance to look at the doctor's library. It is advisable for him to take note of books that may have subject matter dealing with his client's injury. At the trial a most effective cross-examination, worked out in advance, can be conducted by having the doctor admit that certain books are the outstanding authority in the field, and further having the doctor admit that he possesses a copy of the book in his own library. As a result of having carefully analyzed these medical books, the prepared trial attorney will have devised a cross-examination to test any doctor as to whether he is really a qualified expert.

In examining a person's library, you can gain useful information which will add to your store of facts about him: his present and past interests, hobbies, intellectual pursuits, even the extent to which he is able to follow a subject through.

Another quite effective method of short-range preparation is to check records of previous litigation involving the prospective opponent. (These are available through litigation reports, which can be bought.) In addition to finding out if there is any recorded judgment against him, it will prove useful to know all details about any lawsuits in which he was involved. A fruitful source of information is inquiries made of the people who have litigated with your opponent. An amazing amount of useful information can be obtained from these people. They invariably contribute some facts and opinions that are not found in the ordinary record. These same methods of approach can be employed, not only to investigate the party with whom you are going to negotiate, but also to learn more about somebody you may want to enlist on your side in the negotiation.

Almost 90 percent of the information that seems most difficult to obtain can be gotten by a direct approach. Try sitting down with your telephone and asking questions. If you are attempting to locate a person, one of the simplest methods is to call everyone in the phone book with the same last name and state that you want to locate a beneficiary under a will. With this as a reward, it is a rare instance in which you will not receive full cooperation.

A wife wanted to know whether her ex-soldier husband, newly returned from World War II, was using his postal box to receive love letters from a girl friend who lived in England. When she was informed by her private detective that during the previous week her husband had not received any letters from his girl friend, the wife was not fully satisfied. After all, how could she be sure? She insisted on knowing how the detective obtained his information. He reluctantly explained his method. He merely had someone call the post office each day, explain that he was the holder of such and such a box, and ask the clerk to look and see if a very important letter expected from England had arrived. In response to the inquiry, the clerk had each day answered in the negative.

The *Dictionary of American Slang* defines the phrase "to have someone's number" as "to know the hidden truth about another's character, past, behavior, or motives. . . ." This aptly sums up what you are trying to do in your immediate preparation for negotiation. You are trying to know your opponent, you are trying to "get his number." Indeed our era could well be called the "number age." We are saddled with numbers from the day we are born until the day "our number comes up" and we die. We have a Social Security number, dozens of credit card numbers, bank account numbers, brokerage account numbers, stock certificate numbers, passport numbers, telephone numbers, house and street numbers, check numbers, and any number of other numbers. In modern society people receive more numbers than they know how to handle.

And since we all have numbers, it is easy to get information about any given individual. There are many organizations that specialize in gathering credit information, and their charges are quite modest. Large corporations, especially in the retail field, spend as little as one or two dollars for a credit report on a prospective charge customer. Often a simple credit investigation will reveal a vast amount of information about the person with whom you are going to negotiate. This type of research is valuable, and one can sometimes save thousands of dollars' worth of time for a very nominal price.

In researching a situation, always examine and reexamine the rules. How can anyone understand a specific situation without knowing the rules applicable to that situation? How many people read the instructions and bulletins that go with every mechanical device they purchase or even with the medicines they buy? There is the story of the toy manufacturer who starts his assembling manual with: "When all else fails follow the instructions." This being the case, it is not surprising that people who attend an auction or a legal sale have not bothered to read the rules. Sometimes these rules are, unfortunately, learned from experience— usually a bad experience.

You may feel that you already know the rules applicable to your negotiating problem, that it is unnecessary to reexamine them. Then try a simple test. Cover the face of your wristwatch with your hand. Now think, are the numbers on the face Arabic or Roman numerals? Also, how many numerals? Uncover the face and check. Try the same test with a friend. As we go through life we look at the hands of the watch, noting their relative position, abstracting out the other details, never taking notice of the face. We do the same thing with rules. When we consider them, it is only in reference to the specific factual situation. It is therefore necessary to reconsider the rules with each new problem.

An outstanding illustration of this need to reexamine the rules was given by an associate who invited me to attend an auction of a surplus aircraft plant owned by the government. The General Service Administration had put the plant up for auction and it was, supposedly, to go to the highest bidder. Fred, my associate, and I discussed the relative value of the property and determined that we would offer $375,000 for the building and equipment. A hundred or more people had arrived at the auction before us, but Fred, by intuition, was able to look over the crowd, point out a group of three men and say, "There's our competition." He was absolutely right. Brokers and bidders in an audience behave differently. When the bidding began, we started with a bid of $100,000, and they countered with $125,000. We bid $150,000. When they had bid up to $225,000 Fred was silent and we left the auction. I was extremely puzzled; our final bid was supposed to be $375,000. But once outside, Fred explained to me that he read on the offering circular that, according to the rules of this auction, if the government did not feel that the price was high enough, they could reject it. Since we were the second highest bidder, the auctioneer would naturally contact us, tell us that the bid of $225,000 had been rejected, and ask us if we would care to make another offer. We could then counter with a higher price and at the same time ask the government for certain valuable concessions, such as taking a portion of the price in a mortgage. Within seven days this occurred just as if Fred had written the script.

Research supplies information to help anticipate the strategy of the impending negotiation. Such preparation should help answer questions like the following:

1. Are there any penalties involved in this negotiation, such as a penalty for bluffing, or a penalty for giving false information?
2. Have you recognized all of the interested parties to the negotiation?
3. Has anyone placed a time limit on the negotiation, or is there a natural time limit?
4. Who would like to maintain the status quo and who would like to change it?
5. What would be the cost of a stalemate?
6. In this negotiation, what will be the means of communication between the parties?
7. Can many items be introduced into the negotiation simultaneously?

By carefully exploring questions of this type, you will gain fresh insight into the strategy of the negotiation about to take place.

THE NEWER METHODS

In addition to the traditional ways of preparing for negotiation, such as doing your homework and examining the rules, other methods have come into vogue fairly recently. These methods employ the techniques of *group drama* (*psychodrama and sociodrama*), *brainstorming,* and the *conference.* At first glance such techniques may seem far removed from anything to do with negotiation. They were originated by psychologists or by the advertising fraternity. However, they are used to find the answers to problems, and in preparation for negotiation you also are seeking to solve problems. You want to know what the other fellow is going to say, what he is going to offer in response to what you say and do—in other words, what his thinking will be. The use of the group approach has proved to be a highly efficient way to get the answers to these questions. Group therapy and group methods of solving problems owe their efficacy to the power of suggestion and to the giving and getting of feedback. Solving problems through a group judgment has often proved superior to results obtained by individual judgments. This has been recognized in the advertising profession.

The method called *brainstorming* has largely superseded the ordinary conference in certain situations, such as originating a name for a new product or a slogan for a campaign. The method is essentially simple. Suppose that a problem has come up, or a new brand name is to be adopted. The usual practice would be to call a conference of the qualified executives in order to get their various opinions; then a decision would be made on the basis of what had been said. In a brainstorming session, a suitable group of people is brought together, with a secretary. The problem is presented in a clear and concise way. From this point on, the discussion and thinking aloud is permitted to move in any direction. Each person says whatever comes into his mind. No attempt is made to correct or evaluate any statements made, but the secretary takes down every word that is uttered, no matter how strange or outlandish it may seem. The entire transcript of what was said is then turned over to the top executive personnel for evaluation.

What is the theory behind this type of group meeting, and why should it produce results? It is believed that brain activity in a group becomes infectious. Ideas appear to grow by being ping-ponged back and forth. The informal atmosphere of the talk and the strong suggestive stimulus of the group thinking give a feeling of security and relieve inhibitions. Under the influence of group discussion, the individual's thinking is quickened and many fresh, original ideas are obtained that far excel those produced in a conventional conference.

Group psychotherapy, which originated with Freud, has been

subjected to many refinements since its inception, and in recent years J. L. Moreno has made significant improvements in its application. Moreno uses groups of individuals to act together in a form of improvised play to solve individual problems. He calls this *psychodrama*. Psychiatrists use psychodrama to bring out hidden feelings, attitudes, frustrations, and emotions. In essence, the individual acts out different parts in the group setting.

This technique can be valuable in training for negotiation because it permits you to act out the entire negotiation before it takes place. At various times you can play yourself, or an adviser to your side. If you choose, you can assume the role of the other party, or his adviser. Indeed, where the circumstances warrant, it is a good idea to play every one of these roles. It helps you to see what lies before you in the coming negotiation and presents it much more vividly than if you merely talked about it. This method of selecting a definite role and acting it out with a group of other players gives you a chance to try something without the risk of failure. It permits you to bring into focus any important elements that you may have overlooked or ignored. It also permits associates to participate more fully and freely with each member of each side of the group. Furthermore, it facilitates making corrections in your preparation because it lets you put yourself in the other fellow's place. (The police use a technique of role playing when they attempt to reenact their concept of how a crime occurred.) On becoming an attorney, I was fortunate to work in the law office of Lloyd Paul Stryker, one of the outstanding trial attorneys of the day. In his book, *The Art of Advocacy*, Stryker discusses preparation for trial: "I often simulate the witness and ask one of my associates to cross-examine me and to unhorse me if he can. It is great exercise, in the performance of which I have often found that I did not do so well as I hoped. My failures and the reasons for them are then discussed, and I now ask my associate to change places with me and then I cross-examine him. From this, new ideas are developed while all the time the client is looking on and listening."

Before canonizing a saint, the Roman Catholic Church traditionally appoints a "devil's advocate," who is instructed to advance all the *negative* arguments, all the reasons why the person should *not* be canonized.

In another example, week after week during the football season coaches assign substitutes to act the role of the next opponent's star player. A substitute professional quarterback will find himself acting the role of one opponent one week, another the next.

There is an important difference between the "playacting" type of meeting and an ordinary *conference.* In brainstorming a group of people with specified knowledge, experience, and attitudes are called together. Their free and uninhibited participation in discussion can prove useful in solving a problem by group judgment. The individuals called for a conference, however, are not necessarily selected for their special knowledge or experience. A conference may be called for full discussion and fact finding. Guidance or leadership, an unimportant factor in group dramas, plays a vital part in the success of a conference. A conference is for communication, and the communication can be steered in any of three directions: upward, to solve problems; downward, to inform or instruct people; and horizontally, to coordinate or cooperate. Many useful things may emerge from a conference if open communication and a free flow of information are allowed. Certain problems are handled better by the use of the group drama technique, whereas others are dealt with more efficiently in a conference— although we can understand what Tavares Desa, Undersecretary of Public Information for the United Nations, meant when he said, "If you want to get a thing done give it to one man, if you don't want it done give it to a committee."

Group dramas give opportunities for self-analysis. A study of your own motivation and thinking often gives you clues to the probable point of view of your opponent. This gives you the chance to ask yourself exactly what you want from the forthcoming negotiation. A thorough exploration of this question will serve to clarify your thinking on acceptable solutions to the problems to be negotiated, and will also suggest possible compromises that might be made. The answers will not be in absolute terms, but will rather concern the degree of probability of the solution.

CHAPTER 4 APPLICATIONS

1. Make up a list of hypothetical essential ingredients for your next negotiation. Now consider the exact opposite of these elements

of negotiating and see if under certain circumstances they may not be applicable for you.

2. As there are no absolutes in particular methods for preparation, consider how you would conduct a negotiation in which each member of the team might be required to speak his own piece without supervision of the head of the team.

5

ASSUMPTIONS

From the time we are born we begin to form assumptions. Hot things are painful; Mother's arms are warm and comfortable. And, as we mature, we continue to acquire a freight of assumptions at an enormous rate. We could not live without assumptions. When we hand the store clerk our money, we assume that he will give us our merchandise and our change. When we send in a subscription to a magazine, we assume that we will receive it. When we get on a plane to Chicago, we assume that it will land at O'Hare Airport. If we had to question everything, and reason everything through, nothing would get done.

But periodically it is necessary for us to reexamine our super-cargo of assumptions. Some are wrong and must be discarded. Others need to be modified. Still others remain valid.

Assumptions are a vital part of negotiations. In entering a nego-tiation, a man is severely handicapped unless he reviews his own assumptions—and anticipates the assumptions of the other party.

A SOURCE OF MISUNDERSTANDINGS

Justice Arthur T. Vanderbilt advised trial lawyers that when they open to a jury they have to bear in mind the "intellectual environment" of their case and not be dead to the "assumptions of the age" in which they live and speak, for they are not talking in a vacuum to men without previously formed opinions. They cannot flout or ignore public opinion—an opinion that is made up of accepted principles—even though they know that it may often be no more than the rationalized prejudices of the times.

Albert V. Dicey, in *The Relation Between Law and Public Opinion in England During the 19th Century* (New York: Macmillan, 1905), writes, "Above all, bodies of beliefs may generally be traced to certain fundamental assumptions which at the time, whether they be actually true or false, are believed by the mass of the world to be true with such good confidence that they hardly appear to bear the character of assumptions."

Few people realize what a large part of our beliefs is based on unconscious, hidden assumptions. They are not easy to bring out in the open and we frequently fail to recognize their existence. Like the iceberg, nine tenths of our assumptions lie below the conscious level. Assumptions certainly are not learned, in the sense that we learn mathematics. When analyzed, they prove to be odds and ends of information, or usually misinformation, gathered during our lifetime, or dogmas that have their roots in emotional conflicts.

The scrutiny of some "domestic" assumptions can turn up surprising things. A husband was watching his wife as she prepared a roast for the evening meal. After placing the roast on the cutting board, the wife cut the first slice and dropped it in the refuse can.

"Why did you do that, dear?" the husband asked. "I don't know," was the answer. "My mother always did it." The next time he saw his mother-in-law, the husband asked if she always removed the first slice from the roast before cooking it. "Yes," was the reply. *"My* mother always did it." So the husband, intrigued, called up his wife's grandmother. That elderly lady explained, "Oh, yes, I always removed the end slice from the roast because the pan I cooked it in was too small."

The assumption that a long-accepted procedure is valid—without any knowledge of the facts behind that procedure—can lead to meaningless and wasteful activity.

Hidden assumptions are difficult to subject to rational verification. If we make the open assumption that a certain chair will support our weight, we can test its validity by sitting on the chair. If it holds us, then our assumption was correct. If it breaks down, the assumption was false. We would be foolish to keep on repeating this exact same experiment with the same chair. We learn and revise our thinking by testing our assumptions or those of our opponent. It is therefore important to know when we are putting our weight on an assumption, known or hidden.

There is nothing wrong with making assumptions. The problem arises when we act and think as if the assumption is the absolute fact. If we know we are making an assumption, we can be prepared for the unexpected, we are less likely to assert our position dogmatically and, if proved wrong, less likely to be hurt.

As a simple example of a hidden assumption, suppose someone were to ask you what they call the Fourth of July in Great Britain? You might be at a loss to give the correct answer because you had *assumed* that what was asked was, "What do they call Independence Day in Great Britain?" Unencumbered by any hidden assumption, you would give the correct answer. "What else would they call the day that falls between the third and fifth of July but the fourth of July?"

Here is another illustration of a hidden assumption. If someone told you that he saw a beggar walking out of a ladies' room, would you be shocked? Why might you be shocked? Because your hidden assumption of the situation is that the beggar is a man. But he did not say so. It is your hidden assumption that has led you away from the facts.

How often do we assume we know all the facts? This example was popular a few years ago. On a cold January day, a forty-three-year-old man was sworn in as chief executive of his country. By his side stood his predecessor, a famous general, who fifteen years previously had commanded his country's armed forces in a war which resulted in the total defeat of the German nation. This young man was brought up in the Roman Catholic faith, and, after the ceremonies, spent five hours reviewing a parade in his honor and stayed up until 3 A.M. celebrating. Who is it? The facts given were enough to make the average American immediately assume that it was John F. Kennedy. But it was Adolf Hitler.

Our assumptions are a vital part of the human communication system. We must use them continuously in sorting out and trying to make sense of the millions of ambiguous stimuli that confront us. We receive a communication, interpret it, and make a "first guess," an assumption which we stay with until it is disproved. As the Gestalt school of psychology puts it, to probe a hole we first use a straight stick to see how far it takes us. We might paraphrase this and say that, to probe the world, we use an assumption until it is disproved. We should remember that a simple assumption is easy to refute. The hidden assumption, however, is difficult to recognize and correct.

Very often a great deal of time is wasted in a negotiation because both sides have misunderstood the facts of the situation. Perhaps the facts have become distorted because one or both parties are in the grip of hidden assumptions without being aware of it. One should always go beyond the mere words of the negotiator. To find the facts, look to the "outside world" instead of to the words of the opposition. If facts are true they can be verified, and verification leads to a solution and away from misunderstanding. Often the successful function of a mediator is merely to interpret and convey information accurately.

The negotiator must never forget that what he assumes is only a guess or a probability, but if he acts as if the assumption is a certainty, he takes a calculated risk. Therefore, if you can spot the "assumed certainties" of your opponent, you can use his calculated risk advantageously.

A negotiator who fails to understand the immediate situation because he is influenced by a hidden assumption is often stuck with the assumption as a fact throughout the negotiation. This can prove disastrous. An opposing lawyer unfortunately found himself in such a position at a lease closing. This was a conference on an important and complicated lease. Every closing is different, as is every life situation, and as such should be handled as a separate and unique matter. There are printed lease forms known as the Real Estate Board Form Leases. They are considered "standard" forms and are used fairly frequently in routine transactions.

They contain a mass of conditions in fine print. Even a lawyer who had practiced law for fifty years would not remember the significance of each and every item in these forms. My associate in the conference told the opposition lawyer, "Here is the standard Real Estate Board Form Lease. You undoubtedly know it by heart, practicing as long as you have." By this remark he forced the opposition lawyer to assume a role. Instead of analyzing the lease as it applied to the present situation, the other lawyer dispensed with reading the standard printed form. He assumed that examining it would show his lack of experience. He acted out the role into which he had been manipulated, that of having to know every word of the "standard" lease. He passed over the major portion of the lease and spent the remaining time discussing some of the typewritten portions, which, compared with the printed sections, were insignificant. The hidden assumption had been used strategically to his disadvantage. In business, particularly in selling, we have all seen examples of men being "stuck" with assumptions.

Even the vaunted power of the computer to solve problems can be vitiated by a hidden assumption. This was illustrated at an international conference on communication. An outstanding computer expert was reporting on the difficulties experienced in feeding problems to the computer. His company had been employed to determine the proper distance that one automobile should travel behind the car ahead. The following information went into the computer: the reaction time of the motorist, the weather conditions, the nature of the road surface, the friction coefficient of the tires, the air resistance of the car, and so on. Taking all this data into consideration, the computer came up with the following formula: You should allow one car length for each ten miles per hour of speed; for example, at thirty miles per hour allow three car lengths between you and the car ahead; at forty miles per hour, allow four car lengths, and so on.

But, when the experts came up with this formula, they did not realize that they had a hidden assumption built into it. This only became evident when they went on a road test to try out the formula. Then it developed that as soon as they allowed a distance of four, five, or six car lengths between their car and the car ahead of them, cars traveling on the lane alongside them would pass, cut in front of them, and fill in the space they were trying to maintain.

The hidden assumption that invalidated the formula was that cars would travel in a single-lane road and would have the road pretty much to themselves, a condition that did not check with reality.

A few years ago some computer men boasted that they had created a perfect chess-playing machine. Their computer was programed to anticipate—and defeat—any game played against it by even the greatest masters in the world. At least, this was the assumption.

It worked a few times. Then a chess champion, who had studied the computer's previous games, sat down to face his electronic opponent. His opening move was to advance a rook pawn one square. Then he advanced the rook one square. These were wildly irrational moves. The computer's lights flashed, but no answering move was forthcoming. Since the assumption was that the human master would play logical chess, the device had not been programed to combat the illogical game.

Dr. Sydney Lamb, speaking at a Yale conference on computers and the humanities, said, "The computer is not intelligent at all, but very stupid indeed, and that, in fact, is one of its great values— its blind stupidity." But it is scarcely an advantage when human beings build hidden assumptions into the computer's results.

Words themselves frequently embody hidden assumptions. Such words as "sunrise" and "sunset" helped perpetuate the old assumption that the sun revolved around the earth. People have a tendency to label everything prematurely, thus seriously limiting their ability to perceive reality. They also react as though the label described all there is to say about the object to which it is applied. For instance, many people react to the label "contract" as though it could only be the name of a legal instrument. This is far from true. A contract may contain selling devices that have nothing to do with its legal implications. As an example, franchise contracts might make provisions for a volume of business far exceeding the amount that the franchise dealer is likely to earn. On seeing these wildly optimistic figures, the potential customer is likely to assume that this amount of business *will* be done.

S. I. Hayakawa speaks about a still more basic hidden assumption in language when he states, "Underlying our beliefs are unconscious assumptions regarding the relationships between language and reality—a set of assumptions based, among other things, upon not distinguishing between statements about language and statements about the nature of the world." The study of general semantics will help immeasurably in analyzing and dealing with assumptions of all kinds.

CATEGORIES OF HIDDEN ASSUMPTIONS

Making three categories of hidden assumptions can prove useful in negotiating: first, those we make about the *extensional* world, the physical world which exists outside the mind of a human being; second, those concerning our *intensional* world, the world which exists within the mind of each of us; third, the *other* person's *intensional* world.

The first category, dealing with the *extensional* world, contains the largest and broadest areas of hidden assumptions. It concerns the environment, the time and space in which we live. We must try to verify, as best we can, the "facts" of the world around us, rather than accept a mental picture of the world. This was Galileo's intention when he attempted to verify the "logical" belief that a heavy object falls faster than a light one. When he dropped different-size weights from the leaning tower of Pisa, he found that the assumption was wrong.

Most views of the outside world are based upon assumption, hidden or known. We must therefore subject these assumptions to continued verification.

Language is essential in representing the outside world to each of us. It can, however, be misleading in that its structure tends to force us to view the world as having only two values, black or white, good or bad. This is, unfortunately, the viewpoint of Marxian dialectic, and it is not helpful in understanding the world today. The world might be considered as made up of an infinite number of shades of gray, merging successively into one another. It is the great variety of values, the constant flow and change of ideas, that imparts splendor and vitality to our concepts of environment. Assumptions about the extensional world—encouraged by a strict language structure—can lead us to believe that there are absolutes. As such they would not be subject to any further verification. With this in mind, Harry Maynard warns us to beware of the hardening of our categories. The world is a "process," not an unchanging "group of things."

In the realm of the intensional world, we must be careful to realize that our inside world is only a picture of the outside world. We tend to make assumptions about our emotions and thinking. These can confuse us so that we fail to make the distinction between "I *feel* that . . ." and "I *think* that. . . ." The result is that feeling that the truth may be thus-and-so becomes transformed into thinking and believing that it is the case.

The ability to anticipate the other fellow's assumptions can lead to spectacular results in business. Not many businessmen try to circumvent the government legally by anticipating its assumptions, although many of them dream of finding a legal loophole in the regulations to which they are subject.

However, sometimes such schemes come to fruition—and they become classic stories.

The vast experience of the U.S. Customs Authority makes it virtually impossible to create a plan to get around customs regulations—and still remain within the law. But one importer did it. He did it by means of a careful study of the regulations—and by anticipating certain assumptions that the customs people would make.

Ladies' French leather gloves carry a high import duty, which makes them exceptionally expensive in the United States. The importer in this story went to France and bought 10,000 pairs of the most expensive leather gloves. Then he carefully separated all of the pairs of gloves and made a shipment of 10,000 *left-hand* gloves to the United States.

The importer did not claim this shipment. Instead, he allowed it to stay in customs until the period for claiming it had expired. When this happens, the customs branch puts the unclaimed merchandise up for auction—and this they did with the entire shipment of 10,000 left-hand gloves.

Since a batch of left-hand gloves was valueless, the only bidder on the lot was an agent of the importer. He got them for a nominal sum.

By now the customs authorities were aware that something was up. They alerted their men to be on the lookout for an expected shipment of right-hand gloves. They weren't going to let the importer get away with his scheme.

But the importer had anticipated this. He also anticipated that the customs men would *assume* that the shipment of right-hand gloves would arrive in one bulk lot. So he packaged his remaining gloves in 5,000 boxes, two right-hand gloves per box. He counted on the probability that a customs official would assume that, of two gloves in a box, one was a right-hand and one a left-hand glove.

The gamble worked. The second shipment passed through customs and the importer only paid duty on 5,000 pairs of gloves—plus the small amount paid at auction to claim the previous shipment. Now he had 10,000 pairs of gloves in the United States.

The impressions we have absorbed over the years shape our judgments and create bias. Therefore we must realize that ideas do not have the same meaning for other people that they may have for us. We must make the distinction between our intensional world and the other person's intensional world. Without understanding the difference in points of view and interpretation, we would be bound to feel that any settlement in a negotiation would have to be based upon *who is right*. This is not productive. With compromise as a goal, and with due regard to the nuances of meanings, there are an infinite number of solutions available, ranging from the almost positive to the almost impossible.

Here let us comment for a moment on a sophisticated and sometimes dangerous assumption—namely, that you are always *aware* of your own hidden assumptions.

Some years ago I conducted a class in general semantics. In order to demonstrate the hidden assumptions to the students, I would hold up what appeared to be a pencil and ask the class to tell me *facts*—not assumptions—about the object I was holding. Students would call out that the object was a pencil, that it was made of wood, had lead inside, and so on. Then I would bend the object, showing them that it was made of rubber—and that all their "facts" were really assumptions.

A year or so after conducting this class, I myself attended a seminar given by Dr. Bontrager of the Institute of General Semantics. During the seminar, Dr. Bontrager held up an object resembling a pencil and asked his audience to write on an index card the *facts* about this object. I wrote that the object appeared to have six sides, appeared yellow, and so on. I concluded with the statement that I, too, had used a rubber pencil to illustrate the same point to my students.

After the cards were collected, Dr. Bontrager dropped the "pencil" toward his desk. Instead of bouncing high, it gave a metallic ring. The "pencil" was made not of rubber, but of steel.

We sometimes place ourselves at a great disadvantage with hidden assumptions about other people's motivations and actions. For one thing, these assumptions about the intensional world of others are colored by our own views. St. Paul gave us a beautiful example of this when he said, "Unto the pure all things are pure." Our assumptions about others often take on an unreal quality. Instead of listening to what other people are saying, we indulge in wishful hearing. We assume, without any basis in fact, that they have said certain things. Sometimes we go so far as to make assumptions about what a person is going to say before he has had a chance to say it. We interrupt, present our version of what he is about to say, and never give ourselves the opportunity of hearing what he might have said. Thus we deprive ourselves of valuable information. When listening to our opponents we must realize that our view of the world is a personal one, that our value judgments are personal judgments, that our moral concepts are valid for us alone.

The hidden assumption plays a considerable part in all phases of business negotiation.

We must be constantly aware of the possible effects of hidden assumptions on negotiation. This applies to our opponent's hidden assumptions as well as our own. For example, suppose an opponent begins arguing with such heat and vehemence that you recognize his irrational emotional involvement. Do not allow him to push your emotional buttons and cause you to react. Work with him, as a judo specialist would, by not opposing force with force, or as a tugboat that docks an ocean liner. It does not just tug at the line but gradually takes up the slack and then applies even pressure. Continue to try to understand and relate to the "irrational" emotional involvement. The short-fused psychological defenses of negotiators can be overcome by then presenting facts. A fact-finding session may be called to evaluate the facts and establish the facts or even a negotiating objective. It can also be used to get the necessary authorizations from both parties. An authority for the mutual fact-finding approach is Francis Bacon: "One method of delivery alone remains to us; which is simply this: we must lead men to the particulars themselves, and their series and order; while men on their side must force themselves for a while to lay their notions by and begin to familiarize themselves with facts."

A mutual fact-finding session can be of great advantage for resolution. Efforts should be directed to joint evaluation and participation. Facts independently arrived at can be colored with one's own point of view and they remain negotiation items. William James realized this when he pointed out: "Life is one long struggle between conclusions based on abstract ways of conceiving cases; and opposite conclusions prompted by our instinctive perception of them as individual facts."

Facts that are jointly ascertained are the materials of the negotiated solution. If sufficient time is spent in analysis and fact finding, areas of disagreement can be identified and most of the valuable facts in that area established. The differences that then exist are only differences of opinion as to what will happen, and differences possibly as to the significance attached to particular facts. In the negotiating session itself, the negotiation will then be directed toward bringing about changes of ideas or changes in something outside of the facts. The entire negotiation may merely involve certain relative uncertainties and, therefore, the relativeness of the possibilities will be the subject of the negotiation.

In a pre-negotiation conference at which facts are being analyzed, great emphasis should be placed on trying to recognize the issue. If a negotiation concerned only "absolute" facts, there could be no negotiation. It would resolve into a scientific procedure because all parties would tend to agree on "facts." (That is, if they could agree upon the procedures.) It is said you cannot disagree over a fact. You can only be ignorant of it. What a fact is, however, is also subject to disagreement. "Pure truth hath no man seen nor e'er shall know," wrote Xenophanes.

General semantics considers various problems involved in ascertaining "facts." The following are four alternative views of facts which one should be aware of:

1. It is a fact because it conforms to reality and can be verified. E.g., "Some guns are loaded."

2. It is a fact because it is a teaching we believe in. (It is "right.")
E.g., "What is hateful to you, do not do to your fellow men."
3. It is a fact because we feel the same way. E.g., "Children need love."
4. It is a fact because it is valid according to the rules of a system, for example, in the language of algebra. $2x + 2y = 2(x + y)$

Consequently, let us define a fact as information which is known to be both "viewed" and agreed to by the parties according to any one of these four methods. If there is disagreement over a fact, it is disagreement over the source, information, or method.

After some effort, enough outside facts may become available to uncover a possible hidden assumption. The artful negotiator will then be able to utilize the "facts" to the satisfaction of all.

CHAPTER 5 APPLICATIONS

1. Can you think of illustrations where the assumption has proven useful? Where a hidden assumption has helped as well as injured you?

2. In your daily activities watch others making hidden assumptions. Make a list of those that did not serve them adequately. Consider why the individual did not recognize the hidden assumption. Observe their activities and the things they say.

3. Make a list of your own assumptions that at first were hidden but subsequently were brought into your conscious mind. Consider what occurred to bring to light a hidden assumption of yours.

6

WHAT MOTIVATES US?

The satisfaction of needs motivates virtually every type of human behavior. A detailed list of these needs would be infinitely long, and even the attempts to devise classifications can result in an unwieldy number of subdivisions. These classifications do not show how needs overlap. Any such classification can only give a still picture of a living, changing process. When preparing for negotiation, time permits us to study only the broad categories that deal with the essential and predictable.

Professor Abraham H. Maslow of Brandeis University, in his valuable book *Motivation and Personality* (New York: Harper & Row, Publishers, 1954), presents seven categories of needs as basic factors in human behavior. These provide a useful framework for studying needs in relation to negotiations.

Here is Maslow's list:

1. Physiological (homeostatic) needs.
2. Safety and security needs.
3. Love and belonging needs.

4. Esteem needs.
5. Needs for self-actualization (inner motivation, to become what one is capable of becoming).
6. Needs to know and to understand.
7. Esthetic needs.

Physiological needs are common to all members of the animal kingdom. Their goal is satisfaction of biological drives and urges such as hunger, fatigue, sex, and many more. The recently developed concept of homeostasis attempts to define this category of needs more precisely. *Homeostasis* refers to the automatic efforts of the body to maintain itself in a normal, balanced state.

An amusing story dealing with a homeostatic need is told about a financial magnate who lay stretched out on his deathbed. He was under an oxygen tent. At his side stood his loyal subordinate, tears streaming down his face. "Do not grieve," whispered the expiring tycoon, with considerable effort. "I want you to know that I appreciate your faithful services to me over the years. I am leaving you my money, my plane, my estates, my yacht . . . everything I have." "Thank you sir," cried the subordinate. "You have always been so good to me all these years. If only there were something I could do for you in these last moments." "There is . . . there is," gasped the half-dead man. "Then tell me what it is," implored the faithful servant, "tell me!" "Stop pressing your foot so hard on the oxygen line!" the dying man managed to utter.

Homeostatic needs are undoubtedly the most dominant of all needs. A person may lack many things, such as love, safety, or esteem; but if at the same time he is really thirsty or hungry, he will pay no attention to any other need until his thirst or hunger is at least partially satisfied. A starving man has no desire or drive to paint a picture or write a poem. For him no other interest exists except food. All of his capacities are devoted to getting food, and until he gets it, other needs are practically nonexistent.

It should be noted that the entire organism is involved in the gratification of a need. No one says, "My *stomach* is hungry," but rather "*I'm* hungry." When a person is hungry, his whole being is involved, his perceptions change, his memory is affected, and his emotions are aroused by tensions and nervous irritability. All of these changes subside after he has satisfied the hunger need. When one group of needs has been somewhat gratified, however, another set becomes the motivating force.

After the physiological needs are taken care of, the organism is concerned primarily with *safety*. It becomes a safety-seeking mechanism. As with the hungry man, so with the individual in quest of safety. His whole outlook on life is affected by a lack of safety. Everything looks less desirable to him than the achieving of the goal of safety. Safety needs are more easily observed in children, because adults in our culture have been taught to inhibit any overt reaction to danger. But anything unexpected and threatening makes the child feel unsafe, and changes its world from bright stability to a dark place where anything can happen. A child feels safe in a predictable, orderly world; he prefers an undisrupted routine. He tends to feel safer in an organized, orderly world that he can count on and in which he has his parents to protect him against harm.

Adults in our society seldom come face to face with violence, except in war. They are safe enough from such perils as wild animals, extreme climate, slaughter, or massacres. However, the need for safety expresses itself in seeking the protection and stability afforded by such things as money in the bank, job security, and retirement programs. Though human beings no longer live in the jungle, they need protection against the dangers that confront them in the ominous "jungle" of economic competition.

After the physiological and the safety needs have been reasonably gratified, the next dominant need to emerge is the *craving for love and affection*. This longing for friends, or a sweetheart, or family, can take complete possession of a lonely individual. When he was starving or threatened by danger, he could think only of food or safety; but now that these needs have been taken care of, he wants, more than anything else in the world, to be loved. He hungers for affectionate relations with people in general, for a place in his group. In our culture, it is just these needs and cravings that are most often left unsatisfied. Feelings of not being loved, of rejection, of "not belonging," are at the root of most cases of maladjustment and the more severe neuroses. This need for love must not be equated with sex. Admittedly it is a component of the sexual drive, but sexual behavior has many facets and is considered here primarily a physiological urge.

Next in the hierarchy of basic needs is the need for *esteem*.

Actually it is a plurality of needs, all of the same general character. These needs can be divided into two categories. First and foremost is the desire for freedom and independence. Coupled with this is the need for strength, competence, and confidence in the face of the world. The second division comprises the desire for reputation or prestige, the striving for status, domination, and the esteem of other people. Satisfaction of esteem needs helps a person to feel useful and necessary in the world. The most healthy self-esteem is based on respect from others that is deserved, not on unwarranted adulation.

Research and experience continually demonstrate the power of esteem in motivating human beings. Studies of individuals at various levels of the business structure have attempted to find out what makes people feel good about their jobs. The strongest and most lasting "good" feelings come from learning and growing on the job, expanding one's competence, increasing one's mastery, becoming recognized as an expert.

Studying the motivation of salesmen, the Research Institute of America has reached similar conclusions. Many salesmen may respond, when asked casually, that the only thing that moves them is money. However, *self-approval* and *social approval* often motivate salesmen to as great an effort. The pride of craftsmanship involved in making a tough sale—and the possibility of being recognized by other salesmen as a "professional"—spur a man on when the additional money is of relatively little importance.

Even assuming that all the foregoing needs have been adequately satisfied, the individual may still be discontented and restless. What need does he now seek? Most people are not happy unless they are working at something that they feel they are fitted for. A musician wants to make music, an artist wants to paint, everyone would like to do the kind of work that he can do and enjoys doing. Unfortunately this is not always his lot, but insofar as he attains this goal he is at peace with himself. This almost universal need has been termed by Maslow *self-actualization*. Broadly speaking, self-actualization embraces the desires and strivings to become everything that one is capable of becoming. This striving takes various forms and will differ from individual to individual.

In the normal person there exists a basic drive to seek out *knowledge* about his environment, to explore, to understand. We are all motivated by an active curiosity that impels us to experiment and attracts us to the mysterious and the unknown. The need to investigate and explain the unknown is a fundamental factor in human behavior. This *need to know and understand* presupposes a condition of freedom and safety in which this curiosity can be exercised.

Lastly, human behavior is actuated by certain cravings that might be called the *esthetic* need. Some individuals actually get sick in ugly surroundings and are cured by removal to a beautiful setting. The longing for beauty seems strongest among artists. Some of them cannot tolerate ugliness. But Maslow includes in the category of esthetic needs the action of a man who "feels a strong conscious impulse to straighten the crookedly hung picture on the wall." Indeed, the need for order and balance is a basic part of all esthetic expression.

These seven basic needs have been presented in a descending scale of importance. For most people and for most human behavior this fixed order holds true. However, it must not be regarded as rigid and it certainly does not apply to all people. (Any set of generalizations has its limitations.) Undoubtedly there are many individuals to whom the concept of self-esteem is as important as the concept of love, just as there are creative people for whom the esthetic need fulfillment appears as important as a more basic need.

Differences are related to the diversities of human personalities. It is a question of how an individual's personality has developed. A person who has been deprived of love in his early life sometimes loses the desire and ability to give and to receive love. Another factor that tends to change the fixed order of importance is the undervaluation of all needs that are completely satisfied. A man who has never experienced hunger will consider food secondary to all his other needs.

Maslow pictures each successive need as emerging after a prior need has been satisfied. This is not to imply that one need must be 100 percent satisfied before the next one takes over, nor that each emerging need shows up suddenly like a jack-in-the-box. Usually the previous need is only partially satisfied before the emergence, bit by bit, of a new-felt need. Most people are partially satisfied in all their basic needs and, at the same time, partially unsatisfied. For example, if the safety need is only 10 percent satisfied, then the next ranking need, the craving for love and belonging, will not yet emerge. However, if the safety need becomes satisfied to a greater extent, perhaps 25 percent, then the next need will begin to appear in a small way, perhaps 5 percent; and as the safety need approaches 75 percent of satisfaction, the love and belonging needs may emerge 50 percent. This overlapping of one set of needs with the next set, and the constant shifting of emphasis on what a person needs, precludes a state of complete satisfaction of any basic need. Indeed, people seeking to satisfy their needs try to avoid physical discomfort, shun the unsafe, appeal for understanding, abhor anonymity, dread boredom, fear the unknown, and hate disorder.

While money may provide satisfaction of many of these needs, it is not true that the only thing money cannot buy is poverty. Money evaluations sometimes prevent us from realizing that there are other ways to satisfy needs. Job security and money were once all-important motivations in business life. Years of sustained prosperity after World War II have put the bulk of American workers beyond the influences of these gentle persuaders.

Fortune in December 1969 published a survey it had conducted with Daniel Yankelovich, Inc., in which more than three hundred chief executives of companies listed in the *Fortune 500 Directory* were asked questions relating to the handling of key management people. "What strikingly emerges from the survey is that money and position have become less effective factors in attracting good men. . . . The values of this new generation are submerging the money-oriented values of yesterday."

Do not let the dollar signs blind you to the immediate "solutions" they buy. Look behind them. What do they represent? How might the need be satisfied in an alternative manner? If we examine a negotiating situation a bit foreign to our immediate experience, need fulfillment versus dollars may become a little easier to see.

An English mining company that employed thousands of people in an African subsidiary faced a difficult labor negotiating problem. Eighty percent of its employees were black females who had recently left their tribes. The mining company had just been unionized, and the union had made a demand that the company found almost impossible to meet. It demanded that when an employee gave birth she would not be required to work and would be paid 75 percent of her salary for four months after the birth. The African culture permitted multiple marriages and considered children a "bank account" for old age. Therefore, at any given time a large percentage of the women workers would be eligible for this benefit.

If the company had tried to consider the demand on a purely monetary basis, it might have had a long and costly strike on its hands. Recognizing that it was operating within a different culture, realizing its limitations, and understanding the full consequences, the management was forced to pursue the negotiations dispassionately. Management decided to do some fact finding before the negotiation began. In the course of its inquiry it learned that after a woman gave birth she would send the baby back to live with the tribe. The 75 percent of wages she wanted was to pay for the baby's care. The woman always had to return to work. Because the management took a flexible approach, they were not limited to bargaining over money demands. Many alternatives were discussed: the women and their desires, the tribal conventions, and the fact that government laws prevented use of birth control. Hiring only men was impossible. Offering only one month's wages helped no one. Finally a synergistic solution presented itself. The management offered to set up a free day-care center for the children. The offer was gratefully accepted and established a company loyalty from the women workers that had previously been reserved for their tribe.

To sum up, an individual's existence is a constant struggle to satisfy needs; behavior is the reaction of the organism to achieve a reduction of need pressures; and behavior is directed to some desired goal. In short, this is *what* a person does. Our objective is to employ these facts about human needs in successful cooperative negotiation.

CHAPTER 6 APPLICATIONS

1. In negotiating, can you deal with other people on the basis of knowing *what* they will most probably do rather than *why* they may do it?
2. Are there professionals to whom the "why" of a person's actions would be important?

7

THE NEED THEORY OF NEGOTIATION

Needs and their satisfaction are the common denominator in negotiation. If people had no unsatisfied needs, they would never negotiate. Negotiation presupposes that *both* the negotiator and his opposer want something; otherwise they would turn a deaf ear to each other's demands and there would be no bargaining. This is true even if the need is merely to maintain the status quo. It requires two parties, motivated by needs, to start a negotiation. Individuals dickering over the purchase and sale of a piece of real estate, a labor union and management bargaining for a new contract, or the directors of two corporations discussing the terms of a proposed merger—are all seeking to gratify needs.

What these needs are has been explored in the preceding chapter. This information can be put to use in the quest for successful negotiating techniques: knowledge of the Need Theory permits us to find out what needs are involved on both sides of the bargaining table. The theory goes further: it guides our attention to the needs and varieties of application that actuate the opposition and shows how to adopt alternative methods to work with, or counteract, or modify our opponent's motivations. These needs, as we have explained, arrange themselves in a definite order of importance. The Need Theory enables us to determine the relative effectiveness of each negotiating technique. Moreover, the Need Theory gives us a wide variety of choice for our affirmative or defensive use. Knowing the relative strength and power of each need, we can decide on the best method of dealing with it. The technique that utilizes the more basic need in each case will probably be more successful. The more basic the need, the more effective it will be as a gambit.

At this point, let us raise a devil's advocate's objection. Needs are often intangible. People who are satisfying needs act on the basis of emotion—not reason. Since this is the case, isn't it futile to attempt to offer a highly structured theory of negotiation? That question has undoubtedly been partly responsible for the lack of such a theory up to this time.

The answer to the question is *no*. Let us consider religion as an analogy. People are emotionally involved in religion, yet theology need not be unsystematic. On the contrary, although theology starts with an "act of faith," it is one of the most ordered and systematic disciplines we have.

A theory of negotiation, just like any theory of theology, must take into account relative strengths, alternatives, and multiple choices.

The Need Theory provides such a structure in ordering and relating levels, varieties, and needs.

THREE LEVELS OF NEGOTIATIONS

In the Need Theory of negotiation, I have divided the different areas of negotiation into three main levels:

1. Interpersonal—negotiation of individuals.
2. Interorganizational (excluding nations)—negotiation of large organizations.
3. International—negotiation between nations.

It should be noted that organizations of any type cannot act by themselves, independently of people. They must act through people. Remember this when you are dealing with people acting on behalf of organizations. You can recognize two active levels of needs: the level of the organization's need, and that of the negotiator's personal needs.

Individuals, through identification, often transcend the boundaries of their own need structure and mentally become part of a larger organizational-level group. Thereafter, in certain cases a less basic need of the group—for example, esteem—will take precedence over a more basic need—safety, for instance. The great majority of people in most nations do not want war, but their identification through nationalism permits them to be persuaded and propagandized into conflict and thereby to put their safety in jeopardy. Therefore, we should not be misled into thinking that the hierarchy of the need structure does not hold true when an individual willingly risks death (safety need) for national honor (esteem need). It would appear that the esteem need in such instances is taking precedence over the safety need. However, because of identification, this is not the case.

VARIETIES OF APPLICATION

The Need Theory is applicable at all levels of approach. When closely analyzed, the techniques of negotiation under each need are seen to repeat certain forms, called the varieties of application of the need. I have divided them into six groups or categories.

The following variety of applications are placed in an order corresponding to the amount of positive control that we may ordinarily have over each application in a particular life situation. In other words, a negotiator has more control over *his* working for the opposer's needs (1) than letting the opposer work for his needs (2), and so on down to (6), which is the least controllable. The six varieties of application are the following:

1. Negotiator works for the opposer's needs.
2. Negotiator lets the opposer work for his needs.
3. Negotiator works for the opposer's and his own needs.
4. Negotiator works against his needs.
5. Negotiator works against the opposer's needs.
6. Negotiator works against the opposer's and his own needs.

These represent how a negotiator attempts to satisfy his *own* needs. Categories (1) to (6) show increasing risk.

CHART I
VARIETIES OF APPLICATION
(1 TO 6 IN THE ORDER OF
INCREASING RISK AND LESS CONTROL)

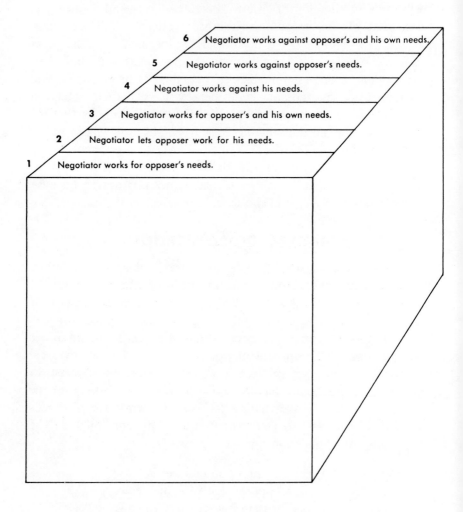

6 — Negotiator works against opposer's and his own needs.

5 — Negotiator works against opposer's needs.

4 — Negotiator works against his needs.

3 — Negotiator works for opposer's and his own needs.

2 — Negotiator lets opposer work for his needs.

1 — Negotiator works for opposer's needs.

Innovative words are being formed weekly for descriptions of applications to diplomacy, to buyer and seller relationship, to business negotiations, to personal, business, and world problems. Here are examples of these new words and definitive words and how they fit into the Need Theory of negotiating matrix:

Varieties of Application	Definitive Words	Specific Applications
1. Negotiator works for the opposer's needs.	Persuade Concede Assure Urge Induce Coax Back Champion Encourage	Freedom from fear
2. Negotiator lets the opposer work for his needs.	Commit Pledge Challenge Incite Motivate Spur Stimulate Excite Trust Uphold Permit Allow Promise	Black is beautiful Beautiful people B.O. (used in ads)
3. Negotiator works for the opposer's and his own needs.	Promote Recognize Embolden Cooperation Confess	Self-determination Alliance for Progress People to people Collective security Building bridges

Varieties of Application	*Definitive Words*	*Specific Applications*
	Compromise	Due process
	Admit	Finalize
	Acknowledge	Involvement
	Authorize	Parity
	Support	Reorientation
	Encourage	Implement
	Foster	Peaceful coexistence
	Help	Soul brother
	Aid	
	Assist	
	Uphold	
4. Negotiator works against his needs.	Forgo	Cease-fire
	Waive	Pacify
	Sacrifice	Bombing halt
	Forswear	
	Recant	
	Disavow	
	Relinquish	
	Surrender	
	Yield	
	Cede	
	Resign	
	Renounce	
5. Negotiator works against the opposer's needs.	Prohibit	Sabotage
	Veto	Defoliation
	Interdict	Containment
	Taboo	Arrogance of power
	Shame	Body count
	Embarrass	
	Betray	
	Abuse	
	Insult	
	Harass	

Varieties of Application	Definitive Words	Specific Applications
	Discourage	
	Hinder	
	Contradict	
	Menace	
	Threaten	
	Imperil	
	Jeopardize	
	Forbid	
	Restrict	
	Force	
6. Negotiator works against the opposer's and his own needs.	Withdraw	Confrontation
	Embargo	Gapsmanship (in
	Renounce	armament race—
	Resign	maintain gap)
	Enjoin	Brinkmanship
	Banish	Armament
	Excommuni-	reduction
	cate	Separate but equal
	Be non-	Balance of terror
	cooperative	
	Thwart	

When Abraham Maslow's seven basic needs were used to explain the Need Theory of negotiation, each basic need was intended as a general classification, not as a pigeonhole. Each one contains many individual terms that might be considered specific needs in and of themselves. It is therefore helpful to consider that each basic need contains clusters of needs. As Bernard Berelson and Gary A. Steiner state in *Human Behavior: An Inventory of Scientific Findings,* "Various writers have constructed lists of motives ranging from very short and highly general lists to more specific ones containing as many as fifty or sixty social motives. One classical scheme reduced social motives to four basic 'wishes'—for security, recognition, response from others, and new experiences."

CHART II
NEED BUNDLES
(MOST BASIC TO LEAST BASIC NEED:
THE MORE BASIC THE NEED, THE MORE FORCEFUL
THE NEGOTIATION GAMBIT)

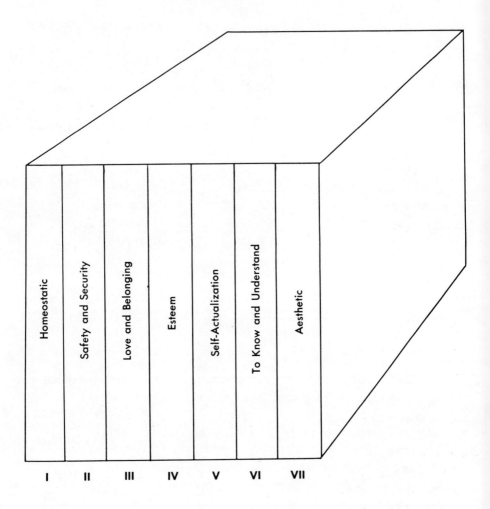

The following is a comparison between Berelson and Steiner inventories and Maslow (Roman numerals refer to Maslow's order; homeostatic needs are not included):

Need	*Definition*
Need Acquisition II	To gain possessions and property. To grasp, snatch, or steal things. To bargain or gamble. To work for money or goods.
Need Retention II	To retain possession of things. To refuse to give or lend. To hoard. To be frugal, economical, and miserly.
Need Aggression II	To assault or injure. To murder. To belittle, harm, blame, accuse, or maliciously ridicule a person. To punish severely. Sadism.
Need Succorance II, III	To seek aid, protection, or sympathy. To cry for help. To plead for mercy. To adhere to an affectionate, nurturing parent. To be dependent.
Need Rejection III	To snub, ignore, or exclude. To remain aloof and indifferent. To be discriminating.
Need Deference III	To admire and willingly follow a superior. To cooperate with a leader. To serve gladly.
Need Affiliation III	To form friendships and associations. To greet, join, and live with others. To cooperate and converse socially with others. To love. To join groups.
Need Conservance III	To collect, repair, clean, and preserve things. To protect against damage.
Need Similance III	To empathize. To imitate or emulate. To identify oneself with others. To agree and believe.
Need Nurturance III	To nourish, aid, or protect the helpless. To express sympathy. To "mother" a child.

Need	*Definition*
Need Blame-avoidance III, IV	To avoid ostracism or punishment by inhibiting social or unconventional attitudes and impulses. To be well behaved and obey the law.
Need Abasement IV	To surrender. To comply and accept punishment. To apologize, confess, atone. Self-deprecation, masochism.
Need Exhibition IV	To attract attention to one's person. To excite, amuse, stir, shock, thrill others. Self-dramatization.
Need Recognition IV	To excite praise and commendation. To demand respect. To boast and exhibit one's accomplishments. To seek distinction, social prestige, honors, or high office.
Need Inviolacy IV	To prevent a depreciation of self-respect, to preserve one's good name, to be immune from criticism, to maintain psychological distance. It is based on pride and personal sensitiveness.
Need Disfavor-avoidance IV	To avoid failure, shame, humiliation, ridicule. To refrain from attempting to do something that is beyond one's powers. To conceal a disfigurement.
Need Defendance IV	To defend oneself against blame or belittlement. To justify one's actions. To offer extenuation, explanations, and excuses. To resist probing.
Need Dominance IV	To influence or control others. To persuade, prohibit, dictate. To lead and direct. To restrain. To organize the behavior of a group.
Need Counter-action IV	Proudly to overcome defeat by restriving and retaliating. To select the hardest tasks. To defend one's honor in action.
Need Superiority IV	Will to power over things, people, and ideas.

Need	Definition
Need Recognition IV	Efforts to gain approval and high social status.
Need Construction V	To organize and build.
Need Autonomy V	To resist influence or coercion. To defy an authority or seek freedom in a new place. To strive for independence.
Need Achievement V	To overcome obstacles, to exercise power, to strive to do something difficult as well and as quickly as possible.
Need Cognizance VI	To explore. To ask questions. To satisfy curiosity. To look, listen, inspect. To read and seek knowledge.
Need Exposition VI	To point and demonstrate. To relate facts. To give information, explain, interpret, lecture.
Need Play VII	To relax, amuse oneself, seek diversion and entertainment. To have fun, to play games. To laugh, joke, and be merry.
Need Order VII	To arrange, organize, put away objects. To be tidy and clean. To be scrupulously precise.

Human organization has been arbitrarily divided into three levels, A, B, C, for simplicity. The needs and varieties of application apply with equal relevancy to each level of approach.

CHART III
LEVELS OF APPROACH

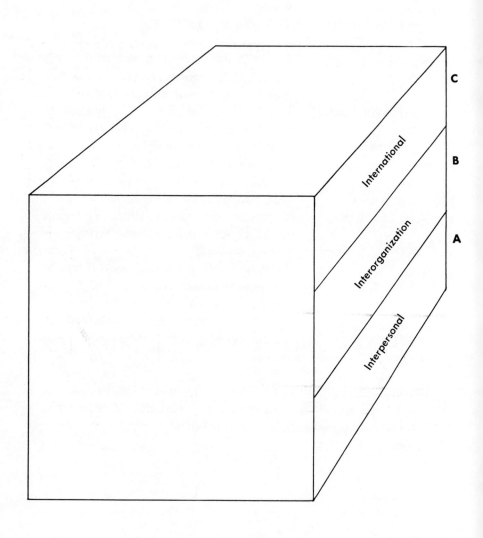

CHART IV
THE STRUCTURE AND ORDER OF GAMBITS
IN THE NEED THEORY OF NEGOTIATING

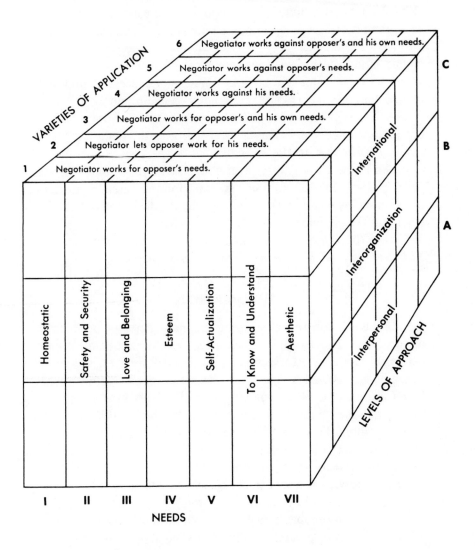

This chart combines the six varieties of application, the seven basic needs, and the three levels of approach. You can use the matrix figure of 126 individual cubes, each of which represents a different negotiating gambit, to help generate creative negotiating ideas. You can calculate the strength and the ease of application of your gambit and your opposer's gambit by ascertaining its relative position on the chart.

The more alternative ways you have of handling a negotiating situation, the greater will be your chances of success as opposed to people who use only two or three methods again and again.

The Need Theory shows the probable order of importance of negotiation maneuvers. Therefore it will give the negotiator a wide choice of methods to use in achieving a solution. Remember, the more basic the need gambit available, the more probable becomes your success in negotiation. If the opposer uses a maneuver involving a less basic need, then you should deal with a more basic need and thus enhance your chances for success.

(For a life illustration of each cube, see Appendix, page 238. This can be read now or referred to for future use.)

SUBLIMATION

Sublimation can reveal seeming inconsistencies in the hierarchy of the Need Theory. Since man is a social-symbolizing creature, his world can offer satisfaction of his needs based on the symbols of his needs, as well as satisfying the actual needs themselves. It is therefore not difficult to conceive of individuals who are prepared to sacrifice their more basic needs for a less basic need on a higher social-symbolic level, as when a soldier is prepared to sacrifice his life for the glory or the esteem of his military unit. In today's world, this is enlarged to where members of a race are prepared to sacrifice their individual lives for the esteem of the race. This could be considered one level above nationalism.

When our more basic needs are continuously satisfied, we go on to achieve still greater fulfillment by satisfying higher needs. In order to achieve such fulfillment, we can often take the risk that more basic needs might not be satisfied, like an artist who, having experienced high-level need fulfillment, will risk starvation for his conception of art.

Another example could be seen during World War II in aviation cadet primary training. Each class had a yearbook. When those yearbooks were dummied up (made ready for the printer), the first page was always left blank for the picture of one of the members of each class of about fifty cadets who was statistically bound to be killed in training. When the cadets were informed of this, as a bunch of nineteen-year-olds, they just looked around and took pity on that other poor fellow who would be featured on that first page of the yearbook.

Motivation to satisfy our needs is not a carefully calculated action, but it is a varying pressure that we experience from moment to moment. We cannot calculate its ultimate effect. Will we put our life in jeopardy if we attempt to satisfy this need? What are the mathematical chances of something of dire consequence happening to us if we attempt to satisfy this need? We respond to each particular pressure as it builds up, taking that course which appears to us at the moment as the most desirable. Some of us who are more mature, older than the nineteen-year-old cadets, will attempt to look into the future to see the consequence, to determine whether that approach should be followed. However, the less mature among us have a tendency to look more for immediate gratification and satisfaction—for example, risk death to satisfy our esteem need.

On the other hand we do not have to look far to find certain mature people who will forgo many personal gratifications for the sake of others. Motherhood is a prime example. Doctors, priests, and nuns give up their own basic needs for the welfare of the sick. During the Sino-Japanese War, wounded Chinese soldiers were being treated by a nun. She was bathing their neglected gangrenous wounds. A reporter observing her stated to another newsman, "I would not do that for a million dollars." The nun, overhearing this, replied, "Neither would I."

History is replete with many stories of people courageously offering themselves (homeostatic need) to sacrifice for the good of their office and their country (esteem need). One such story concerns Alexander Hamilton. When Secretary of the Treasury, he was approached by a blackmailer who attempted to induce him to use his influence on the extorter's behalf by threatening Hamilton with the exposure of his amour with a Mrs. Reynolds. Instead of acceding to the blackmailing scheme, Hamilton went to President

Washington and told him of his predicament, then told the cabinet, and published the details of his relationship. This displayed his high ideal of public responsibility and permitted no suspicion of impropriety in his conduct of the Treasury. As a direct result of this disclosure. Hamilton's wife ended up in an insane asylum and his son was killed in a duel defending his father's honor.

NEED FULFILLMENT AND DEPRIVATION

A seeming inconsistency in the hierarchy of needs involves deprivation. Young people today who have been brought up in affluent homes are able to worry more about the social consequences of their careers than about the material benefits that may flow from those careers. Children from affluent families also appear to be more likely to develop into hippies, with their ability to withstand deprivation, than poorer children. Many secure young people sacrificed themselves in the Peace Corps. They were placed in a deprived situation and some were able to withstand the limited satisfaction of their basic needs. Still other volunteers got what is known as the Albert Schweitzer Complex. For although their work was exciting and the surroundings picturesque, sometimes, after they had been on the job for three or four months, they found their environment no longer picturesque or quaint. They became frustrated and decided to go home, having experienced what is called "culture shock." Being able to withstand this shock would seem to depend on what their satiated needs were at that particular time. If they have had, as Maslow said, gratification in the higher and lower needs, such people will value the higher needs more. They will withstand the lower-level deprivation for satisfaction on higher need levels.

The United States government has studied the ability of Marines to withstand deprivation of needs in an experiment that consisted of depriving some of them of full satisfaction of their more basic needs by subjecting them to simulated combat conditions for a period of time, while a similar group was not put under the strain and had all their basic needs satisfied. Then both groups were put into actual combat to determine which one was now better able to withstand the new deprivation of their needs. It was decided that the men who had had their needs satisfied stood up better than those who had been deprived. This was at variance with the belief that men would be better able to withstand deprivation if they had been previously conditioned to it.

This seems to be consistent with what has been observed in the manner in which large American businesses deal with executives. How to dehire an executive has been a problem that American business corporations have had to face. They would prefer that he resign because this would not have a disastrous effect on his colleagues and their feeling of security. The methods that they follow seem to coincide with a reverse order of the hierarchy of needs. They tend to withdraw satisfaction of needs at the highest level first, hoping that the executive will take the hint and hand in his resignation. Where an executive seems to be more secure in his basic needs, having not been deprived of them, he will promptly react to a withdrawal of the higher-order need satisfaction. However, where he feels in jeopardy, where he feels insecure about his basic needs, he will not react when his higher need satisfactions are withdrawn.

Here are some of the severing methods that corporations use in reverse need-level order, expecting the executive to resign after each ploy.

Esthetic level. One day the executive will come into his office and find that his carpet has been removed, or perhaps his secretary has been replaced with one substantially less attractive.

Knowing and understanding level. The company makes him take part in every meeting and conference throughout each day so that he cannot take care of his own work, or they may not permit him to attend any meetings whatever, or they may move his office continually so that no one can locate him, or ask him for recommendations, then not acknowledge or follow them.

Self-actualization level. The company removes his responsibilities, possibly kicks him upstairs and gives him an empty title.

Esteem level. They take back his men's-room key or assign him to degrading duties or take away his parking space or remove his special lunchroom privileges.

Love and belonging level. They will speak to him about other companies and other jobs that may be for him, and might go so far as to have a specific job offered.

If he has not quit, the company may have to work their way down to the safety and security level. They may call in the company physician, who, after an examination, shakes his head and says he would not object if the executive put in for early retirement.

If the executive has been so uncertain as to his capabilities to satisfy his homeostatic need—that is, to make his salary—that he will not allow any of these actions to deprive him of his job, then the corporation must resort to summarily superannuating the employee.

EMOTIONS AND NEGOTIATIONS

Things, positions, and situations can be negotiated, but it is more difficult to negotiate feelings. It is advisable in an emotional situation to try to get beyond the feeling, to move to the levels of the things and actions that caused the emotion. This is particularly true of an unsatisfactory marital situation. If there is no emotional love, the partners may merely have negotiated themselves into a truce, where they live in a state of suspended hostilities with each other. We can anticipate these problems before they occur and can find methods of handling them. We need to look for creative alternatives so that we can avoid a dead-end situation. No matter how gloomy the future may appear, imagination for an alternative point of view may shed new light.

There is a story of a railroad examiner who was testing a man for a switchman's job by trying to place him in a dead-end situation.

"Suppose," he asked, "that you were on a mountain and saw one train speeding in one direction and another train about a mile away speeding along the same track toward the first train, unable to see one another. What would you do?"

"I would fire my emergency signal gun in their direction."

"Where did you get an emergency signal gun?"

"The same place that you got the two trains."

How can multiordinate terms be useful in considering emotional situations? Multiordinate terms, or multiordinate satisfying terms, are things that are capable of satisfying one's needs on all the levels, from the most basic, homeostatic, to the least basic, esthetic. One such term is money; another is sex; also, to some, faith. After you have considered the multiordinate term, the following questions are posed. At what level are you seeking sexual satisfaction now? Are you being satisfied only on the most basic need level—homeostatic? Are you using it to give you security, safety? Are you using it for love and belonging? Or esteem? There are people who use sex not only to get satisfaction at the lowest level but through all the need levels up to the highest level, the esthetic. Now consider on what levels you are seeking satisfaction from the use of money. Recognizing multiordinate terms and their capabilities of satisfaction on all need levels can supply you with additional creative alternatives.

THE USE OF THE NEED THEORY IN MOTIVATING CREATIVE PEOPLE

The person who manages people must be able to motivate them to meet the company's objectives. How can you create a climate to motivate creative people? Satisfy their more basic needs so that they can work on a higher level—at least at level five, self-actualization. It is only after meeting the basic needs that the more creative aspects of a person can be realized and released. A creative person does not suffer from a shortage of new ideas but from difficulty in having them considered. Harshly judging an unusual or even an unworkable idea deprives him of the atmosphere which encourages the use of intuition and insight.

Behavior tends to become less creative and more routine under great stress. People tend to respond in a habitual or familiar way, and their ability to act creatively with an improvised or differentiated response is greatly reduced. Behold the turtle. He makes progress only when his neck is out. Let the creative employee stick out his neck.

Creativity is considered one of the most important elements of a successful negotiation. It has been said, "Don't give children cut flowers, but teach them how to grow plants."

CHAPTER 7 APPLICATIONS

1. Read over the definitive words of the variety of applications. Go through them carefully to see which ones you have used during your negotiating experience. Do not continue reading until you have finished this. When you have done this you should recognize that the ones you *have* used represent your negotiating styles. However, there is no reason why in your negotiating each and every one of these applications may not be appropriate in one or more of your life experiences. Under certain circumstances they all can be used.

2. Think of an additional word describing the different needs in each need-bundle classification.

3. Think of an additional definitive word describing a variety of application.

4. People and nations have a tendency to repeat negotiating styles and usually have only two or three to choose from. On the international level, certain nations are identified with particular styles (which will be discussed), for example, forbearance for the Chinese, deadline for the French, "I must report to the Kremlin" for the Russians, compromise for the United States. Can you think of other national negotiating styles that your study of history has demonstrated to you? Can you think of some negotiating styles that are used by members of your family? Used by your business associates? Used by your business opposer?

5. Give an illustration from your personal experience of each one of the needs and each one of the varieties of application on a personal level in your attempt to fill these particular needs, not necessarily in a negotiating experience.

6. In the next negotiation that you enter, evaluate the needs that your opposer is dealing with as far as you are concerned and the variety of application that he is using.

7. Analyze various television advertisements and classify them according to the gambits of negotiating that are used, in regard to the needs that they involve and the varieties of application.

8

THE USE OF QUESTIONS

To know what your opposer is thinking and striving for, you must turn detective, you must apply various methods and techniques to your primary objective of recognizing his needs. The problem involves communication, how to get through to people. The excellent book *Getting Through to People,* by Jesse S. Nirenberg, can serve as a valuable guide. The seasoned negotiator is ever on the alert for tip-offs on the mental processes of his opposer, for clues that will reveal his motivations. He listens carefully to what the opposer says and meticulously observes the way he acts. His mannerisms and gestures, his recurrent phrases and modes of expression, are all clues to his thinking and his desires—his hidden needs.

The usual way to get information, of course, is to ask a question. Questions are windows to the mind. In an appropriate situation I have often asked my opponent, "What do you want from this negotiation? What do you expect? What would you like to accomplish?" Through such straightforward probes, in addition to other information, I often succeed in finding out my opponent's needs, what he is after, and then guide my future negotiating accordingly.

The use of questions in a negotiation as a means of recognizing needs generally involves three decisions: *what* questions to ask, *how* to phrase them, and *when* to ask them. The effect on the opposition is also an important consideration. The importance of properly phrasing a question is well illustrated by the following story. A clergyman asked his superior, "May I smoke while praying?" Permission to smoke was emphatically denied. Another clergyman, approaching the same superior, asked him, "May I pray while smoking?" To the question thus phrased, permission to smoke was granted.

It is equally important to know when to ask the question. Many a committee has been tied in knots and many a jury has been hung when the chairman or foreman started off the consideration with, "Let's find out where we stand before we begin the discussion," or "What do you think of this plan?" The timing of this question tends to freeze people into an immovable position.

Before asking people to take a position, it would be more advantageous to have everyone involved ask one or two questions. Postpone any commitment of position. Sincere questions requiring information should be sought. Leading questions suggesting an answer should be avoided. Questions should be used to make all participants familiar with available facts and assumptions upon which to base their conclusions.

Under Anglo-Saxon jurisprudence, questions are used in both direct and cross-examination as a means of getting at the facts of a case. Until the Glorious Revolution of 1688, prisoners in treason and felony cases had no counsel, but even when counsel was finally allowed, the attorney was not permitted to address the jury, although he was allowed to cross-examine. Said Sir James Stephen: "Their cross-examination, therefore, tended to become a speech in the form of questions, and it has ever since retained this character to a greater or lesser extent."

A lawyer in cross-examination tries to stay away from types of questions where the answers are uncontrollable,

The use of questions is a powerful negotiating tool and must be employed with discretion and judgment. The question determines the direction in which the conversation, argument, or testimony will move. The proper use of the question can often command an ensuing negotiation. The question you ask also controls the amount of information that is likely to be given back to you, much as turning the water faucet controls the flow of water. Questions stimulate the opponent to think, and often to start thinking critically about your proposition. By asking a specific question such as "What time is it?" or "Do you like watermelon?" we are demanding only a limited amount of specific information. Such questions are easy to answer, and in essence we are guiding or controlling the thinking of the other party. However, if we go to the other extreme and ask a general question such as "Why did you do it?" or "How did you do it?" then the answer is more difficult. Answering such questions forces your opponent to think a great deal more—with increasing risk that he will reexamine his premises or more critically reevaluate yours.

By the judicious use of questions you can easily secure immediate attention, maintain interest in the item under discussion, and direct the course that you want the conversation to take. Very often, by questions, the opposition can be led toward the conclusion you desire.

However, the use of questions raises several problems. One may innocently touch some emotional chord with a question and arouse considerable antagonism. I experienced this early when I asked a woman the simple question, "When were you born?" We were filling out a questionnaire and my query was perfectly routine; at least, so it seemed to me. But the woman was obsessed with the fear of growing old and the sense that life was slipping away from her. She reacted violently to what I considered a harmless question.

That woman taught me a lesson. I now proceed in this fashion: "On this Motor Vehicle form, they require a statement of your age. Some people prefer to state 'twenty-one plus.' Do you have any preference?" Experience constantly shows that it is necessary to prepare the ground before asking questions.

Indeed, it is good practice to explain the reason for asking a question wherever this is feasible. It avoids trouble and embarrassment. Another way of avoiding unnecessary or unpleasant emotional response is to avoid asking forcing questions like "What is your excuse?" A nonforcing question, such as "How do you feel about the matter?" permits full and continuing discussion.

Preparing the ground before asking a question reminds me of the observation made by an architect friend. He was discussing communication, but his analogy applied to the asking of questions as well. Communication, he said, was like erecting a building. Information corresponds to the supplies for the building. If you sent the supplies to the site without plans having been previously furnished, the workmen might easily go ahead and put up any type of structure, not knowing what the architect had in mind. The correct procedure is for the architect to send the plans of the building to the job site first, and then, when the supplies arrive, the workmen will (we hope) put everything in its correct place, according to the plans. In questioning, you should give the other party a plan in advance of what you intend to gain from the conversation. If they have the plan first, then you can feed them the information, asking questions as you see fit. Ask questions and they will respond with much if not all of the information, in a proper perspective.

A further problem in asking questions involves their form, which was touched on in the smoking story about the two clergymen. Do not ask questions that carry any vague implications, or that can easily be turned to your disadvantage. Tone of voice and wording should be given very careful consideration. This is important in the interest of clarity and in order to avoid any false inferences. Questions should be asked, not to score an advantage over your adversary, but for clarification. Well-conceived questions—concise and directed to the point under discussion—are a powerful negotiating tool for discovering the motives and recognizing the needs of the opposition.

Questions may also be used to control discussion in a negotiation. This is well illustrated in an article by Irving L. Lee in the *Harvard Business Review,* January-February 1954, entitled "Procedure for 'Coercing' Agreement." The problem involved the management group of a fairly large corporation, which seemed unable to formulate policies and reach meaningful decisions. It bogged down in basic disagreements between department heads. After much study the problem was solved by adopting a special procedure for the meeting. Mr. Lee's article explains:

The chairman was to proceed as usual until he sensed an impasse, a situation in which conflict was well marked. This was likely to be any period when the talking seemed to accentuate differences, when there was evidence that the vote would be close, when the minority view was well stated, when people were contradicting each other. At this point he was to announce that the chair was raising a Question of Privilege for the Group *and until further notice all talking which expressed any difference of opinion would be out of order. The chairman then would give the floor to any proponent of the view that aroused the controversy, who would be invited to state or restate the position without interruption. No counterstatement was to be permitted. The opposition's role was to be limited to the asking of questions. . . .*

The opposition may ask Questions for Clarification. *Questions of this variety are permitted: "What exactly is your procedure again . . . ?" "You said . . . ; did you mean this?" This process is supposed to forestall the impulse to disagreement until there is an effort at understanding. . . . It is also a way to emphasize the belief that a proponent is entitled to every consideration in making his position clear, and that it will not be argued down before it is adequately stated. If listeners can be encouraged to wonder about what speakers mean, that may open rather than freeze the disputed position.*

The foregoing procedure works remarkably well. The use of the proper question technique steered the meetings into successful decisions and "coerced" the management group into agreements. Lee's article gives a marvelous insight into the use of questions for the purpose of guiding and influencing negotiations.

AFFIRMATIVE STATEMENTS

Skillful questioning can unearth a hidden assumption that is the basis of violent emotional reaction. Under such circumstances, it would be good strategy to make the simple statement, "I understand how you feel." This type of statement can remove the necessity for defiance because you are telling the opposer that he has been heard and understood, that you comprehend the validity of his point of view. Furthermore, telling him that you grasp his mental image may induce him to examine yours.

The proper use of statements is a way not only to control a negotiation but to present your opposer with the information you want him to have. Above all, try to maintain complete emotional control over any statement. Do not avoid emotional statements, but make sure that they advance—rather than stop—the negotiation. Machiavelli offers sound advice on how *not* to use statements: "I hold it to be a proof of great prudence for men to abstain from threats and insulting words toward anyone, for neither . . . diminishes the strength of the enemy; but the one makes him more cautious, and the other increases his hatred of you, and makes him more persevering in his efforts to injure you."

When a negotiation appears to be headed toward an impasse, it is good strategy to clear the air by a flat statement such as, "It's the best we can do under the circumstances." This appeals to the opponent's need to know and understand, and forces him to reconsider the situation. You may decide that it is better strategy to take a less hard line or to compromise on a point. In this event you might say, "I don't think we'll have much trouble with this point if we can get the other one settled right." The statement shows a definite intention to make a concession on the first point, facilitating the progress of the negotiation. This is considered tacit communication and is a way of protecting one's position while at the same time indicating a possible adjustment. Another such illustrative statement is, "If you will lower your demand just a little, I'll do everything I can to sell it to my associates." However, if no concession or adjustment can be made, such statements will probably lead to a breakdown in the negotiation.

The proper use of statements demands close attention to the choice of words and phrases. Sometimes one word loaded with emotional significance can be disastrous. For example, one of the lawyers in a preliminary conference once used the adjectives "happy" and "rich" with unexpected results. He was trying to argue the benefits of a certain point that he claimed would make my client rich; somehow he also worked in the adjective "happy." In discussing the case later, my associate and I agreed that had the other lawyer used the comparative forms, "happier" and "richer," he would not have aroused our client's antagonism and stopped the negotiation. Even an important person who fancies himself as *happy* and *rich* does not mind being told, "This will make you *happier* and *richer.*"

Here is an incident that by understanding the relative positions of the parties and using the proper words, one side can force the other to make the opening move.

J. P. Morgan once wanted to buy a large Minnesota ore tract from John D. Rockefeller. Rockefeller merely sent John D., Jr., around to talk.

"Well, what's your price?" Morgan asked.

"Mr. Morgan, I think there must be some mistake," John D., Jr., said. "I did not come here to sell. I understood you wished to buy." (You may recall that I stole a leaf from Mr. Rockefeller's book on behalf of my client in the old office building being demolished—Chapter 2.)

Good technique involves much more than finding out your opposer's needs. The knowledge you have gained must be used in the most effective way. Webb and Morgan, in *Strategy in Handling People,* show how a master politician, Mark Hanna, exercised his skill in influencing a young businessman. It is an example of Need Theory in action.

The well-known politician, Mark Hanna, in 1896, when Mc-Kinley was running for President, organized the greatest Republican campaign in American history. He was attempting on a certain occasion to influence William Beer, a young New York businessman. The response he wished was loyal Republicanism from Mr. Beer. He took advantage of the fact that the instinctive drives are always present in the organism, ready to be stimulated, and, since their responses are not fixed, may lead to various adjustments. The instinctive drives he stimulated were associated with family loyalty, a learned pattern involving more direct instinctive tendencies. The stimulus he used was a series of conversational remarks about Beer's father. He asked first, "Are you the son of Judge Beer in Ohio? You have an uncle down in Ashland, haven't you?" And so on about these great men, his relatives. Soon he had Beer talking and kept him discussing business for an hour or more. In this way he made a good friend of the younger man and held him for the Republican cause. He attached Republican adjustment to the parental and gregarious drives.

This interview between Mark Hanna and Mr. Beer should be regarded as a negotiation. Certainly Hanna had a definite goal—to persuade the young man to work for the Republican cause. The strategy Hanna employed appealed to the young man's need to belong, to be a part of his family group.

There are, of course, many ways of saying the blunt word which we all have to say—"no." The agent says, "Don't call us, we'll call you." In turning down an invitation to speak, a prominent man writes, "I am trying to keep down all outside activities to a barest minimum and it is on occasions when I have an invitation to do something as interesting as your proposal that I have to strengthen my character."

The unsold prospect says, "I'll think it over," or, "I'll have to talk it over with my associates." The negotiator may say, "Let's lay that point aside for a moment—we'll come back to it later."

HOW TO FORMULATE QUESTIONS

Subconsciously your opposer realizes the tremendous force that is potentially contained in questions. Therefore, if the questioning process is not handled in an understanding way, it can cause great anxiety in the person being questioned. This anxiety is a sign that one feels that one's self-esteem, self-regard, or person is endangered. If your opposer shows signs of anxiety during the questioning process, you should do something about it—you should act immediately to remove the source of discomfort. You can progress into another area or eliminate the uncertainty of the question by making your purpose clear. As Dr. George Gallup points out, "When you start asking questions, the other person immediately wonders, 'Why does he want to know?' "

Creating anxiety can also be avoided by giving attention to transitions. When it is necessary for you to change subjects, know in what direction you want to proceed, making sure the shift is smooth and logical. Finally, be sensitive to the knowledge that the questioning process causes reactions in the other person's mind and be aware of his reactions. Comprehend what you are trying to evoke in the other person's mind. Don't ask questions haphazardly without regard to possible consequences. Remember the story of the young lawyer who had a witness on the stand.

"Did you see the alleged fight start?"

"No."

"You did not arrive on the scene until the altercation was over?"

"That is correct."

Rather than be satisfied with his cross-examination and stop it there, the lawyer continued, "Then how do you know that the defendant bit off part of the plaintiff's ear?"

"I saw him spit it out."

As has been discussed, some people have divided questions into categories: what questions to ask, how to phrase them, and when to ask them. They have said, for example, that if a question was put one way you might get a worthwhile contribution; put another way, however, the question might infuriate or confuse the opposer or cause him to pull away. Let us consider these arbitrary categories briefly. They permit some useful insights, in spite of the fact that they do not actually help us to formulate a particular question for a specific requirement.

WHAT

Questions should not offend. They are not disciplinary measures, nor should they show signs of leadership. Questions should be relevant to help form new meanings and insights and help provide new "experiences." When an employee comes in late and you say, "Do you know what time it is?" you do not really want to know what the time is, you want to discipline him, you want to show who is boss. An entirely different way to handle the situation is to start by asking, "Do you have any problem that is causing you to be late, and can I help with it?" Perhaps difficulty at home has caused his tardiness.

HOW

Questions should be nonforcing; they should not put a person in a spot. St. John reminds us, "It is the modest, not the presumptuous inquirer, who makes a real and safe progress." As I have mentioned before, if you lay a foundation as to why you want the information, you will help to eliminate anxiety. If you are dealing with a question concerning the future, it is important that you recognize what you are looking for: Are you asking in terms of *evidence* or in terms of *estimates?* The one asks for facts, the other for opinion. Finally, phrase your questions so that the answer that you want is easier; for example, if you are selling soda, ask, "Do you want the large glass?" rather than "Do you want the small or large glass?"

WHEN

If you want to gain control of a conversation or overcome an interruption, a question can be used. First, incorporate the interruption into your next question. Let us say a telephone call from the buyer's wife interrupts a fifteen-minute sales talk just before the close. You cannot start the sales presentation all over again. You might say, "Look, the big decisions we reserve for our wives, but we still have to make the little business decisions, don't we? We still have to decide whether to buy three hundred tractors this year. As I was saying, with three hundred tractors . . ."

Secondly, if you incorporate the last statement of a group with your question, this can lead the group thinking back to where you want it applied. You will find it a very useful questioning process. For example, you have called a conference for the purpose of getting some information on a *production* problem. For an hour after the conference has started they are still discussing the *supply* problem. Try at the appropriate time saying where you honestly can, "Jim, can you apply the same insight you have shown for the supply problem to the production problem?" You have them back on your track.

As useful as a classification approach to questions seems to be, it fails to show how to formulate questions for your conversations. Let us consider a different method. What purposes does a question serve in the communication process? This avenue can provide useful insights and can be helpful in enabling you to compose questions.

FIVE FUNCTIONS OF QUESTIONS

Questions appear to be able to be divided into five basic functions.

I Cause attention. Provide preparatory conditions for the operation of the other's thinking. Example: "How are you?"

II Get information. Provide questioner with information. "How much is it?"

III Give information. Provide the other with information. "Did you know you could handle this?"

IV Start thinking. Cause the other's thinking to operate. "What would your suggestion be on this?"

V Bring to conclusion. Bring the other's thinking to a conclusion. "Isn't it time to act?"

There are advantages to this form of approach in considering the questioning process. Understanding that a question can serve one or more of these functions allows you to prepare a series of functional questions which can be used during the course of a negotiation. Having a reserve of functional questions ready at any time will permit you to direct the stream of conversation in any manner you want. You can make up several questions that will help guide your overall strategy. At the same time, under each individual tactic, have several questions ready for moment-to-moment guidance. Even where the opposer is doing most of the talking, you can safely permit this because with the use of a question you can always obtain conversational control. Let us consider each separate function of questions:

FUNCTION I. TO CAUSE ATTENTION.

When the commuter that you meet asks you the question "Beautiful morning, isn't it?" this is more or less devised to break your preoccupation. Many of the ritual questions (i.e., "How are you?") that are asked are under this function. Here are some specific examples: "Wouldn't it be wonderful . . . ?" "Would you mind

. . . ?" "Could you help me . . . ?" "By the way, how often have
I . . . ?" "How many times have I . . . ?" "May I . . . ?" "Could
you tell me . . . ?" "If you would be kind enough . . . ?" You can
see that in this function of questions there is little that would cause
any anxiety.

FUNCTION II. TO GET INFORMATION.

These are questions designed to obtain information. Some words
that lead off this type of question are as follows: *who, what, when,
where, should, shall, could, is, do, for instance, will.* Anxiety can
be caused if the reason for wanting the information cannot be
ascertained.

FUNCTION III. TO GIVE INFORMATION.

We know very well that many times questions contain and give
a great deal of information in spite of the fact that they might seem
to be grammatically structured to get information. For example,
take the desperation questions "Why was I born?" and "What is
there to live for?" These contain a great deal of information which
anyone listening to them can readily understand. Questions can
accuse. There is the story of an automobile that ran down a hill and
hit the side of a house. The mother inside immediately looked for
her young son. She shouted the question, "George, where are you?"
A timid voice replied, "Mother, I didn't do anything." Other
questions serving this function might be used to bring hidden objections out into the open: "All right, why don't you want to go?"
Some other illustrations are: "Do you like being pushed?" "Was it
also . . . ?" "Can *any* of *your* problems be solved?" "Oh, really?"
Sometimes you want to sustain the interest of the other person and
say: "Have you ever . . . ?" Or perhaps you want to put the
listener on the defensive: "Isn't it so . . . ?" Some words that are
used in these forms of questions are: *because, if you, did you,
would you.*

The questioning process itself is a way of supplying information.
Questions have a kind of educational force that carries through.
They carry information along with them. People who are asked
the same question twice may answer differently a second time because their attitude has been changed by having been asked the
question the first time. Questions asked in a certain series have

a tendency to carry information—e.g., "Is there justice in the United States?" "Is there justice for all?" "Is there justice for the blacks?" Follow-up questions tend to give more and more information.

Anxiety is caused by function III when the replier feels that the information given is threatening.

FUNCTION IV. TO START THINKING.

These are such questions as: "Have you ever . . . ?" "Are you now . . . ?" "How much would you guess that sells for?" "Aren't we lucky to . . . ?" "To what extent . . . ?" "If I were to . . . ?" "Is there . . . ?" Some of the words used in these questions are: *how, why, did, would, describe.* Anxiety can be a by-product of the thinking if the replier feels endangered.

FUNCTION V. TO BRING TO A CONCLUSION.

This function can cause anxiety when you want to lead the listener where you want him to go and where he might not want to go. This may happen when you start out with questions such as: "Isn't it true?" "Which do you prefer?" "Is this the only way?" "Where would you rather eat, here or there?" "Was it also because . . . ?"

QUESTION MATRIX

To enable the reader to consider the large variety of questions that can be created by combining the different functions, the following five question matrices are presented. Each question in the matrix contains two different combinations of the five functions—offering a total of twenty-five different types of questions.

	I (Cause Attention) Provide preparatory conditions for the operation of other's thinking.
I. Provide preparatory conditions for the operation of other's thinking. (Cause Attention)	(I-I) "Excuse me, could you help me?" "Excuse me, may I help you?"

II. Provide questioner with information. (Get Information)	(I-II) (Treat Classification Question) "Would you be kind enough to tell me how much it costs?"
III. Provide other with information. (Give Information)	(I-III) "May I ask how many times I told you to cross at the corner?"
IV. Cause other's thinking to operate. (Start Thinking)	(I-IV) (Planned Classification Question) "Could you tell me what would be your suggestion on this?"
V. Bring other's thinking to a conclusion. (Bring to Conclusion)	(I-V) "I hope you don't mind my asking you, do we have a deal?"

II
(Get Information)
Provide questioner with information.

I. Provide preparatory conditions for the operation of other's thinking. (Cause Attention)	(II-I) "Do you have the time, by any chance?"
II. Provide questioner with information. (Get Information)	(II-II) "Where should I eat, and how do I get there?"
III. Provide other with information. (Give Information)	(II-III) "How do you spell *swimming,* with two *m*'s?"
IV. Cause other's thinking to operate. (Start Thinking)	(II-IV) (Open and Leading Classification Question) "In what direction shall the company go after you give it your proper consideration?"
V. Bring other's thinking to a conclusion. (Bring to Conclusion)	(II-V) "Could we go when you make up your mind?"

III
(Give Information)
Provide other with information.

I. Provide preparatory conditions for the operation of other's thinking. (Cause Attention)	(III-I) "Did you ever make a time purchase, may I ask?"
II. Provide questioner with information. (Get Information)	(III-II) "Because my check bounced, you insist on cash?"
III. Provide other with information. (Give Information)	(III-III) "Did you know you could handle this if you let yourself try?"
IV. Cause other's thinking to operate. (Start Thinking)	(III-IV) "If what I'm telling you is true, why shouldn't you do it?" "The answer is obvious, don't you think?"
V. Bring other's thinking to a conclusion. (Bring to Conclusion)	(III-V) (Association Classification Question —brings important association into the question) "The president likes this; don't you?" "Look over the agreement and see if it is correct; if so, would you sign here?"
	IV (Start Thinking) Cause other's thinking to operate.
I. Provide preparatory conditions for the operation of other's thinking. (Cause Attention)	(IV-I) "How would you react to that suggestion, by the way?"
II. Provide questioner with information. (Get Information)	(IV-II) (Cool, Window, and Directive Classification Questions) "To what extent do you think we could afford it?"
III. Provide other with information. (Give Information)	(IV-III) (Filter Classification Question— brings to light the state of the other person's mind) "Have you ever heard of the Robinson-Patman Act?" "Did I ever tell you how intelligent you are?"
IV. Cause other's thinking to operate. (Start Thinking)	(IV-IV) (Implied Alternative Classification Question) "Will your methods be accepted outside the state as well as they are in the state?" "Will you either cool down or get out?"

V. Bring other's thinking to a conclusion. (Bring to Conclusion)	(IV-V) "Why don't you let me decide on the restaurant when you tell me whether you like French or Italian food?"

V (Bring to Conclusion) Bring other's thinking to a conclusion.

I. Provide preparatory conditions for the operation of other's thinking. (Cause Attention)	(V-I) "Don't you know that this is the only way, if you don't mind my telling you?"
II. Provide questioner with information. (Get Information)	(V-II) "Your considered opinion, then, is that according to the law, I would be in violation of antitrust?"
III. Provide other with information. (Give Information)	(V-III) (Hypothetical Classification Question) "What would you do with a yacht?"
IV. Cause other's thinking to operate. (Start Thinking)	(V-IV) "Isn't it true that because of his political attitude you didn't like him?"
V. Bring other's thinking to a conclusion. (Bring to Conclusion)	(V-V) (Double-barrel Classification Question—two concluding ideas) "Do you prefer to negotiate with a large team and a large company or with a small team and a small company?"

THREE OR MORE FUNCTIONS IN A QUESTION

A question can also contain three functions. Sometimes such questions can be misleading or dangerous; they become rather confusing since they are loaded with so many functions. For example, "Do you think that the sale of old police horses to meat packers should go through or not?" In this case a "no" answer and a "yes" answer can mean the same thing. "No" might mean that the sale should not go through. "Yes" might mean that the sale should not go through. A typical three-function question would be gaining attention, giving information, and asking for a conclusion. The telephone receptionist's question was an example of this. Many salesmen's closing questions are three-function types: "Would you mind looking this over to see if the information is correct, then would you sign here?" It contains I, IV, and V functions.

OLD QUESTION CLASSIFICATIONS AS COMPARED TO NEW USE OF QUESTION FUNCTION

Let us compare some of the question classifications and see how they reveal the functions they contain. The following are a list of question classifications: the first group are questions that have been classified as manageable; the second, classified as difficult. You will notice that the first group have I, II, and IV functions, while the second group tend to have III and V functions. This does not imply that you should not use questions with III or V functions, but merely that it is more difficult to give the listener information and make him come to a conclusion by the questioning process than it is to get information, start thinking, and gain attention.

QUESTION CLASSIFICATIONS THAT ARE MANAGEABLE

Functions

IV   *Open-end questions* cannot be answered with a simple "yes" or "no." They usually begin with *who, what, when, where, why,* or *how*—e.g., "Why did you do it?"

II-IV   *Open questions* invite the other person to express his thinking freely. It gives him latitude in answering. "Will you tell me, Tom, how this looks to you?"

II-IV   *Leading questions* give the direction of the reply. "Then couldn't you send a letter to Tom?"

IV-II   *Cool questions* have little emotion involved. "Now, what would you say that the next step in the solution of this arithmetic problem is?"

IV   *Planned questions* are part of an overall logical sequence thought out in advance. "And after you take care of the first part what would your suggestion be on this?"

I-II   *Treat questions* let the respondent know that he can help when he expresses his view. "Could you help me, Joe, with one of your excellent suggestions?"

IV-II   *Window questions* help you look into the other
             person's mind. "Why do you feel that way about
             her?"

IV-II   *Directive questions* focus on a particular, understood
             point. "How excessive do you think the cost might
             be?"

IV   *Gauging questions* give feedback about the state
             of the other person. "How do you feel about that?"
             "How does that strike you?"

QUESTION CLASSIFICATIONS THAT CAN CAUSE DIFFICULTY

Functions

III-V   *Close-out questions* force the other person into your
             preconceived point of view. "If you were convinced
             that the action was destructive for you, you wouldn't
             take it, would you?"

III-V   *Loaded questions* put the other person on the spot,
             whatever his answer may be. "Do you mean to tell
             me that your solution is the only solution to this
             problem, and the right one?"

III-V   *Heated questions* reflect a good deal of feeling
             toward the respondent. "Having already spent a
             great deal of time discussing your problem, don't
             you think we should move on?"

I-V   *Impulse questions* just occur to questioner. "By the
             way, what is your impression of how your boss
             would handle this situation?"

IV-V   *Trick questions* would appear to require a frank
             answer, but are actually going to put the respondent
             on the spot. "What are you going to do about your
             marital problem—get a divorce, separation, or an-
             nulment?"

III-V   *Reflective or mirror questions* simply reflect another
             point of view, or your own. "Here's how I see it,
             don't you agree with me?"

V-III   "You think this plan would not work because it is
             too costly?"

GRAMMATICAL QUESTIONS AND THE FUNCTIONS

There are four ways of grammatically structuring a question, and some of these structures lend themselves more easily to one function of a question than another. First, by placing the subject after the auxiliary verb we can make a function IV-type question: "Are you going?" Or a function II question: "Did you study last night?" The second way of making a question is by using an interrogative pronoun or adverb: *who, which, where, how.* These usually are a function II or IV question: "Who studied last night?" The third type of question is formed by adding an interrogative statement to a declarative statement: "You did study, didn't you?" These can be used for a function V question. The fourth way of making a question is by putting a question mark at the end of a declarative statement: "You've been studying?" This can be used for function V questions.

Any of these four ways can be used for the function I questions and the function III questions. Further, when we consider speech emphasis and content, we can see how almost any one of these grammatical structures can be used for any of the five functions of questions.

PROCESS OF QUESTION CONSTRUCTION

Understanding the function of a question is still only one aspect of a process. The framing of a question requires other abilities. It involves your intuitive feelings for the situation and your ability to devise a question that takes into account a number of conscious and unconscious clues that the situation bears at the moment.

Many examples of forms of questions have been provided. Still it must be borne in mind that the form of any spoken question can be varied by accent, innuendo, emphasis, and the other speaking devices that we use to carry on and emphasize aspects of conversation. The full context of a written message can also be varied in similar manners.

The simple use of the question "How are you?" can be changed from one function to another by emphasis:

"How are you?" No emphasis on any particular word. Causes attention. (I)

"How *are* you?" Get information. (II)

"How are *you?*" Gives information. (III)

"How are you?" Starts thinking. (IV)

"But how are you?" Brings to a conclusion. (V)

Then there are situations in which a question can serve all five functions as example. Have you ever been in a restaurant when the waiter would like you to sign the check? He comes over and asks, "Another drink?" He is doing this basically to gain your attention (I), and also at the same time he wants information (II) to another function. He may want you to leave (III). This question could start you thinking (IV), and finally it could have you come to a conclusion (V). Therefore when you question, remember, in the context of the situation and of the moment it is capable of being interpreted as serving any function by the listener. The responsibility is on the speaker. If the conversation misfires he must be prepared with understanding and alternatives.

HOW FUNCTIONAL QUESTIONS OPERATE

It would appear that we cause much less anxiety by the functions I, causing attention, II, getting information, and IV, starting the other person to thinking, rather than III, giving information, and V, bringing the other person to a conclusion. Let us see how this operates in day-to-day situations. Let us say that it is possible to ask another person his opinion without putting him on the spot or forcing him to respond, as: "Would you like to add anything further?" (a I- and II-function question) rather than "What is your opinion?" (a V question), Another example: As a door-to-door salesman, you ask, "Would you like to buy the Encyclopaedia Britannica?" That is a V question. The answer may be "No," and the door slams in your face. Instead, you might start off "Do you have any children in school?" to gain the attention of the person and get information (I and II functions).

The telephone company spent millions of dollars sending representatives around to suggest different methods of answering the switchboard. Some receptionists, they found, answered the phone with "Who's calling?" That tends to be antagonistic to some people. They feel that the person will only be in to certain people (III function). The suggestion was made that the receptionist ask instead, "May I announce who's calling?" This gains attention (I), and more or less gives the other person a choice in answering. Another way of answering the phone might be "May I tell Mr. Smith who's calling?" This is a multiple-function question, containing a I, a III, and a V function. It gains attention, provides you with information that Mr. Smith is there, and allows the caller to come to a conclusion. You have the right to say "yes" or"no."

Let us compare other types of questions as illustrations. "You're not working now, are you?" has a III and a V function. Another way of handling it would be "Are you looking for a job right now or waiting for a while?" This contains two IV functions. Another illustration, "Do you quarrel to settle your domestic conflicts?" is a III and a V function. Another way of handling this might be "When conflicts arise, how do you try to settle them?" which is a III and a IV function.

In an interviewing situation, there are questions that you as an interviewer should ask. Your purpose is to gain attention, certainly to get information, and to start thinking. Therefore questions designed around these three functions are quite useful, and if you find that functions III and V are coming through, then you should re-examine the type of questions you are asking. Let us assume that we were using the type of question we should not ask, as "I assume you wouldn't smoke pot?" That is a question that contains a V function and a III function. It might better be asked, "Mr. Smith, would you care to discuss your opinions on marijuana?" This contains a IV and a II function. Another way is "Can you tell me anything I've missed that you might like to bring out?" That is a IV and a II function. The open questions, which are II and V functions, also fall into this category. In interviewing, the II and IV functions are all-important.

THE IMPORTANCE OF FUNCTIONAL QUESTIONS IN PREPARING FOR NEGOTIATIONS

To reemphasize, in the course of a negotiation set up an over-all group of functional questions, questions that cover the entire negotiation from start to finish, each one performing its various functions at the particular time. I.e., at the start of any lengthy negotiation, ask attention-causing questions, then questions which get information, later questions which start thinking, and finally questions which bring the thinking to a conclusion. Also have small clusters of functional questions that can serve the immediate purposes and move the negotiation tactically over your entire strategic plan. You can then let your opposer do almost all the talking. You can control the direction of the negotiation by thoughtfully interjecting a question now and again.

STATEMENTS AS QUESTIONS

Very often people make statements that are really requests for information. Used consciously, statements as questions can serve the same functions as direct questions. However, from the time we were children, we have used such statements almost unconsciously. Such statements can indicate uncertainty, pretending to know something that is not known, or simply one's inability to ask questions. These "questioning" statements should be listened to carefully. They are valuable insights into your opposer's needs. Treated as a III-function question by adding a question mark, "Nobody loves me" can be a helpful means of drawing closer to a person. Treated as a statement, it carries emotional dynamite.

Indirect questions are statements that require an answer. Sometimes they can serve the purpose of questions more diplomatically than a direct question, such as, "The chairman wants to know when you're coming," instead of, "When are you coming?" A president of a corporation might want a potential buyer to get the idea that the firm is quite desirable and is being pursued by other buyers. The president's statement, "Guess who asked if the company was for sale," will usually elicit a response, but one over which the president has no control. The buyer's answer might range from the facetious to the brutal. "You would never guess who asked to buy the company" permits more control because it is probably going to be answered with "Who?" or "No." With this answer one can continue and probably get the reaction he wants.

The indirect question (as III function) helps one to make a running commentary. (Example: "How do the people of the United States feel about this?") It makes additions and corrections to what is being said; it implies what you want to know or suggests the information that you desire, and it helps you to be reasonably certain of what is being communicated.

Begging the question is a statement in which the premises are assumed to be true and not needing additional proof. Such statements are prefaced by such phrases as "It stands to reason that . . . ," "Let it not be denied that . . . ," "Everyone knows . . . ," "It is self-evident . . . ," "You don't have to worry that . . ." Begging the question is a useful device that politicians have raised to a fine art.

Statements can tell, report, describe, explain, or answer and serve some of the same purposes as a question. The imperative mood is a still more forceful way of using a statement as a question. These statements command, make a request, or give directions: "Be careful!" "Kindly come as soon as possible." "Take the next turn." They are used with such verbs as *come, go, speak, do,* and *be.* Add these additional conversational tools to your negotiating vocabulary.

SELF-QUESTIONING

Experienced newspapermen have frequent recourse to a quotaiton from Rudyard Kipling's *Elephant Child* which lists the six standard question words: "I keep six honest servingmen; they taught me all I know; their names are What and Why and When and How and Where and Who." Remembering this stanza helps reporters get all the information that is necessary for a standard story. "Who," "what," "when," and "where" questions are II-function, low-order abstractions, closer to reality, and their answers leave little room for interpretation. "Why" questions, IV function, at the other extreme, do ask for interpretations, and "how" questions, IV function, fall somewhere between the two extremes.

All of these words in questions, however, can be used to stimulate imaginative thinking in negotiations, yielding creative alternatives.

Still another self-questioning method used to help an orderly development of your ideas and negotiating strategies is the repeated use of "when": (1) when you are trying to define your ideas, (2) when you are trying to collect information, (3) when you are trying to gather ideas, (4) when you are trying to evaluate your ideas.

"How" questions, on the other hand, can lead to ideas of alternative ways of putting strategies to use: how to adapt, modify, magnify, minify, substitute, rearrange, reverse, combine. Asking yourself these "how" questions can usually stimulate a flood of ideas. It is important to remember when questioning yourself that you ask, Where does this statement, or this question, have unquestionable meaning to me? Einstein defined creative questioning as "the driving spirit of inquiry." He surely included the concept of self-inquiry among the aspects of creative questioning.

LEVELS OF QUESTIONS

Human beings tend to organize their concepts and classifications of the world into levels. Language structure encourages and enables this to happen. The study of general semantics, which refers to it as the process of abstracting, is useful in understanding how this occurs. This important study also considers the ways that people deal with the different levels. As an illustration consider an event that is occurring at the moment. From this event we abstract the things that we perceive and are concerned with. This is called a first-level experience. On the second level, we describe the experience; it is what we say directly about the experience. What we say about what we said about the experience, more or less our interpretation of the event, is on the third level. On a higher level, the fourth level, we reach a conclusion or a generalization about what we said about what we said about the experience.

When we couch a question on one of the various levels we should be aware of the fact that the answers that come back to us will usually be on a similar level. If, for example, during a strike we ask, "Are the employees of my firm loyal?" we are asking a very high-order question that calls for an answer that may be quite irrelevant in meaningfulness and probability. If the question were worded, "Has the personnel department recorded specific instances of employees' actions which caused actual physical damage to company property?" the answer we would get might be more meaningful and useful. In France an applicant for a Ph.D. was asked in his oral examination by a professor, "Why does opium put people to sleep?" The answer: "Because it contains a dormative principle."

This is an illustration of changing the level of an answer to a higher level and of course avoiding the question.

Another example of the use, or misuse, of a high-order question is when the atheist challenges the Christian minister with "You say that God created man. Then who created God?" This often proves effective before an audience, but the basic inconsistency of this high-order question is that it blends time and eternity into one without the necessity of carefully making a distinction as required in a low-order question. If we carefully choose questions whose structure more adequately fits the specific area with which we are concerned, we will become more effective in dealing with people by receiving and acting on more relevant information closer to actual experiences.

HOW TO ANSWER (OR NOT) WHEN QUESTIONED

Professor Chandler Washburne in an excellent article in the general semantics magazine *Etc.,* March 1969, on the vital subject of how to answer when questioned, ends his discussion with, "The future of this much-needed science is in your hands." I would like to propose a similar statement to you and show you some of the various applications that might be considered. These are not offered as suggestions to follow but merely as examples of alternatives that you may have been subjected to or used on others. The field may be divided as follows: (1) leave the other person with the assumption that he has been answered, (2) answer incompletely, (3) answer inaccurately, (4) leave the other person without the desire to pursue the questioning process further.

(1) LEAVING THE OTHER PERSON WITH THE ASSUMPTION THAT HE HAS BEEN ANSWERED

In the questioning process we deal with two sets of assumptions—those of the questioner and those of the person questioned. In answering we should try to handle the questioner's assumptions and attempt to leave out our own. An army captain once made the wrong assumption when faced with a question. He had been in charge of his company's officers' club funds, which he had slowly misappropriated over a long period of time. While in the PX one day he was accosted by two military policemen. One put his hand on the captain's shoulder and said, "Captain, would you come outside with us?" The officer replied, "Could you excuse me for one moment?" He went into the men's room at the rear of the PX and shot himself. The MP's were astonished. They had come in to tell the captain his jeep was parked by a fire hydrant. He would be alive today, but possibly behind bars, if he had made an effort to consider the question on the basis of the other person's assumptions rather than his own. He might have answered the MP's question with a challenging "Why?" and acted accordingly.

(2) ANSWERING INCOMPLETELY

An incomplete answer is one in which we cover a much more limited area than the questioner intends. Let us say you have just had dinner at the home of a newly married friend and his wife has cooked the meal. The next day the husband asks you, "Well, how did you like my wife's dinner?" Your answer might be, "She certainly sets a beautiful table. The silver was especially fine. Was it a wedding present?"

Use restricted meanings to the questions asked. Sometimes in a negotiation if details are presented and both sides are concerned that they could never agree on the specifics, they will ask questions which are subject to restricted answers rather than obtain an absolute rejection which they do not want. When, for example, the question was asked of the manufacturer, "Could you handle this order?" the manufacturer, considering a restricted meaning, said, "Certainly we can handle an order of this sort." Neither side was asking or receiving an answer to the question of when delivery could commence.

As previously stated, you should ask questions considering the level that you wish to receive answers on. If you ask a high-level question you will probably get a high-order, abstract answer. A lower-level question will elicit more precise, detailed information. In answering questions, however, this process can be reversed. When you are asked a high-order question, you can give a low-order answer by prefacing your answer with, "Well, to be more fundamental . . ," When the question is asked, "How do you think the disarmament talks are going?" the answer might be, "As skilled diplomats, our representatives are in direct and constant communication with the representatives of the other side." A low-order question can be given a high-level answer, as when asked, "Why didn't the president of Columbia take more immediate action against the S.D.S. students when they started their disruptive activity?" The answer might be, "Rugged individualism is dead in the United States." There was a man fishing in a bayou in Louisiana. Two men came up to him and asked if there were any snakes in the water. The fisherman assured them there were none. After the men had taken a swim, one asked the fisherman, "How come there aren't any snakes?" "The alligators ate them all," he answered.

Another method of answering incompletely is to sidestep the question. Let us say that you are a salesman and are in the middle of your presentation. At this point the customer asks, "How much does it cost?" Your object is not to answer at this time; you wish to complete your presentation before revealing the price. You might reply, "The dollar value is what I'm sure you're interested in. Therefore, let me round out the details and present the various costs so that I may more fully be able to answer your question." You might also say, "When I've finished my presentation of the entire article, I'm looking forward to asking your opinion of the price." Sometimes use of the restricted meaning can be of assistance; tell him the price of the part that is being demonstrated at the time, then go on with the presentation.

(3) ANSWERING INACCURATELY

Use an analogy beginning "As I understand your question . . ." and then set forth your own version of the question; or begin with "A similar situation . . ." and state a situation that you are prepared to compare it to; or set forth a typical analogy to which you would like to relate the question. You can also change the question by substituting a different question. Suggest that you are going to answer and deftly change the subject: "I thought you might say that, and you deserve an answer. But before I reply, let me ask this question." "Yes, I agree with the intent of the question, but let me rephrase it slightly." If the questioner is still unsatisfied and says, "I don't think the answer is pertinent," your answer might be, "Perhaps you're right. How would you phrase it?" or, "How would you have stated it?" or, "Would you prefer that I put it this way?" or, "How would you like me to say it?"

(4) LEAVING THE OTHER PERSON WITHOUT THE DESIRE TO PURSUE THE QUESTIONING PROCESS FURTHER

State many answers without committing yourself to any one. For example: "Why can't we improve railroad service?" Answer: "When we consider shifting population, the change in the economic conditions of people in various sections of the area, the failure of the state to supply necessary funds, the federal government's preoccupation with supersonic jets, labor's inclination to give as little for the dollar as possible . . ."

State that the answer to the question is that the question cannot be answered: "That's one of those unanswerable questions." "The future holds the key to that problem." "It would serve no purpose in this instance to speculate on the future."

Give a "nothing" answer: "That *was* a dinner." "*What* a dress."

Use disarming praise: If the mother of a girl asks a reluctant bachelor, "What are your views on marriage?" he could answer, "If I could only be sure that all mothers looked as charming as you. Tell me, how do you manage to do it?"

If the question cannot be refuted logically, use a remark designed to stigmatize the opposer's point of view as being below notice: "Isn't it the duty of government to assist its needy citizens?" Answer: "Do-gooders are taking away people's initiative."

Use humor in answering questions: "Who were the first people to discriminate against you?" (This was asked of a Jewish comedian.) Answer: "My parents."

Counterattack on a point quite irrelevant to the point at issue: "Isn't it the duty of government to assist its needy citizens?" Answer: "Some people want to destroy free enterprise."

Don't answer. The method used can take many forms: you are distracted; you cause a distraction; you intentionally continue creating a distraction by choosing another question or appointing someone else to answer the question.

Consider what occurs when a person asks a question. He has problems too—and look at the interrogator's problems! He lacks the depth and the knowledge of the circumstances that the other party may have to answer the question and he may even lack knowledge of the vocabulary used to describe the circumstances that are involved. He may not really have decided on what he wants to know, and he is not at ease in asking his question. The inquirer may also feel that he cannot reveal the true question because of its sensitive nature. He may also have prejudices against various groups or occupations and consequently may avoid giving a true picture of his own feelings. And finally, the inquirer may lack the confidence in the respondent's ability to deal with the question. These elements must be considered as natural barriers in the questioning process.

NO QUESTIONS ASKED

We have generally been talking about how to handle a question during a business meeting. If one controls the meeting, questioning is automatically disposed of. My interest in this particular field was aroused by Alfred Fleishman's article "How to Sabotage a Meeting," *Etc.,* September 1967. I have used the various strategies outlined in Chapter 9 to show you how a meeting can be disrupted. These also are not given as suggestions but merely to show the possible situations that one may encounter and be prepared for.

- (a) Forbearance. Keep the meeting going; outlast the opposer.
- (b) Surprise. Interrupt the meeting; proper timing is necessary for this to be effective.
- (c) *Fait accompli.* Adjourn the meeting before the opposition has finished speaking.
- (d) Bland withdrawal. Walk out.
- (e) Apparent withdrawal. Do not appear until it is too late for others to accomplish anything.
- (f) Reversal. Call a different meeting at the same time and place.
- (g) Limits. Apply parliamentary procedures; ask for a point of order, etc.
- (h) Feinting. Inform members of the opposition that the meeting was called for a different time and place.
- (i) Participation. Stack the meeting; bring friends.
- (j) Association. Obtain the assistance of associates with a

similar purpose. They enter discussions for their purposes.

(k) Dissociation. Challenge the speaker's veracity or integ-
rity. Indulge in name calling.

(l) Crossroads. Create a diversion; change the subject; bring
in new subjects.

(m) Blanketing. Load up the meeting with friends so the
opposition members cannot get into the room.

(n) Randomizing. Challenge the opposition to a game of
chance. Flip a coin.

(o) Random sample. Throughout the meeting, offer limited
"facts" that the other side cannot verify or disprove immediately.

(p) Salami. Divide the announced purpose of the meeting
into smaller parts and assign each segment to a committee for decision.

(q) Bracketing. Keep suggesting that the meeting was called
for purposes beyond the intention of the opposition, then
short of the intention. Conclude at the midpoint or real
reason.

(r) Shifting levels. Conclude the meeting for the purpose of
calling a smaller—or larger—group together.

CHAPTER 8 APPLICATIONS

1. After reviewing the question matrix, make your own matrix
with five functions of questions on top and five on the left-hand
side. Now draw lines and make twenty-five empty boxes. Fill the
boxes with your own illustrations of questions containing two functions, I-I, I-II, I-III, I-IV, etc., using examples given in this chapter
as a guide. After you have done this you should be able to form
skillful questions that work for you in any negotiation.

2. Make an outline consisting entirely of questions, using the
functions of each question to achieve a desired result in a simple
relationship with a child, salesman, customer, and husband or wife.
Use functional questions so that the end result will be the closing
question.

9

HOW TO RECOGNIZE NEEDS

A GOOD LISTENER

Now consider the other means that can be employed—aside from asking questions and making statements—to recognize the needs of the opposer. One method is listening carefully to the words uttered by the opposer, his phrasing, his choice of expressions, his mannerisms of speech, his tone of voice. All give clues to the needs behind the statements he makes.

But if you would be a good listener, you must bear in mind that conversation or negotiation between individuals can proceed at various levels of meanings. Freud postulated that a dream can be interpreted on three different levels. Similarly, in many instances, a person's conversation or statement has several levels of meaning. For example, the opposer's statement on one level is the message that he *seems* to be trying to communicate. On a second level, it may be the message that we can infer from the way he speaks and the words he uses. On a third level, it may convey a meaning to us because it is linked with his manner of approach to the subject.

Listening is as much a persuasive technique as speaking. A successful listener must keep an open mind and strive to be free from bias and preconceived notions. Every statement can have at least two meanings. George Orwell, in *1984*, gives certain slogans that, at first glance, would seem inconsistent. However, in agreement with Anatole Rapoport, we can see how, under certain circumstances and within certain limits, they make sense. Orwell's fictional slogan, "Freedom is slavery," can be true if there is no restriction on an individual's whims, because then the individual becomes the slave of his whims. His dictum "War is peace" makes some sense if we think of the unifying effects of war on the people of a nation: they are at peace with each other by being united in defense of their country.

Once you are ready to be a good listener, free of bias, anxious to learn something worthwhile about the needs of your opponent—what may you expect to hear?

Sandor S. Feldman, in his book *Mannerisms of Speech and Gestures in Everyday Life* (New York: International Universities Press, Inc., 1959), mentions many common mannerisms of speech that can be important in negotiation. Sometimes they may be attention-getting devices, sometimes they may mean the exact opposite of what the person appears to be saying. However, they give us some insight into the psychological factors present.

We frequently hear the expression "By the way . . ." The speaker wants to give the impression that what he is about to say just entered his mind. But nine times out of ten, what he says is very important and he is only pretending when he gives the casual introductory phrase. When a person begins his sentences with such words as "to be honest," "to tell the truth," "frankly," or "honestly," the chances are that he is *not* being frank or honest. Such expressions are used very frequently as a cover-up.

"Before I forget" is really a nonsensical phrase. If a person is going to forget something, then he will never say it, it will be out of his mind. But if he hasn't forgotten and is going to say it, why introduce the matter with such a phrase? This expression is similar to "by the way," and in both cases there is a pretense that the matter that follows is unimportant. It is actually very important to the speaker and his fear of forgetting is untrue.

If a wife asks her husband, "Do you still love me?" and the hus band answers, "Of course I do," the chances are that the wife will not be satisfied. The phrase "of course" is suspect. It has a shadow of doubt: it implies, "Sure, I love you, but not like in the old days." Had the husband answered with a simple "yes" it would have meant that he really loved her as always and his wife would have been contented. ("More than ever" would be an even better answer.) "Of course" indicates an absence of absolute assurance and the need for self-reassurance.

The term "naturally," so often used, is very similar to "of course" in meaning and implication.

The foregoing speech mannerisms are but a few of the more than 100 given by Dr. Feldman in his book. It should be understood that these phrases have psychological significance. They give us a clue to what is going on in the mind of the opponent. For this reason, listen attentively whenever your adversary makes a statement, and always be alert to spot hidden motives and needs revealed by seemingly innocent recurring phrases.

Sometimes you can become aware of a change in attitude on the part of the other person, not by *what* is said, but by *how* it is said. Assume that the negotiation has been going along smoothly, in a pleasant atmosphere, with all participants calling each other by their first names. Suddenly there is a switch to the surname, "Mr. Jones" or "Mr. Smith." This change is a sign of tension. Even worse, it may signal that an impasse has been reached.

NONVERBAL COMMUNICATION

Besides listening to your opponent in an attempt to learn his desires and needs, you must also closely observe his gestures. For example, in a friendly conference, if one member suddenly sits back and folds his arms with some abruptness, you would know at once that trouble had arrived. Gestures are tremendously important. They convey many shades of meaning, and have their psychological undertones and overtones. Therefore, observe the gestures of your opposer carefully and continuously to gain a clue to his thinking.

We are using the term "gesture" in the broadest possible sense. It includes much more than simple body motions. Tension can be shown by any number of signs such as blushing, contraction of the facial muscles, fidgeting, undue preoccupation, strained laughter or giggling, or even just staring in silence. Actually these are nonverbal means of communication. Dr. Sandor Feldman analyzes over fifty different gestures and other nonverbal expressions. These include bodily movement, posture, facial expression, and mannerisms of all kinds.

In any negotiation you are, of course, talking with your opposer. At the same time you are looking at him and seeing him. Psychologists make a distinction between *looking* and *seeing*. When we examine our outside world, we *look*. It is a form of spying and is objective. But when we *see*, we take in, we absorb, we comprehend the general impression subjectively. Suppose you meet a beautiful lady wearing a low-cut dress that displays the charm of her body. She wants you to *see* her and she will feel hurt if you do not register admiration in some form. But if you give her a look that's a stare and show that you particularly notice the low cut of her dress, then you are spying on her, you have offended her and she will feel compelled to withdraw. You are no gentleman.

Coughing frequently can have many implications. In some instances it has proved to be a form of nervousness, something the speaker depends on to help him go on talking. Often it is used to cover up a lie, or it serves to express doubt or surprise on the part of the listener if someone talks about himself with too much confidence or conceit.

Facial expressions are obvious means of nonverbal communication. But the "poker face" confronts us with a total *lack* of expression, a blank look. This very lack of expression tells us that a man does not want us to know anything about his feelings. In spite of the assumed mask, we can read his intent.

Blinking is a protective reflex action to keep the eyes moist and to remove accumulated dust particles. However, studies have shown that the rate of blinking is higher when we are angry or excited. Normal blinking is hardly noticeable, but when it becomes a mannerism it attracts our attention by its frequency and rapidity. In this abnormal state, blinking has been found to be connected with feelings of guilt and fear. It is used to hide something, and some research indicates that excessive blinking can serve as a lie detector.

Gestures, of course, can be used consciously and effectively in place of words, especially if the words themselves might not be tolerated or allowed. For instance, a lawyer may want to show his disagreement with the judge before a jury, or a soldier may want to indicate a difference of opinion with his top sergeant. But sometimes gestures are *too* expressive. They may reveal more than you want them to. The police claim they can always pick out the top man at a Mafia gathering by observing the extreme deference the others show him.

The skilled negotiator always keeps his eyes and ears fastened on his opposer. As Francis Bacon says in his essay *Of Cunning,* "It is a point of cunning, to wait upon him with whom you speak, with your eyes; as the Jesuits give it in precept: for there be many wise men that have secret hearts and transparent countenances." Emerson stated, "What you are speaks so loudly I cannot hear what you say."

However, no matter how closely you "wait upon him" with your eyes, you cannot completely gauge the emotional state of your opponent. Nevertheless you must always be cognizant of the fact that emotions are lurking in the background whenever two or more people meet and talk. If you are dealing with an emotionally mature person, so much the better. Such a person can accept facts, even unpleasant ones, as concrete situations, to be handled as a means toward a solution of problems, rather than to be hated and thrust aside. It is the emotionally immature person who chooses techniques of negotiation for sheer emotional satisfaction, rather than for achieving a settlement.

The factors that affect emotions may be intangible. The room and setting in which a conference is held can have an effect on the emotions of the conference. The English political leader Ernest Bevin stated, from the experience of a lifetime spent in conferences, that he found that the ones held in cheerful, bright-colored rooms were more successful. The arrangement, location, and details of decoration can have an important influence on negotiation.

Aside from the surroundings, you can learn something by observing the way people move about in the conference room. If a person is interested in what is going on at the conference table, he will lean forward and become part of the group. The moment that he loses interest, he will withdraw or back away from the table.

Silent actions, gestures, and movements of all kinds have something to tell if you can read them correctly. In a situation where you want people to look to you as a person of authority, try to sit at the head of the table. Another seating arrangement involves two groups negotiating at a conference table. Try to sit on the side of the table with the opposing group. Then attempt to take issue with certain propositions proposed by your group, siding with the opposition. In minor things this appears to work, because the opposition begins to consider you as a member of their team. Thereafter they will listen most agreeably to your proposals for solving the points of disagreement.

The difficulty in evaluating nonverbal forms of communicaton is that they are connected, to a great degree, with the subconscious as well as the emotions. In coping with this, use your intuition (which I would define as a half-conscious blend of innumerable minute observations). Men defer to "a woman's intuition." And while woman's intuition might be nothing more than man's transparency, women do, at least, seem more intuitive. A woman looks for the small details and observes them more accurately. Also, any woman who has brought up a child has had to communicate with the infant for two years on a nonverbal basis; this contact with the child from birth further develops intuition in women. We would all be better negotiators if we could acquire the skill in understanding gestures, the ability to observe details, and the intuition that seem to be innate in women.

However, to avoid any generalizations, let me relate this story. A jury was being picked in a criminal trial. As they started the selection, a prospective woman juror rose and told the judge that she wished to be excused. When she was asked why, she stated that one look at the accused had convinced her that he was guilty. With this the judge asked her to sit down and be quiet. The person she was pointing to was the district attorney.

Inborn gestures are very much the same in all parts of the world, but acquired gestures vary in different societies. In the United States, a man usually stands eighteen to twenty inches away when conversing face to face with another man. If talking to a woman, he will back off an additional four inches. But in Latin America men feel comfortable at thirteen inches. This is also true in France. Therefore, an American woman, let us say, in Paris, would feel imposed upon talking to a Frenchman at a distance of only thirteen inches, and he would feel most rejected were she to back away to twenty-four inches. (Could this be a reason why many women believe that Frenchmen are naturally aggressive?)

Cultural differences affect not only our use and interpretations of gestures but also our ways of thinking, and our attitudes toward the social structure. We have different ways of saying things. In English, the clock "runs"; but in Spanish, *el relo anda*, the clock walks. In Spanish, a worker does not miss the bus; the bus left him. According to Stuart Chase, one conflict between the Indians and the early American settlers was due to a difference in the definition of property rights. To the Indian, no individual had exclusive "rights" in fishing or hunting lands. When the Indians sold land for a few knives or beads, they thought they were transferring additional hunting rights only. Naturally, when the palefaces exercised exclusive ownership over the lands, the Indians were bewildered and angry. The Europeans, on the other hand, regarded the Indians as cheats and liars who were not living up to their signed agreements. It was all due to different cultural concepts causing a breakdown in communication.

A cultural difference in the use of the word "no" causes endless trouble between Japanese and American businessmen. The Japanese businessman feels that if he answers with a complete negative he would cause the Americans to lose face. The American businessman, unaware of this, is often forced to negotiate without getting what he would feel is a clear response. Again, this is a breakdown in communication connected with cultural differences.

If you pump a German's hand more than once you confuse him. In India the color of a gift is quite significant: certain shades of green, for example, may give offense to the recipient. In the United States it is the custom for neighbors to call on a new arrival, but in France it is just the reverse. The new resident is obliged to call on the old ones.

Nor are habitual gestures merely a matter of ethnic difference. A man puts on a coat right arm first—a woman puts on the left arm first. When a man helps a woman to put on her coat, there is often a slight awkwardness.

The point is this. To the negotiator, as the old song has it, "every little movement has a meaning all its own." The slight raise of the eyebrow, the tilt of the head, the sudden movement of the hand—all this is a language that the man who deals with people must understand.

It would seem, then, that successful negotiation demands smooth and unobstructed communication at all times. However, do not confuse communication with understanding. In more optimistic times it was believed that if people "understood" each other, there would be fewer breakdowns in communications. We do not have to "understand" people to communicate. Understanding and empathy are long-term goals. But in our time it almost seems that failure to communicate occurs *because* the parties feel they understand each other too well. As in the distinction between looking and seeing, understanding is the nervous (subjective) response to our communication (objective) attempts. I would, however, agree with Dostoevsky, in *The Brothers Karamazov:* "If people around you are spiteful, callous, and will not hear you, fall down before them and beg for their forgiveness; for in truth you are to blame for their not wanting to hear you." This failure in the communication chain is in oneself.

We must negotiate so that our opposer will reveal himself to us. We seek to recognize his needs, his motives, and his desires. We accomplish this by asking questions, by noting his mannerisms and context of speech, by observing his telltale gestures and other nonverbal communication, by allowing for emotional stresses and cultural differences.

CHAPTER 9 APPLICATIONS

1. There are several books on nonverbal communication, such as *How to Read a Person Like a Book* by Gerard Nierenberg and Henry Calero, that give detailed analysis of nonverbal communication. Could such an analysis be useful in your next negotiating session in reading your own gestures as well as reading the gestures of the opposer?

2. Make a list of at least five cultural differences between any two or more cultures with which you are familiar.

10

NEGOTIATING TECHNIQUES

When we have thoroughly prepared—when we have probed the assumptions existing on all sides—and, most particularly, when we have translated our knowledge into an understanding of *needs,* then we have mastered the "pieces" in negotiation.

How we deploy them on the board is a matter of technique—strategy and tactics.

Those two words—strategy and tactics—are clearly differentiated in definition. In practice, however, it is often hard to tell whether a particular move is a bit of strategy or a tactic. In fact, the word *stratagem* seems to combine the idea of strategy and tactic.

So in this chapter we will consider *strategy* as comprising the techniques used in the actual process of negotiation and *tactics* as devices used to implement the strategy.

Many of life's situations may be likened to the techniques we use when we dance in a crowded ballroom. When we move, where we go, how fast we go—all are determined by certain definite conditions: the tempo of the dance music, the partner, the other couples, our mental state, the presumed mental state of the other people, subsconscious adherence to traffic rules and regulations, and so on.

Our strategy, for example, may be to circle the outside of the floor, or it may be to penetrate to the center. The tactics we use—a particular step or change of direction—are governed by that strategy and also by the conditions around us at that moment.

The strategies set forth here are all designed to implement the Need Theory, which we have discussed at some length.

In studying the techniques of successful negotiation, we may think of them as so many tools which we learn to use. The Encyclopaedia Britannica defines a tool as "an implement or appliance used by a worker in the treatment of the substances used in his handicraft, whether in the preliminary operations of setting out and measuring the materials, in reducing his work to the required form by cutting or otherwise, in gauging it and testing its accuracy, or in duly securing it while thus being treated."

In this definition the phrases "preliminary operations" and "setting out and measuring the materials" are analogous to what we do in entering upon a negotiation. Our "preliminary operations" include research, consideration of needs and assumptions, and past experiences in the area under survey. We seek to gauge or measure in advance the hopes and goals of our adversary and ourselves, and their relationship to the conflict and frustrations of the problem being negotiated. During the course of the negotiation we employ other "tools" to accomplish our aims.

The inexperienced negotiator's strategy will be limited to a few simple and obvious devices. The expert negotiator, however, will employ a variety of means to accomplish his objectives. These means will involve "when" strategy or "how and where" strategy.

"When" strategy essentially involves a proper sense of timing. It is easier to use in a negotiation when a new element enters the picture rather than when all elements are static. But properly applied, it can change a static situation into a dynamic one. "How and where" strategy involves the method of application and the area of application. Often it is advantageous to use two or more strategic approaches in the same negotiation. The more familiar you become with various strategic techniques, the better the chance of success in negotiating. Above all, do not rely on the behavior described in "Empedocles on Etna" by Matthew Arnold:

> *We do not what we ought;*
> *What we ought not, we do;*
> *And lean upon the thought*
> *That chance will bring us through.*

The following are examples of a double strategy called "low-balling." This overall strategy combines apparent withdrawal and reversal, two of the basic strategies which will be fully discussed later in the chapter. It is applied on three levels: interpersonal, interorganizational (corporate), and international.

Selling automobiles is a highly competitive business. Many potential buyers try to take advantage of this by going from dealer to dealer with the request, "Just give me the price." Sooner or later the buyer will be hit with a "low-ball" price, one that is too low to be realistic and may even be below the dealer's cost. After the buyer has completed his appointed rounds, he will return to the low-ball dealer. He will expect that since he has completed his negotiation, there is nothing more to talk about. But the negotiations have just begun. The salesman will assail him with "extras" and high-priced financing. He may take the order and never deliver or switch to another car. The low-ball price will be blown to bits.

On the corporate level, the roles can be reversed. This time the seller is the victim, but the strategy is essentially the same. It is used when a business is in dire straits and must be sold immediately. The potential buyer offers a price or a deal that he knows is un-realistically good. He stalls but continues to offer the lure until all other potential buyers have lost interest. Then he offers his real price on a take-it-or-leave-it basis that the seller must accept.

On the international level, "dumping" of surplus goods is an "honest" form of low-balling. The selling price is low, so low that it drives the competing industries in another nation out of business. Then the rival nation enjoys a monopoly position and charges monopoly prices.

"WHEN" STRATEGY

"When" strategy can be separated into several of the following: *forbearance, surprise, fait accompli, bland withdrawal, apparent withdrawal, reversal, limits,* and *feinting.* Here are a few examples of these types of strategy.

Forbearance ("Patience pays"). When you hold off, suspend, put off an answer instead of giving in at that moment, do not answer a question, caucus, or take time out to decide, you are using the strategy of forbearance. Waiting so that your people can think and letting the other side have time to think about it also come under this heading. Younger people call it keeping your cool; in labor relations it might be referred to as a cooling-off period.

The Quakers furnish an example. When members of a Quaker meeting find themselves divided on a question, it is customary to declare a period of silence. If the division still persists, the clerk postpones the question for another time or a later meeting. This can go on indefinitely until the question is resolved. Forbearance thus avoids a direct conflict and eventually achieves a settlement.

Franklin D. Roosevelt used to tell a story about the Chinese use of forbearance, based on four thousand years of civilization. Two coolies were arguing heatedly in the midst of a crowd. A stranger expressed surprise that no blows were being struck. His Chinese friend explained, "The man who strikes first admits that his ideas have given out."

Knowing when to stop is another element of forbearance. The salesman must know when to stop talking. The attorney must know when he has sufficiently cross-examined the witness. Earlier in this book we related the story of the last tenant in the old office building. This negotiation was probably carried past the point where it would have been wise to stop. Benjamin Disraeli recognized this factor when he said, "Next to knowing when to seize an advantage, the most important thing in life is to know when to forego an advantage."

Surprise. This strategy involves a sudden shift in method, argument, or approach. The change is usually drastic and dramatic, although it need not always be so. Sometimes, in fact, the change can be ushered in by as insignificant a sign as the alteration of the tone of voice during a negotiation. Where you have carried on the entire negotiation in a calm, even voice, one blowup can effectively make the point. Surprise can be used as a tactic in negotiation when new information is introduced or a new approach is taken. For example, in the middle of a negotiation it is sometimes effective to substitute a new team leader. Of course, this has its disadvantages, but it can serve the same purpose as substituting a new pitcher when the old one has lost control of the ball. When, during a negotiation, one party flies off the handle and acts completely irrationally, he is very probably using the surprise tactic. The seemingly irrational person feels that this behavior will make it more difficult for the other side to cope with the situation. However, the truly mentally unbalanced person is the most difficult of all to deal with; his behavior never ceases to amaze. He is even more difficult than the inexperienced negotiator.

An Anglo-American company opened a new mine in Zambia's copper belt and brought in workers from a nearby province. The workers and their families were housed in temporary dwellings built near the Kafue River. The company had great, paternalistic plans to build a substantial village with modern housing, electricity, and running water. They assured the workers and their union that building would start "soon." The temporary housing was not satisfactory; not only were the quarters flimsy but the only source of water was the river. The workers and their families had to go down to the river to bathe and to draw water for personal use. To the great distress of management, several children and an occasional wife would turn up missing while bathing in the crocodile-infested river. The obvious solution appeared to be to put in water pipes immediately so that no one would have to go near the river. At the same time management decided to chlorinate the water as a health measure.

After they had announced their "obvious" solution, management was surprised when the union official came and said, "Look, we don't want those water pipes." "Be reasonable," management argued. "You're losing a lot of people. Just accept these pipes temporarily. They're in your better interest. We're even chlorinating the water and getting rid of the fluke, which is causing a severe problem among the workers and their families. We're doing all of this for the workers, and you, Mr. Union, don't want it. Why?"

The union official refused to discuss the matter, so management investigated. They found that the union believed that if the water pipes were installed temporarily, management would never get around to building permanent housing. They feared that unless pressure was brought on it, the company would not make the capital investment that a permanent village would require. They were quite prepared, even at the cost of human lives, to accept the present conditions if that would put pressure on management and expedite the building of permanent housing.

Management decided to ignore the union's protest and installed the pipes. Two weeks later all the piping was smashed and, of course, the workers and their families returned to the river for water. Management found that the union had spread a rumor in the village that the chlorine in the water was used specifically as a birth-control measure so that the women's work in the mine would not be interrupted.

Although management tried again to reason with the union, it was to no avail. The union by its intransigent position forced the management to build permanent housing at a considerably faster rate than they would have if the workers and the crocodiles could have been separated. To the surprise of the management, the union worked against its own people's short-term interests to force management's hand.

Fait accompli (*"Now it's up to you"*). This is a risky strategy but there is often a temptation to use it. It demands that you act, achieve your goal against the opposition, and then see what the other side will do about it. Those who employ this strategy must make an appraisal of the consequences in case it should prove to be a failure. An illustration of the unsuccessful application of this strategy was the attack by England, France, and Israel upon Egypt during the Suez crisis. They acted without prior consultation with the United States and hoped to present the world with a *fait accompli*. The United States intervened, however, and forced them to abandon the attack and to withdraw.

In direct examination of an unsavory witness a lawyer will sometimes bring out all the bad things that can be said about him before the opposition can cross-examine and make his past seem even worse. The other side is presented with a *fait accompli*.

In the mergers of conglomerates today, we can often see the use of this tactic. If, before the merger actually takes place, the Justice Department indicates that it might object, quite often the conglomerate will go ahead with the merger and present the government with a *fait accompli*. In effect the conglomerate says, "It's done. Now what are you going to do about it?" The government may feel that breaking up the merger is more trouble than the "illegality" is worth. Of course, to be concluded successfully, a *fait accompli* requires recognition by the other party. If no action is taken, the user is likely to find himself in the position of Chief Justice John Marshall when he presented President Andrew Jackson with a ruling Jackson refused to accept. "John Marshall has made his decision," the President said. "Now let him enforce it." It was never enforced.

The *fait accompli* is useful in other situations. If a contract is sent to you which contains a provision you do not agree with, cross out that portion that you do not want, sign the contract, and send it back. Your opposer, confronted with a *fait accompli,* can either return the contract and reopen the negotiation, or accept the deletion. Quite often he will accept the changed contract.

Bland withdrawal ("Who, me?") A company located in the East decided to build a factory in Texas. Plans called for structural steel to be used in the building. After meeting with their board and discussing their problem, the management realized that they would have to use structural steelworkers, most of whom were members of a strong Texas union which commanded high wages and was not easy to deal with.

Rather than pay union scale, the company used its own workers to begin construction. The factory was well advanced before the steelworkers' union caught up with the situation. "You can't do that," they protested. "That's nonunion." The management said, "What? We didn't know. We thought that we could bring our own construction workers to Texas. We'll hire only authorized union workers from now on."

The union was satisfied that the problem was so easily solved; the company was more than happy to have put the most costly part of the construction work behind them at a considerable saving over the Texas union labor costs.

In the franchising field, bland withdrawal has been used with varying success. The franchisor has an obligation to his franchisee to anticipate in the operation manual any situation that may arise in the course of running the business. The franchising firm often takes years to work out operational situations to prepare in every way to meet the unexpected and to try to give the franchisee the benefit of experience. One such careful planner was a motel-chain franchisor.

He told me the following story: A guest at a franchisee's motel had found a bedbug in his room and, incensed, wrote an indignant letter to the operator of the motel. The operator replied promptly, using the form letter suggested by the franchisor. It dwelt at length on the pleasure it gave management to hear from the motel's guests; it stated that it was their obligation to keep the lines of communication with the customers open, that the customers paid his salary, that management was delighted to hear even of such unusual situations as the one described in the letter; that however rare the situation might be it would be looked into personally and taken care of forthwith. The guest was suitably mollified as he finished the operator's letter, but then he discovered that his own letter was inadvertently attached to the response. On it in red pencil was boldly printed: *"Send bedbug form letter."*

Apparent withdrawal ("The man who wasn't there"). This strategy is made up of a mixture of forbearance, self-discipline, and a little deception. The aim is to convince your opponent that you have withdrawn, but without his knowing it, you are still in control of the situation. I used this strategy with a certain degree of success in litigation involving the Rent Commission of the City of New York. The Rent Commission had determined that a hearing be scheduled at a time that was arbitrary and would prove detrimental to my client. The New York Supreme Court agreed that the scheduling of the proposed hearing would be detrimental. However, instead of granting an injunction, which had been requested, the court merely suggested to the Rent Commission that it should postpone the hearing. In spite of the request of the court, the Rent Commission went ahead with the hearing, I attended this hearing, but before it began, I had the official stenographer take down a statement for the record: "I warn everyone in attendance that this hearing is being held against the wishes of the Supreme Court; I will see to it that the court is so informed and I will follow this matter through to its normal consequences. Moreover, I will not be a party to this hearing at this time." Having made this statement, I stalked out of the room. My withdrawal apparently was complete. However, unknown to the hearing officer of the Rent Commission, an associate of mine remained in the hearing room. Seated with a group of witnesses that had been called, he was prepared to take over in the event that the Rent Commission chose to go ahead with the hearing. This strategy, fortunately, was effective. The person in charge of the hearing was unsure of how to proceed. He called the rent commissioner for advice and was told to adjourn the hearing. Thereafter the commissioner was persuaded that landlords are members of the community, and important ones, and that no one can be victimized without harm to everybody.

In the field of acquisition, an illustration of apparent withdrawal would be where a public company receives word that another corporation is trying to acquire them. The effort has already begun in the marketplace and stock is being bought up. Then after the public company has taken one retaliatory action or another, whether effective or not, the acquiring corporation withdraws. It seems to have been stopped or frightened off. The withdrawal is only apparent, however; the acquiring corporation is now working behind the scenes, going to mutual funds or optioning the stock of those who have heard of their attempt to buy control and who have come to them sub rosa. This continues for a time, then suddenly the public company wakes up to find that the acquiring corporation has been working underground and has gained control. The reason for the apparent withdrawal, after making known that they were interested in the acquisition, was that this allowed the public company's alleged friends to approach them with less fear of discovery and help them in their task.

Reversal (*"You can go forward, backward"*). In this strategy, you act in opposition to what may be considered to be the popular trend or goal. Bernard Baruch once said that people who make money in the stock market are those who are the first in and the first out. By this he meant that you should buy when everyone was pessimistic and sell when the prevailing atmosphere was optimistic. This strategy may sound easy to execute, but in reality it is exceedingly difficult. Were it not so, we could all immediately become rich and powerful.

Gertrude Stein reserved a popular concept about Wall Street when she said that the money remains the same, it is merely the pockets that change.

In the days following World War II the left-wing American Labor Party was prominent in New York politics. The ALP had formed an extreme aversion to a certain Brooklyn state senator, and had decided to "go after" him. They entered a candidate in the

Democratic primary in the district, and there was a possibility that they might not only beat him, but gain control of the Democratic Party in that district.

The senator refused to knuckle under and work for the endorsement of the American Labor Party. His problem was to prevent the ALP from "making an example" of him.

The senator and his staff decided on a strategy of reversal. They would make a bid to take over the American Labor Party in that district by entering a candidate in *their* primary. Squads of workers went out, and in two days enough signatures were accumulated to make an ALP primary fight feasible. Then the truce flag went up. The American Labor Party agreed not to fight the state senator if he would withdraw from the primary. The strategy worked perfectly.

Reversal strategy permits you to think of new alternatives. There is nothing that states a priori or even logically that if the company makes more money it must pay higher wages to its union workers. The union would most certainly not accept as absolutely necessary the concept that if the company's profits are lower, its workers will receive less money.

A few years ago on a visit to Brazil, a friend went to an art dealer in Rio, looking for a painting to take home. He was particularly drawn to a painting—the biblical battle of Jericho done in primitive style. The pictures in the gallery were selling for $100 to $150, but when he asked the dealer the price of this particular painting he was told, "Five hundred dollars." Although it was a fine painting, he was amazed at the difference in prices and asked the reason. My friend insisted on knowing why and at last was told the story.

It seems an Indian from the northern Amazon jungle came to the shop one day, bringing with him three paintings. The dealer recognized their merit and was immediately willing to pay as much as he paid established artists in Rio—about fifty dollars a painting. He asked the Indian how much he wanted, and the Indian replied, "Two hundred and fifty dollars for the three paintings."

"That's impossible," the dealer said. "I couldn't possibly afford that much."

They discussed the matter for a time, but the Indian would not budge from his original demand. The dealer began to get angry and, seeing this, the Indian went outside, deposited one of the paintings in a trash can and set it on fire. This was too much for the art dealer to bear. He rushed outside and shook the Indian. "What are you doing?" he said. "You've destroyed a beautiful work of art! Why don't we come to terms? How much for the remaining two paintings?"

The Indian said, "Two hundred and fifty dollars."

The dealer refused to believe the price and tried to reason with him, but the Indian obstinately refused to consider any other offer. When it became clear that the matter would not be solved, the Indian marched out again, burned a second painting, and waited impassively for the dealer to come to him. "Please," said the dealer, "don't destroy the last painting. How much do you want?"

"Two hundred and fifty dollars."

And that is the reason, my friend told me, that he paid a retail price of five hundred dollars for the biblical battle of Jericho he brought back from Brazil.

Some people take to reversal strategy quite naturally. One such man read that smoking was injurious to health, so he decided to give up reading. In another case a business was in a unique field and, being without competition, it had become highly successful. At a meeting of the board of directors it was determined that the company would set up an independent competitive company before someone else did so.

The Trollope ploy is a form of reversal strategy. In it two messages are received from your opposer. You accept that message which you think is advantageous and ignore the other one. What we might call the double Trollope is more complex. In using this strategy, you intentionally send two messages forcing the opposer to accept the less onerous one. For example, if mild demands are first made and then are followed by stronger demands, the other side will react to and be more likely to accept the milder demands.

Double reversal has its advantages. For example, a few years ago a major airline was building a large complex in New York City and wanted lower electric rates than Con Edison charged. Con Edison turned them down, saying that the Public Service Commission would not permit it, that the rate schedule would not sanction it. The negotiations came to a standstill. The airline then engaged a group of engineers to determine costs for an independent electricity-producing facility. The airline saw that the cost was not too high and that the investment could probably be amortized, so they were ready to go ahead and build. When Con Edison heard of this, they reversed their position at once. They applied to the Public Service Commission for a much lower rate for this type of user. The Commission immediately approved the new rates. To Con Edison's consternation, the airline would not now buy at the new rate but insisted they were going ahead with their plans for a generating plant. Con Edison reversed itself a second time, went back to the Commission, and obtained a still lower rate. Only then were they able to close a deal with the airline. The airline, however, was not the only beneficiary of these negotiations. Now all commercial users of large quantities of electricity in New York City are entitled to the same reduced rates that Con Edison offered the airline.

Limits ("This is the absolute end"). Limits can be of many types. There are communication limits, those placed on each negotiating-team member as to what he may talk about and to whom he may talk; time limits; and geographical limits—as a proposal applying to only one section of the country or only to one company. When a party sets a limit, there is no reason why you must be restricted by it unless it suits your purpose to conform. In legislatures, when a limit is reached—let us say, December 1, at midnight—discussion will stop. If some legislature members still want the opportunity to speak, the clock is stopped before midnight while discussion continues. In negotiation, if you choose to ignore a limit, try to save face for the person who has set the limit. Humor can often be helpful in this regard. Once when a limit was set at 5 o'clock, the other side drew a cartoon of a clock face without the numeral 5. This released the tension and the negotiations continued.

One experienced negotiator if possible calls meetings three days before Christmas or Thanksgiving. This sets a natural time limit. The other side does not want the negotiations to go over so that they will miss the opportunity of being with their families. I have seen this strategy solve a problem for the management of a public company that was interested in a merger. The majority of the stockholders favored a merger, but the minority stockholders did not have the rosy optimism of the majority and threatened to bring suit. In order to solve the problem, majority stockholders gave the minority a "put"—that is, in the event that the stock went below a certain price the minority stockholders were guaranteed the higher price. A limit was set as to any possible loss that they might experience. In consideration for this the minority agreed to the merger.

Sometimes negotiators limit communications coming from the negotiation when the issues involved should concern only the parties to the negotiation and not be used for publicity value.

Finally, limits of many sorts may be employed merely to test the strength of your position. If your opposer pushes you to the limit you know that he does not consider your position to be a strong one or he may be testing you. It is of importance to have other counterstrategies available.

Feinting ("Look to the right, go to the left"). This involves an apparent move in one direction to divert attention from the real goal or object. It can also involve a situation in which you give your opponent a false impression that you have more information or knowledge than you really possess. This strategy has been successfully used in criminal trials. The district attorney is duty-bound to tell the court all of the information and facts that he has in his possession. He may not withhold from the court any evidence that may be pertinent to the case even though it may not help the prosecution. He does not always do this. Feinting strategy by defense counsel may lead the district attorney to believe that counsel is in possession of "all" the information and, therefore, the district attorney may feel the obligation *now* to tell the court all rather than continue to withhold pertinent facts.

Today, because of the speed of communication, a prepared governmental decision can be tested by feinting. The decision is released by "a reliable source" as a trial balloon before it is actually made. This gives the government an opportunity to test the different responses that might occur when and if such a decision is actually made. Then, if opposition develops, it can either develop a strategy to counteract adverse responses or decide upon a new solution to the problem.

In Buffalo, New York, one of the largest hotels in the city for many years was the Hotel Buffalo, the first big Statler hotel. Statler himself intended to keep it that way. When he built the first hotel, he had complete plans drawn up for a second hotel which were always ready for use. Whenever word would reach him of a group of hotelmen coming to Buffalo to look at potential sites, Statler would file his plans with the Building Department and make sure that word of it got to his potential rivals. On learning of the filing of the plans, the hotelmen would abandon their project because of Statler's feint, and Statler would withdraw his plans to use them another day.

In the course of a negotiation, feinting can be useful if you are giving in on a point that is not especially important to you. Make the concession sound very important, however, and if you are dealing with someone who does not have awareness of the entire situation, be sure that he works for the concession before you grant it. Feinting can be used when you want to cover up important elements. Ignore the important and stress the things that are not important to you.

"HOW AND WHERE" STRATEGY

Some of the principal forms of "how and where" strategy are *participation, association, disassociation, crossroads, blanketing, randomizing, random sample, salami, bracketing, agency, and shifting levels.*

Participation (*"We are friends"*). In this form of strategy you strive to enlist the aid of other parties in your behalf, to act either directly or indirectly. International alliances like NATO or the Warsaw Pact are good examples of this form. Each participant will probably assist the other with his individually different strategy. This includes "me too," strategy, such as has been used in the maritime labor relations field. As reported in *The New York Times,* August 28, 1965: "Almost every [Maritime] Union has a clause in its contract that if something better than what the contract terms delineate is later granted to another union, it will be automatically added to the first contract." The *Times* stated that "this is one of the chief reasons why the Merchant Marine strike went through its 73rd day without a settlement." It would appear that this strategy of the union backfired.

If you reach a deadlock at the negotiating table, it is often helpful to persuade both sides to assign two team members to participate separately, away from the negotiating table, try to resolve the difference, then come back to the negotiation later.

Coalition bargaining is an expansion and refinement of participatory negotiation. The National Labor Relations Board has ruled that an employer cannot be forced to bargain with all the unions involved at the same time. However, members of other unions can sit in while one particular union negotiates a contract with the employer. In this way the other unions get a good idea of the employer's strategy and may even be able to hold the employer to certain proposals he has made or cite his reasons and excuses for not giving in on a particular issue when their own negotiations come up subsequently. Other names given to this procedure are coordinated bargaining or conspiratorial bargaining, depending on which side of the table you are on.

Participation need not be one-sided. Both employer and union officials can sometimes benefit by acting together. A construction-industry executive once used this strategy to solve a difficult problem. He was offered a subcontracting job involving many buildings. Other subcontractors were reluctant to become involved because, they said, the union would force them into a form of contract that would be a straitjacket. They claimed that anyone would lose money on that job. The executive decided to take a chance anyway.

When the union presented its rather harsh contract demands, the contracting executive, instead of opposing them, tried to get the union officials to participate with him. He examined the offered contract clause by clause and asked the officials how they would handle the situation, how, by participating with him, they could show him ways to comply with the regulations and still be able to make a reasonable profit. The union officials got into the spirit and showed him that it was not so difficult. From their "real" experience they would show him, first, how to comply and, second, how to benefit from compliance.

One clause that seemed unbearable to him stated that no one but a teamster could drive a truck on the job. He, for example, had only to bring a small cake of ice onto the job site, yet to comply with the clause the subcontractor would have to have a teamster on duty all the time. This, the executive said, was clearly unreasonable. The union officials saw it differently. "Why don't you merely subcontract this one-hour job to one of the other major subcontractors? They have teamsters on their payroll. That would be compliance as far as we're concerned." So it went throughout the discussion. Instead of opposing the union officials, the executive made them participators and was able to handle the job successfully.

Participation can be especially important when you are contemplating a merger or acquisition. One of the ways of using this strategy is to let the seller know that you will continue to operate in the same tradition and manner in which the business has been run. After the merger, buyer and seller can participate together and run the business on a mutually satisfactory basis. This is a useful negotiating technique when you are trying to buy a family business with a long tradition of service.

Association ("You and me, kid"). Attorneys and other consultants are asked many times to accept less than their standard fee because the people or project they will be involved with are considered "prestige." After the consultant has been around for a while he knows that in many instances he is being taken advantage of. But still he gets clients who say, "This is a very unusual case [or project]. If you take this case it will be a feather in your cap." The client uses the strategy of association, attempting to get the consultant associated with the project for prestige, not mere dollars. I once heard an experienced attorney answer such a plea with "Look, if I took all the feathers off my cap and put them on my tail, I could fly around this room."

The celebrated Domino Theory that has dominated the thinking of many U.S. policy-makers for more than twenty-five years is also an example of association. Also called the Chain-reaction Theory, it rationalizes that if one country falls to communism, other countries will fall in a similar fashion.

One night a businessman was seen by his wife with a young lady. When he came home later, his wife asked, "Who was that girl you were with tonight?"

When he replied, "My mistress," his wife flew into a rage and ordered him out of the house.

"Hold your temper," he said. "Don't you have a wonderful family, a beautiful home, furs, your own car, and everything your heart desires? You don't want to throw it all away. Anyway, you know what tomorrow is?"

"Yes," she whined, "it's our anniversary."

"Well," he said, "we're going to a great restaurant and show. So let's have a good time."

The next night at dinner, while celebrating their anniversary, the wife looked across the room, then turned to her husband.

"Isn't that your partner from the office?" she asked.

"Yes."

"Who's the young lady with him?"

"That's his mistress."

She looked at her husband and said with self-satisfaction, *"Our* mistress is prettier than *his* mistress."

This technique is used extensively in the advertising field. Testimonials assert that a famous person uses and endorses a certain cigarette, soap, hairdressing, or some other product. These testimonials associate the product with the rich, important, powerful personages who endorse it. Many people identify themselves with these personalities and begin to use the product.

Many businessmen who feel that they would be too sophisticated to be influenced by this advertising tactic fail to realize it is related to the business device of electing famous military, scientific, or political figures to the board of directors of corporations. The corporation is now supposed to benefit from the "halo" effect of these famous people.

Disassociation (*"Who is your friend?"*) Obviously this strategy is the reverse of association. A product, or more frequently a cause, is discredited by showing that unsavory characters are connected with it. This is a form of strategy that is often used in politics by both the extreme left and the extreme right. It calls the attention of the general public to the kind of people who are associated with a particular movement, cause, or proposal. It is hoped that the assumed reputation of the people connected with the movement will steer the public in the opposite direction, away from the association.

The American Tobacco Company contended that it wanted to expand its operations and had in truth become a conglomerate and therefore would change its name to reflect its new interests. The new name, American Brands, did suggest a wider interest, but it must be said that the timing of the move indicated the company was also concerned with the bad connotations that "tobacco" had acquired during the 1960's and wanted to dissociate itself from them.

Sometimes strategies in negotiation come up inadvertently. For example, the Japanese embassy in Washington, in order to comply with a request for American-made machinery, invited representatives of two companies to meet with the purchasing agent of the Japanese concern. One of the sales representatives was a garrulous man, the other was rather quiet. The talkative man dominated the conversation, leaving the quiet one on the sidelines unable to do more than nod his head in agreement with the pleasantries that were offered. He could not help feeling, however, that he had lost the sale, when the other American said, "I love your country. I can't wait to come back on a more extensive visit." The Japanese purchasing agent politely asked him when he was last there. "In 1945," the talkative man said, inadvertently revealing that he was part of the American occupation forces in Japan. When he also disclosed he had been a U.S. Air Force bombardier in the Pacific during the war, the silent salesman knew he could relax. He had the order. Dissociation worked for him.

Crossroads (*"Intersect, entwine, and entangle"*). In this form of strategy you may introduce several matters into the discussion so that you can make concessions on one and gain on the other. Minor issues, however, should be handled carefully. If you take too much time with them, the other side will start fighting back as if they were large issues. Then as the opponent gives in, he does it expecting a concession on a major issue. It also covers the situation where you bring forces, arguments, or pressures of some kind to bear on a particular object of the negotiation. This corresponds to a military tactic in which machine guns are placed so as to create a devastating crossfire and cover an area more thoroughly. In chess, this approach is used where pressure from many pieces is applied to one of the opponent's pieces or spaces.

The crossroads strategy can also be used to raise a counterdemand as a temporary issue when your opposer has made what you feel is an uncalled-for demand. For example, if the union negotiators should say, "We now want a shorter workweek," the employer might reply, "In view of the fact that you are now asking for a shorter workweek, on that basis we want you to give up several of the extra holidays that we had previously agreed on."

Raising a secondary (straw) issue to conceal your main concern might be considered under this heading.

Blanketing (*"Shotgun coverage"*). In blanketing, one technique is to try to cover as large an area as possible to achieve a breakthrough in one or more places. In reverse order, to avoid a breakthrough by your opposer, you can cover a large segment with more force and more pressure than might be necessary. The Rockefellers with their tremendous investment in New York real estate were anxious to keep land values high by bringing as many prestigious institutions to New York as they could. John D. Rockefeller, Jr., felt that one such prize would be the establishing of United Nations headquarters in the city. The story is told that William Zeckendorf, who was a real estate broker at the time, discussed the project with Rockefeller and was authorized to put together a parcel of land that would be suitable for the U.N.

With Rockefeller money behind him, Zeckendorf used the blanketing strategy. He looked over a parcel of land on New York City's East Side. It contained mainly run-down slaughterhouses and meat-packing plants. He had estimates made of the value of all the pieces of property as closely as he could and made sure he had a good idea of what each owner would sell for. Then he offered to buy for double that price. This assured the assembling of the land rapidly before prices ballooned as the owners learned that they had a claim on Rockefeller money.

Another aspect of blanketing is where you want to prevent your opposer from knowing where you weakness lies. You can inundate him with evidence or information in an attempt to hide that area which you consider your weak spot.

Frequently when the union and an employer are ready to negotiate and the union has many demands, the employer will try any number of devices to prevent the union from setting forth its demands first. One employer systematically came into the negotiation room early each day, set up a blackboard, and filled the entire board with *his* demands. He did not leave a single open space on which the union could write. This visible reminder of the employer's demands took the initiative away from the union and prevented it from immediately setting forth *its* demands.

There is a certain group of businessmen who are called "deal men." They are in a sense business brokers, trying to bring together the buyer and seller or other elements required. Different techniques are used by the more sagacious. However, the ordinary deal man uses the "shotgun" method. Without regard to the consequences, he brings together as many people as possible, hoping that two of them may match up and permit him to make a commission. I myself prefer the "rifle" method.

Randomizing ("Outbluffing by chance"). In this strategy, you make use of the law of chance to defeat the "bluffing advantage" in a game. For example, I had become quite proficient in the game of "guess which hand the coin is in." By sleight of hand I fooled my son over and over again. He continually made a very high percentage of wrong guesses. Then he decided to base his guesses on the law of chance. He tossed his own coin to decide his choice. When he did this he guessed right at least 50 percent of the times, over a long period of guesses and tosses. Randomizing, using the law of chance, improved his score by making my bluffing useless.

There will always be those fortunate people—the clappers in the bell-shaped curve—who can deal with statistics and the laws of probability to ring the bell. One such person was Baron Long, a famous gambler in the 1920's. Baron Long made his big killing at the Agua Caliente racetrack in Mexico. He used the maneuver of "building."

"Building" calls for a system of betting in which offtrack bookmakers pay at track odds. The track odds are, of course, based on the total amount wagered at the track on each horse. When the offtrack bookies pay at track odds they are able to keep for themselves the percentage taken off by the track for expenses and taxes.

To make his killing Baron Long had to rig the track odds so that the payoff on the fastest horses—the favorites—was far greater than the risk involved. To do this he had a large group of associates line up at the track betting windows. They kept the public from betting the favorites. At the same time they were upsetting the odds by wagering on the poorer horses in the race.

Meanwhile, other associates were making huge bets on the favorites with the offtrack bookies. The favorite won, at track odds approaching 1000 to 1. The bookies who did not go out of business were forced to pay off at that price.

After this the bookies changed their strategy to prevent a recurrence of this maneuver. Nevertheless, the same trick was worked in Great Britain in 1964 at a greyhound track. The mastermind, a gambler named John Turner, lined up his men in front of the windows, *à la* Baron Long. They manipulated the odds on the race so that the payoff on the winning combination was 9875 to 1. The bookmakers, who operate legally in Great Britain, went to court—but in 1965 a High Court judge found nothing illegal in the stratagem. The judge described it as a battle of wits in which Mr. Turner had come out on top. Obviously even bookies who learn from the past are doomed to repeat it.

There was once a particular type of con man known as the "Murphy man." The Murphy man used the strategy of randomizing. In the 1920's, the name and game originated in the area west of Times Square known as Hell's Kitchen. This section was heavily populated by Irish immigrants. The technique of the con man was to approach a stranger in the area, offering, for a price, to obtain a girl for him. If the victim gave him some money, the con man would then take him to a tenement house and instruct him to "ring Mrs. Murphy's doorbell," the odds being that there was a Murphy somewhere in the building. You will note today that this con game is still in existence. The names have changed but the game is the same.

Random sample (*"Fibbers can figure"*). This involves picking a sample and assuming that the sample that has been chosen will represent the whole. Political parties use this quite frequently to show the general public that a survey they have taken indicates that their candidate will be the winner. The deception consists in planting the people who take the survey in carefully selected areas. Statistics presented in negotiations are often based on random samples and must be closely scrutinized. How to detect biased samples, deceptive averages, and other irregularities is set forth in *How to Lie with Statistics* by Darrell Huff and Irving Geis.

There is the story of the traveler who was reluctant to fly in an airplane because he heard about people carrying bombs on planes. Discussing his fear with a friend, a statistician, he asked him, "What is the probability of a bomb being on the same plane that I might take?" The statistician figured it out and came up with something like 1 in 10 million. The traveler thought awhile, and then said, "What is the probability of two bombs being on the same plane?" The statistician worked it out and replied, "I wouldn't be concerned. The probability is so remote, it could never happen in your lifetime." A year later the traveler met the statistician and the statistician asked him how things were going. "Oh, I've been flying all over. Now I'm no longer concerned about someone bringing a bomb aboard the plane that I'm on. I always carry a bomb with me." Hijacking and searching have outdated this story.

Difficult as it may be to believe, a story has it that the Beatles owe part of their early success to the strategy of random sample. The late Brian Epstein, their manager, recognized the group's potential long before the general public knew of their existence. The Beatles' initial popularity was limited to the Liverpool area. Their records did not show up on the overall hit charts.

Brian Epstein decided to change all of this. He sent his agents into the various towns in England where the record charts were compiled. Within a concentrated period of time they bought up Beatle records (which Epstein then resold in his own record shops). The Beatles' popularity rating zoomed—and they were off to the races. One result of this strategy is that Britain was helped to balance its books for some time.

In the fall of 1967, when President Johnson's popularity was at a low ebb, certain backers arranged for polls to be taken. The polls were restricted to areas where Johnson was likely to be very strong. Furthermore, they pitted him against not too strong opponents. The results were then publicized as an upturn in the President's popularity. The research firms involved were chagrined, but the backers of the polls had accomplished what they had set out to do.

A large firm wanted to spin off one of its subsidiary wholesale companies. Before they made the move, however, management decided it would be advantageous for them if they could prove some market dominance of the subsidiary. They called in a respected research agency and suggested that a survey be done in the wholesale area. The holding company narrowed down the survey guidelines so that no competitive products were in the particular area chosen. Needless to say, the conclusion reached by the independent research agency was that the subsidiary had a 70 percent market dominance in the area. This made the spinoff wholesale company seem most desirable.

Most of the time when you get a random sampling, you have no idea where the sampling or the control sample came from. Even if you know, the bias inherent in the sample still might not be obvious. A humorous advertisement on television once claimed that nine out of ten doctors ate a particular brand of chop suey. Then they presented a picture of the ten doctors. One was white and nine were Chinese.

Salami ("A slice at a time"). This strategy involves taking something bit by bit, so that you eventually get possession of the entire piece. Mátyás Rákosi, General Secretary of the Hungarian Communist Party, is credited with having given this technique its name. Rákosi explained the "salami" operation to his collaborators as follows: "When you want to get hold of a salami which your opponents are strenuously defending, you must not grab at it. You must start carving for yourself a very thin slice. The owner of the salami will hardly notice it, or at least he will not mind very much. The next day you will carve another slice, then still another. And so, little by little, the whole salami will pass into your possession." This nibbling process has been very much in evidence in the actions of the Communists since World War II.

In line with this approach, never make it appear that you are trying to take anything away from your adversary, no matter how slight. A good salesman in the nut store does not overload the tray with nuts and then remove a portion of them in order to get the proper weight. He gradually builds the order up to the proper weight, adding, never subtracting.

The salami tactic enables you to get your toe in the door. Large firms understand that an initial selling stage is to create an opening, do something for a potential customer, get a small slice of the action. A good example of the salami tactic was in the mortgage redemption insurance business. In past years insurance companies sold insurance to people when they took out mortgages on their new homes. The insurance would be used to pay off the mortgage in the event that the wage earner died or was disabled. One insurance company was a Johnny-come-lately to the field. Its salesmen found that the management of the largest savings-and-loan banks were not interested in giving their leads to more than one company. To meet the situation the new company instructed its men to try a new tactic.

"Look," they would tell the bankers, "we're offering you a new type of service. We are not going to solicit customers personally as your old company does, and we're not going to call on the customer when he first makes the loan, as they do. We're going to service your accounts in an entirely different way. We will use direct mail exclusively and we want only the names of customers who have not bought insurance from your present insurance company. We feel that you owe it to your bank and mortgagors to be given a double opportunity to protect your investment with insurance." The bank was forced to agree. The mail solicitation was extremely successful. The holders of the mortgages were in a better position to buy insurance after they had owned their houses for several years. They had more responsibilities, were more mature, and were better able to afford it.

Before much time had passed, 90 percent of the mortgage insurance went to the new firm. As soon as they reached this position, they went to the banks and said, "We now have ninety percent of the business. Don't you think that the type of service we are giving warrants our covering your customers one hundred percent?" Soon they were the sole surviving insurance company servicing the savings-and-loan associations in their area. They used the salami tactic in other areas with equal success and ended up servicing many of the banks throughout the United States.

The U.S. government uses the salami tactic to withdraw from certain defense manufacturing areas. Instead of cutting off the defense industries completely, they use a more subtle approach. They call it "phasing out," which really means that slowly, a slice at a time, they decrease their orders with a particular manufacturer until he is supplying nothing to the Defense Department.

Bracketing ("How to make and hit the mark"*).* This expression is taken from the old artillery term in which the first shell was arranged to fire above the target, the second below the target, and thereafter this bracket was split successively until reduced to an on-target distance. An executive of a large business firm explained his ability to retain his top position by saying he used the strategy of bracketing. His duties require him to make many decisions. He does not spend all of the decision time trying to be "right on target." He is satisfied if he is in the right area. Thereafter he merely cuts down the degree of error.

When a debtor has not paid a bill, try billing him for a larger amount than due. He will usually call to dispute your figures, verify the correct amount that he owes you, and probably be quite reasonable about settling the smaller debt.

An employer had a contract with a tailoring union. Although the contract recognized four classifications of workers, all were paid the same standard rate. In the opinion of the employer the standard rate was a high one. However, this did not stop the union from asking for still higher wages. The employer had a counter-proposal: he was willing to increase the wages—of course, not as much as the union wanted—but he wanted the job classifications to be redefined. Instead of four, he wanted six classifications. The union, in consideration of the wage increase, did extend the classi-fications. The employer was willing to agree to a grandfather clause —that is, none of the employees then on the payroll would be subject to the new classifications—and to pay still higher wages to top expert tailors. However, he would also over a period of time pay lower rates for less skilled labor. By bracketing, paying a lower rate and a higher rate, he was able to average out the wages with the median wage right on his target.

Agency. The possible uses of an agent in negotiation are so im-portant that they are being presented here as a separate strategic topic. It has been contended that partisan zeal should be every attorney's byword. It should also be the byword of every agent representing parties to a negotiation.

Sometimes it is expedient to let an agent conduct your negotia-tion for you. Certain circumstances may force you to such a de-cision; it can occur in any negotiation. Francis Bacon, in his essay *Of Negociating,* wrote of agents:

It is generally better to deal . . . by the mediation of a third than by a man's self. . . . In choice of instruments, it is better to choose men of a plainer sort, that are like to do that that is committed to them, and to report back again faithfully the success, than those that are cunning to contrive out of other men's business somewhat to grace themselves, and will help the matter in report for satisfaction sake. Use also such persons as affect the business wherein they are employed; for that quickeneth much; and such as are fit for the matter; as bold men for expostulation, fair-spoken men for persuasion, crafty men for inquiry and observation, forward and absurd men for business that doth not well bear out itself. Use also such as have been lucky, and prevailed before in things wherein you have employed them; for that breeds confidence, and they will strive to maintain their prescription.

Here is an instance in which the role of an agent was played with good results.

A conference had been arranged between my client and his adversary. His attorney and I were also to be present. My client failed to show up at the appointed time. After waiting for him quite a while, I suggested that we begin the negotiation. As our talk went on, I found that I was being singularly successful in getting the opposition to make commitments; but every time they asked me for a commitment, I would say, "Well, I'm sorrry, but I only have limited authority." By serving in the role of an agent, I secured many concessions for my client without committing him in any way.

The technique of giving the negotiating agent only limited authority or tying him down to specific instructions beyond which he dare not commit himself has proved extremely advantageous in many cases. The opposing party, realizing that the agent is bound to live up to his instructions, is more restrained in his demands.

In certain cases the agent may have an additional individual incentive to secure a favorable settlement. For example, when an insurance company represents a defendant in an automobile accident case, it is acting as an agent on behalf of the defendant. It also has an incentive to get the best possible settlement because it will have to pay for any damages awarded to the plaintiff, together with court costs.

Sometimes it is judicious to delegate all authority to an agent. Businessmen do this when they place their employees under fidelity bonds. Should any case of theft or dishonesty arise, they are relieved of the task of prosecuting or condoning the crime. They do not have the authority to act because they have placed or delegated full authority in the hands of the insurance company. This arrangement saves them from having to make many troublesome decisions. One man I know achieves almost the same degree of protection and avoids involvement as well—without the expense of bonding his employees. He requires every applicant for a job to fill out the regular bonding form, which he then simply files away without taking out a bond. The employee is under the impression that he has been bonded and is deterred from committing a dishonest act by the thought that he would then be up against the bonding company, which would be a lot harsher with him than the employer is likely to be.

Although an agent is often desirable in one's *own* cause, it also follows that in negotiations it is best to avoid dealing with the adversary's agent. If at all possible, deal with the principal. A corollary to this is, Never take for granted that you are actually dealing with the principal or even the proper party.

A pertinent case, which occurred some time ago, gives a bizarre illustration of the main point and its corollary. My client's father had vanished for approximately six months after the United States entered World War II. It was only by chance that a relative discovered that the father had been working as a cook for a construction firm that had a contract to do some defense installations in Iran. Since the father was an accomplished linguist, it seemed strange that he should take a job as a cook.

Some years later my client related the story to me and said that he had been trying unsucessfully to collect the proceeds of an insurance policy provided for all employees of the construction firm. The attorney who had been handling the case for my client heard many different stories explaining the father's conduct. One that seemed most convincing was that the father was working for the OSS and was sent on a secret mission to Iran to ascertain what was going on along the Russian border. Having obtained the information, he wanted to get home quickly. Therefore, he started a fight with a superior. He was summarily discharged and was placed on a steamer sailing to the United States. Somewhere in the Atlantic, the steamer was torpedoed and sunk by a German submarine. There were a few survivors. From their written statements it was ascertained that the father was last seen floating on a raft. These circumstances, plus the passage of several years, were enough to establish the fact that he was dead. However, the construction firm for whom he worked told the attorney that they had discharged him prior to his death and therefore were no longer responsible. The lawyer pointed out that the man might have been a government agent. In answer the construction firm said that this was all the more reason for not paying any claim. Three years of threats, claims, and lawsuits were unproductive. This was the situation when I was introduced into the picture, being retained and substituted as attorney.

After an initial investigation, it was determined that the construction firm had worked in Iran under a cost-plus government contract. If the firm could be made to pay any money, they would be reimbursed by the federal government. Therefore, I determined that my approach would be to circumvent the construction firm and go directly to the government agency that had employed the firm. I presented my claim there.

The government agency to which the claim was made was receptive. Within one week after I had exhibited all the necessary documentation and evidence, the U.S. government paid the full claim. I never did find out if the man was or was not with the OSS. However, it is my firm belief that the father was indeed one of those heroic men who had sacrificed both their identities and their lives during World War II.

The lesson to be learned from this case is always to deal with the man who signs the checks.

International corporations now use bicultural people as a type of mediator or agent. Such companies are now familiar with the kinds of cultural conflicts they meet when they set up operations in a foreign country. For example, in India a local executive will tend to hire people exclusively from his particular area. Since employment is priceless to the Indian, this sort of regional nepotism is hard to combat. The local man is constantly beset by his employees—who are also his neighbors. They feed him the "inside story" about the "others."

Bicultural managers, who have been born in India but have lived abroad, are better able to cope with this situation. They have a broader perspective and can be trusted by all parties. Thus they interpret the conflicting parties to each other.

Life, in its capriciousness, can bestow the role of mediator on one who was previously uninvolved. During the great blackout of the eastern United States in 1965, young boys in midtown New York were permitted full authority over all traffic when they jumped into the snarled intersections and began to help out.

Shifting levels (*"It looks different from here"*). Shifting levels deals with a strategy or tactic in which you change your involvement in the problem to a higher or lower level. It may also consist of dividing the problem into different parts, redefining the situation, or rehandling it. As an example, if a man has been dealing with the problem, let a woman handle it. When a government agency and a subcontractor cannot agree on a final negotiated contract, they might change from one type of contract to another—from a price contract, in which full price is being negotiated to a cost contract, one in which each element of cost is considered separately. From this new perspective, the buyer might even be able to help the seller reduce the cost elements involved.

Let us look at different examples of this tactic. On the personal level, in the Ocean Hill–Brownsville School District dispute in New York City, whatever suggestions the Mayor of New York made to settle the problem between the district and the teachers' union, one side or the other rejected. Therefore, when Mayor John Lindsay proposed a new solution, instead of having it apply specifically to the Ocean Hill–Brownsville section, it applied alike to all the school districts in the city. Each side was able to accept this without loss of esteem.

In a labor dispute a strike might be called. Rather than deal with the union committee, the employer might send a letter stating his position into the homes of his employees. He is going back to the source of the union's power. An opposite shift would be to go over a person's head. This can be especially effective when you are dealing with an agent who says, "I do not have the authority." He is practically asking you to go beyond him. You must realize that when you are dealing with such a person he may have limited flexibility and be unable to take the initiative. In addition to this, the information of what is going on in the negotiation is bound to become distorted as the limited agent passes it on, because he will tell his principal only those things he thinks his superior wants to hear and therefore the superior will have misconceptions about what alternatives are available in the negotiation. All these factors should be considered when dealing with an agent and most certainly when you decide that going over the agent's head may be the only way to resolve a dilemma.

The late Walter Reuther, gifted negotiator, shifted levels when he insisted that negotiation be conducted on a national rather than a regional union level. In spite of that fact, after an agreement was reached, even he was unable to get the local unions to accept the agreed-on terms. The contract was rejected. This same problem was experienced in a West Coast maritime negotiation. However, in this instance, the employers insisted that observers be chosen from the individual locals and that they be permitted to sit in on the negotiaton. After the observers had experienced the give-and-take of the meetings and in caucuses, they made clear their positions to the union officials and let the officials negotiate the local problems. Toward the end of the negotiation, the observers went back to their locals and were very effective in bringing them the full message and gaining the acceptance of the contract by the entire membership.

Changing the view of the problem is a form of shifting levels. To illustrate this, let us see it in action. John is pacing the floor in the middle of the night. His wife wakes up and asks, "What's the matter, John?" He says, "I can't pay Henry the ten thousand dollars I owe him." The wife picks up the telephone and calls Henry. "Hello, Henry, John can't pay you the ten thousand dollars." She hangs up. John looks at her and says, "Why did you call up Henry at three A.M.?" "Well," she says demurely, "you can go back to sleep. Now it's Henry's problem."

Some employers use this technique in dealing with unions. When a union makes demands for larger pensions, for example, the employers reexamine some of the assumptions that were built into the pension plan. One assumption, let us say, was the rate of earnings of the pension fund. When the plan was set up, the assumption was that the fund would earn 3 percent. With higher earnings possible today, the fund can safely be assumed to earn 4 percent or perhaps more. While the physical assets of the fund have not changed, the formula can be, and this will help meet the union demand that more money be paid out without the employer having to add to the fund.

Another approach to shifting levels, by changing the viewpoint, can be used when there is dissension within the union's ranks. The younger members want high wages, the older ones want bigger pensions. Instead of attempting to satisfy both groups the employer might make a package proposal of a dollar amount and tell the union to divide it up any way it likes provided that the dollar package is ratified immediately and that the union can within three or six months decide which way it will divide it. "Now, it's the union's problem."

Merely by shifting levels you can change the entire direction of what you are doing or attempting to do. You may find that you are not selling newspapers but, rather, news; not life insurance but security; not glasses but vision; not awnings but shade. Have you considered what business you are really in? Asking this question periodically could change your life's concept. If a doctor asked himself the question during his career, might not the answer change from "curing the sick" to "maintaining health"? A teacher's answer might change from "teaching" to "helping people grow and mature." Check on your ability to shift to a higher level when you ask yourself the question, "What business am I in?"

The reason it is important to ask this question at intervals throughout life is that as a life situation or a business situation develops it reaches different plateaus. Life has a pattern of constant change and often the people involved are not even aware of it. A head of Food Fair supermarkets realized he had hit a plateau when he stated he was no longer in the food business but in the real estate business. His object from that time on was to open more food stores rather than to concern himself with methods of selling food.

One caution is necesary. When shifting levels, I would not view it as the Rand Corporation allegedly did. It moved from a high abstraction to a low abstraction and found that the low abstraction was far more challenging. As reported in *The New York Times* in 1969: "The Rand Corporation, one of the country's oldest and most prestigious think-tanks, is in its second year of analyzing New York City and is now convinced that its past studies of the nation's defense systems were far simpler by comparison.

" 'This has certainly been an education for the Rand Corporation,' Douglas Scott, information director of the New York City office, said last week. 'There are certain comfortable simplicities about research on defense,' he explained, 'but not here. The complexity of the human element, the complexity of the fiscal and political element, the plain complexity of New York City are something we haven't encountered before.' "

This is the problem for a great many people when they reach a high abstraction level. How could Rand possibly have considered the defense of the United States without taking into account the basic problems of the cities and states and people which, after all, make up the United States? It would appear that instead of considering the whole, Rand isolated a segment of life and treated it as though it were a whole. Instead of confronting the entire life situation, they used a case example, taking one system out of many possible defense systems and saying that this was the system by which an abstraction, the United States, should be defended. Then it appeared that the problems of New York City were more complex.

If you are a salesman, consider what shifting levels may mean to you. The door-to-door salesman no doubt expends the same effort in closing a sale as does the millionaire real estate salesman, yet the rewards to each are disproportionate. Just as the value levels of the products they are selling are different, so are the rewards similarly different. Diamond Jim Brady, who amassed a fortune selling railway equipment, realized that if you choose to make your living from selling, you should sell expensive things.

College administrators could also benefit from shifting levels. Instead of negotiating on a low-order level, as, for example, with students who object to the food, the teachers, or the curriculum, they should try to go beyond these problems to meet the demands on an entirely different level. By doing so they could transform the discontent of the students from preoccupation with petty details to a creative dialogue about the quality of education and its relevance to today's world and today's society. When discussions are held at this higher level, each and every one is encouraged to join in and work toward a common goal.

AN OPERATIONAL EXAMPLE OF CREATIVE ALTERNATIVES AND STRATEGIES AND TACTICS

Some years ago a large furniture plant was built on the outskirts of a small Southern town. It provided good employment for many of the people of the community. The town fathers saw the great advantages in industrialization and went so far as to give tax incentives to other firms that moved into the area. As the years passed the furniture plant grew and finally found it necessary to build an extension. After it was built, however, the furniture plant's insurance company refused to provide fire insurance for the extension unless it had a full sprinkler system. It was then discovered that the present water main leading into the plant was inadequate for the proposed system. An additional main would have to be put in.

The management of the furniture plant went to the town council, but the council said it could not put in the water main because it would be kept in only a standby condition, no water would be used, and the town would never be repaid for the installation. Management attempted to negotiate with the council in many ways. At a council hearing they presented a good case to show that the number of workers they would employ in the new extension would use more water and that, overall, there would be a benefit to the town. The council countered, however, with the statement that it did not have sufficient funds, and that was correct. The town had weakened its financial condition by giving tax breaks to encourage new industry, and there was not enough left in the treasury to finance the new main (a *fait accompli.*) The furniture executives walked out in a huff, stating they would shift their entire operations to another area (apparent withdrawal), saying they could even get tax considerations from another town (association).

Through the local newspaper the management of the plant took their case to the people of the town (shifting levels). They presented the facts as they saw them—that without a main to supply water to the sprinkler system, they could not get insurance and so could not operate in the new addition; that other towns were willing to finance fully a development of this sort because of the opportunity for employment it would give the local people (appeal to need to know). The town council began to realize that the management was not feinting. The merits of their statements in the newspaper had had a very powerful effect. However, this realization did nothing to improve the condition of the town treasury.

Management then suggested that the council borrow against future tax credits (creative alternative), but the councilmen saw that they would only be postponing an eventual problem and would not go along with it.

At this point a creative approach to the problem that everyone would accept had to be found. A mutual fact-finding session was suggested. An investigation into the actual construction of the main revealed that the factory could finance it alone. By so doing, it could reasonably expect to sell water to the developers of housing for the new factory employees on land along its right-of-way. A water main would thus enhance the value of the land. The factory would be repaid for the cost of the main and also show a profit. Consequently, the plan applied for and received a franchise to lay and operate the water main as a local water company.

Since the town would not have to lay out any money and the furniture plant would have a new asset, everyone thought it was a "good" solution. At this point, however, the condition of the money market changed. The plant did not have sufficient funds to start the installation of the pipeline and could not borrow it. Stalemate again.

One company officer reexamined the problem and came up with still another alternative. He realized that the sprinkler system, which had been the point of departure for the problem they faced, was designed to protect the building, but the building itself was far less valuable than the contents of the building (shifting levels). On further investigation, management discovered that another way (creative alternative) to protect the contents of the factory was by use of a foam system that was being used by aircraft manufacturers. The disadvantage of a sprinkler system is that the water runs into other floors and can produce damage to the contents amounting to millions of dollars. In certain types of industry the sprinkler system is vital for protection, but in the furniture industry the advantages of the foam system far outweighed those of the sprinkler.

After the foam system was installed throughout the plant, other members of the plant's trade organization realized its advantages (association). They formed an independent group, with this plant as the leader, and became self-insurers of their own plants (participation). The money that was saved on insurance premiums and the new method of fire protection was used for further expansion.

This story shows in operation the multiple use of different strategies and tactics. Life situations rarely give opportunity for the use of a single type. Always keep your mind open to the various alternatives.

CHAPTER 10 APPLICATIONS

1. From your own experience or something that you have read or heard about, give an illustration of each strategy included in the chapter. This will permit you to reexamine each one of the labels which were used as designating titles as parts of an overall process. Before each negotiation, it is advisable to examine the entire list of strategies and tactics to stimulate thinking of creative alternatives.

2. In your next negotiation have at least three strategies in reserve.

11

CREATIVE-ALTERNATIVE ATTITUDES

The term *alternative* does not necessarily mean a choice of one of two methods. Some people automatically limit themselves to seeing only two alternatives—for example, when they are asked to compare two things. Try it out on yourself. Place two objects before you and make out a list comparing them. When that is done, look at the list.

Have you dealt with only the similarities involved? Have you dealt with only the differences involved? Or have you given a balance of both? Comparison can be broader than the either/or method.

In olden times the Chinese regarded all negotiations as having three alternative solutions: a bag of gold, pushing your opponent off a cliff, or committing suicide. Similar limiting approaches have been used in Western negotiations: You get your opposer to concede by force, by compromise, or by concessions.

First, in using force, you deal entirely with your strengths and emphasize your opposer's weaknesses, so that the solution of the negotiation ultimately is the balancing of force which hopefully leads toward a reasonable agreement. It is difficult to see a reasonable agreement resulting from this type of negotiation. The other side is asked to make a sacrifice; it does not appear that he is gaining anything, and therefore he has no stake in making the agreement a stable condition. The loser will work for a change in the situation. Any businessman relying on force is merely setting the stage for a relationship in which the other side is interested in one thing: When does his turn at bat come?

What about compromise as another method of reaching agreement? Usually in this case each side is seeking a shortcut in the negotiating process. Agreements so reached probably are not satisfactory to either party. When a person says, "I'll split the difference," this is too arbitrary a statement. He is not just splitting the difference. Instead he is setting forth a new position from which he wants to work. In most instances a person must justify a change in position to his opposer by the use of reasoning. This does not take place when both sides rely merely on compromise.

The last way is by making concessions. This, however, must be balanced by the giving of concessions by the other side. If this type of orderly process takes place, the various positions each side has taken are changed. But concessions will not be accepted gratis unless they are preceded by the various reasons for making the changes. One side must justify a change of position to another. In both compromise and concession we have a process of yielding to greater points of reasonableness. Can we use reasoning in a negotiation to gain a mutually advantageous and lasting solution?

The answer is yes. In explaining how this might be possible, an effort will be made to try to avoid applying Foley's Law. This law was explained, as was only right, by an official of Irish Airlines. "Any problem, no matter how solvable, can be rendered insolvable when you generalize it sufficiently." An explanation will be given in which we will attempt to avoid generalities.

The problem can be restated as: How to change an opposer's win/lose stand into a creative-alternative attitude.

CREATIVE ALTERNATIVES CAN CHANGE
WIN/LOSE STANDS

Robert R. Blake, a trustee of the Institute of General Semantics, in the 1961 Annual Alfred Korzybski Memorial Lecture helped stimulate some of the following thoughts. The win/lose approach in negotiations can be replaced with an attitude that there are creative alternatives, an infinite number of solutions for the problems. Some of these solutions may be better, some may be worse, but they should be examined by each of the groups concerned for the mutual advantages of both sides. This is in opposition to the win/ lose approach, where a fixed position is taken and you try to force your opposer to embrace your solution.

There is no doubt that we all have the urge to win, and when we are part of a group this urge becomes a drive. If a disagreement occurs with another group, this is seen as a disaster rather than an opportunity to utilize creative thinking, which enables us to re-examine our position and possibly bring about a satisfactory solution for all concerned.

When we are part of any negotiating coterie, our needs blend in with the group's needs. Even in a simulated negotiation, one can see how each member strongly identifies with his team's position and downgrades his competitor. The either/or orientation of the win/lose approach interferes with realistic true-to-life reasonability. With that type of attitude, cooperation between opposing sides is not possible. Even the ability to open one's mind to the opposer's belief is lost. Positions are often reached during a negotiation where the motive to win is equated with your loyalty to your other team members, or to the organization which you represent. You are disloyal if you do not press to "win." This can very effectively eliminate the possibility of working together with your opposer to solve the problem by mutual effort. If, with this distrusting win/lose attitude, an arbitrator were to be called in, members of the team would regard it as an inability to resolve anything by themselves. If a judge were to make a decision and the decision was adverse, the judge's attitude and comprehension would be criticized. If they should perchance "win" the negotiation with this one-sided attitude, the other side would be made to feel that they were the losers. It would then only plant seeds for future retaliation.

Before we can fully explore the answer to the initial question, a second problem arises. Can we maintain the advantages of competition and at the same time bring about a collaboration in which all parties move toward mutual solutions of their joint and separate goals? Again the answer is yes. Not only is this possible, but it is feasible even if only one of the two parties has this creative-alternative approach in mind.

The first step is to realize that there must be a better way than the win/lose approach. Let us examine our own attitudes when we are involved in a win/lose situation. What we find occurring within us undoubtedly occurs within our opposer. In the event that we are negotiating with someone who, we feel, wants to win and make us the losers, we find this only strengthens our will to win and forces us to fight harder. Compare this to the reactions that you may have to one who you feel is truly showing you respect and truly attempting to work with you, proposing a number of creative alternatives for consideration to help bring about a resulting solution that might be beneficial to all concerned. Which attitude would you prefer to create after you get over your suspicion?

The pressures on both sides and by the group on the people within it are the same—all of them prodding the person to "win." If we can take that type of group pressure off the individual and off each side we might engender within all an openness to help look for a solution in the infinite area of possible creative solutions rather than in the win/lose approach.

We must check ourselves for Merton's principle of the self-fulfilling prophecy. The prophecy is fulfilled not because it is an accurate prediction but because our actions and beliefs cause counterreactions within other people that are of the same nature as those we predicted. Our behavior, therefore, brings about the predicted behavior in the other person. We help make it so. If you would like to find a mutually beneficial solution in a negotiation, the other side must be able to judge from your actions that you are sincere in your desires. Your total conduct must be persuasive of your anticipations. Cooperation must be your goal. It can then become a shared goal. Even secrets can be shared.

C. W. Morris observes, "The increase of communication may not only fail to give agreement in valuations and modes of conduct but may actually be used to increase conflict, competitiveness, and slavery. For sharing a language with other persons provides the subtlest and most powerful of all tools for controlling the behavior of these other persons to one's advantage—for stirring up rivalries, advancing one's own goals, exploiting others."

In "Defense Level and Influence Potential in Small Groups" * Jack R. Gibb states, "If one is to make fundamental improvement in communication, he must make changes in interpersonal relationships." One way to achieve such an improvement is to change defensive behavior into supportive communication that minimizes your opposer's anxieties and enables him to concentrate on what you are saying and attempting to do. Gibb cites six pairs of defensive and supportive categories:

Defensive Climates vs. Supportive Climates

1. Evaluation	1. Description
2. Control	2. Problem Orientation
3. Strategy	3. Spontaneity
4. Neutrality	4. Empathy
5. Superiority	5. Equality
6. Certainty	6. Provisionalism

These six pairs are interactive. Since interpersonal attitudes are often, and sometimes necessarily, evaluative, it may be possible to counterbalance them with attitudes and words expressing empathy, for example. Questions, Gibb points out, often produce defensiveness. This is why it is almost essential to understand the Five Functions of Questions explained in Chapter 9 and the ways they can induce or reduce anxious or defensive behavior.

Attempts to control your opposer through speech as well as through nonverbal communication provoke defensive attitudes, while descriptive speech that does not seek to change your opposer but to give him background information provokes no one. Problem orientation also, when it seeks to define a problem and elicit the help of your opposer in solving it, is permissive and allows him to reach his own conclusions. This is the exact opposite of pursuing a devious, manipulative, and selfish strategy. Fully utilize fact finding as an initial procedure.

In short, as Gibb states, "One reduces the defensiveness of the

* *Leadership and Interpersonal Behavior*, L. Petrullo and B. M. Bass, editors, 1961.

listener when he communicates that he is willing to experiment with his own behavior, attitudes, and ideas. The person who appears to be taking provisional attitudes, to be investigating issues rather than taking sides on them, to be problem-solving rather than debating, and to be willing to experiment and explore, tends to communicate that the listener may have some control over the shared quest or the investigation of ideas. If a person is genuinely searching for information and data, he does not resent help or company along the way." We should discuss our mutual problems, not each other's demands.

Knowing that problems do exist in negotiations between groups, recognizing reasons for their existence, and being understanding of these conditions are useful but they do not help you solve the problems in your negotiations. You must know about and be able to take certain concrete steps to bring about active cooperation between the parties.

The first such phrase is referred to as fact finding. This results from both parties working together to determine the facts. Facts should not be made the subject of negotiations. If they can be initially and independently agreed on, this will eliminate a tremendous number of personalized, emotion-laden attitudes causing conflict. The initial state that tends to separate the two parties is the result of both parties independently arriving at their separate opinion of the facts. Joint fact finding linked to outside criteria should be the beginning step. Mutual action, in this stage, would facilitate an onward movement in the negotiation.

In taking the second negotiation step, one side should not be requested to present, nor should it present, the "best" or "only" solution to the problem. It should set forth as many creative alternatives as the other team might work with. This in turn will stimulate the other side to approach it in a like manner, and possibly so continuing, the end product will be satisfactory to both. Starting with a mutually beneficial approach in negotiation automatically encourages creativity. Group action is stimulated to looking for alternative ways of coming up with a feasible solution. The knowledge and talent of each member of each group is unlocked, and at the same time each side is prepared to present its needs while helping to meet the needs of the other. Even one-sided disclosing of secrets encourages the other side to be supportive.

During this stage, rather than expressing the fact that differences exist, as suggestions and alternatives are proposed, look for the similarities. Latch on to these similarities and build on them. In most instances, fertile ground for such growth immediately exists.

Bring about involvement of everyone concerned, all members of your team as well as members of the other side. The more people involved in suggestions, the more alternatives set forth, the more successfully differences will be brought out and resolved. When you involve people in seeking a solution to a problem and they make contributions toward its resolution, they can easily become committed to working for its fulfillment.

Attempt to keep the entire group informed of the progress of the negotiation. Let them go through the mental gymnastics that each step entails. We cannot expect members of the opposing group to jump to a conclusion which may have been reached by other members of their group merely because it has been arrived at through the process of negotiation. If they are part of the process and follow the steps through, examining the alternatives and concessions as they occur, the final solution will be realistically accepted.

Having a member of your team who is able spontaneously to recognize a potential stalemate before it occurs or as it is occurring, who is able to step in, suggest alternative ways that might be examined, and state them in a rather abstract, nonevaluative manner so that they do not arouse any emotion, will be of great assistance in working toward a solution. In this role the expert negotiator should not be involved with the contents of what is being negotiated but rather with the alternatives. He should also be able to point out where various courses of action might lead.

To recap the steps:

1. Recognize the shortcomings of and the alternatives to a win/lose approach.
2. Understand defensive and supportive climates.
3. Engage in joint fact finding.
4. Get mutual suggestions of creative alternatives.
5. Involve everyone on both teams.
6. Have an open observer ready for spontaneous, problem-oriented courses of action.

If you ask, Can this be achieved by me in my negotiations? remember the story of a young man newly arrived in New York City. He stopped an older man on the street and asked, "How do you get to Carnegie Hall?"

"Practice, my son, constant practice."

CREATIVE ALTERNATIVES FOR MUTUAL ACCOMMODATION

Being able to come up with creative alternatives is seen as one of the basic concepts of successful negotiation. This allows mutual accommodation where all parties can be the winner. A creative alternative should satisfy some need of each participant in a negotiation, not, however, in the way that some governments have claimed to be responsive to the needs of the people. We can trace such alleged attempts back to ancient Roman times. Rome received most of her grain from North Africa. During a naval battle between rival claimants to the throne, half of the grain fleet was destroyed and as a result the proconsul was asked what should be done. He said, "Half of the shipment would not eliminate the food shortage in Rome. Unload all of the wheat and load the fleet up with sand because a starving people will need the circus in the Colosseum."

We can switch the misconstruing of needs to today and understand how people who offer allegedly creative alternatives have even become specialized. One group refers to its members as "washroom consultants." They are prepared to advise how to set up the washrooms in an organization, whether a restaurant, theater, or office. On first hearing this, it might seem rather remote that alternatives could be offered in this situation. But let's consider some of their more successful techniques. They assert that the cost of paper products in the washroom can be cut by almost 50 percent. An alternative suggested is hanging the paper towels higher. People will then use fewer. With some thought, we can appreciate their suggestion. When our hands are dripping wet, the higher we raise them in order to reach the towels, the more the water will run down our sleeves. Now for the toilet paper. They suggest that the most propitious place for cutting down the use of toilet paper is by placing it directly in the rear rather than alongside the toilet. The more difficulty people have in reaching for the toilet paper, the less they use. Could this explain some of the graffiti on the walls?

True creative alternatives sometimes come from necessity. Before Central Station Alarm Companies became the popular business that it is today, some people could not afford to have their store linked by telephone lines to a central station. In the event that someone attempted a burglary in a business so protected, an alarm would go off in a central station office and the police and guards would respond. Some poor but enterprising storekeepers had figured out another way of handling the situation. When they were leaving their stores for the night they would dial all but the last digit of their home telephone number. They would put their finger in place on the dial, turn the last number all the way around to the dial stop, but prevent it from returning to the original place by putting a cork in the finger hole behind the dial stop. This would prevent the call from being completed. They would then attach a string to the cork, attach the other end of the string to the front door, and go home for the night. If anyone tried to come in the front door, he would pull the string which would pull the cork out of the dial, and the dial would then return to its position, completing the phone call and ringing the proprietor at his home. He then knew that someone was burglarizing his store. An unfortunate side effect of this system was that the proprietor and nine other people in his telephone exchange would not be able to receive any phone calls during the evening. A section of the phone exchange dialing system would be tied up. The phone company later changed the circuits so that this will no longer work today.

Being able to seek alternatives is like playing golf with a full set of clubs. No professional would think of playing golf using the same club over and over. He would find the club most appropriate in the situation for which it was constructed and the way he felt at the moment.

Suggestions for creative alternatives should be made by either side in a negotiation. In one union situation the employer, when faced with particularly tough demands, discussed each one separately with the union negotiating committee. He explained his point of view—how difficult it was for him to comply—and asked them if they would alleviate some of the difficulty or at least show him how they could have compliance without undue hardship to him.

When approached in this manner, the union out of professional pride showed the employer creative alternatives to achieve compliance.

The title given to the next creative alternative episode is "The Phantom $7 Million." The highest settlement in an antitrust suit was recently made by members of the drug industry for an antibiotic monopoly. The settlement was for $100 million. It was the result of class actions on behalf of forty-three states and certain cities representing the general public and also on behalf of the wholesale and retail druggists. Of the $100 million, $3 million had been allocated to be paid to the drug wholesalers and retailers. It was felt that the wholesalers' and retailers' claim was slight in that if they had been forced to pay more money for the antibiotics, their mark-up was higher—if they had paid less, they would have made less. But after publicity of the settlement came out, the attorneys for that class felt that their clients' claim was worth at least $40 million. After some concentrated negotiations between the lawyers handling most of the claimants and the lawyers representing the wholesalers and retailers, the figure asked for by the wholesalers/retailers was reduced to $10 million. However, this was $7 million more than the allocation in the full settlement.

The drug companies paying the money, when asked for more, refused to go any higher than the $100 million. Other plaintiffs representing the classes of the public refused to give up one cent of the monies that had been allotted to them. A change in the original distribution would have required the further ratification and approval of each different class representing the forty-three states, plus cities, involved in the original settlement. It would have been a long and difficult process. The problem boiled down to how to raise $7 million to complete a final settlement for the $100 million.

This instance called for creative alternatives. A method which seems to stimulate creativity is trying to think in terms of what are the most basic elements that make up the transaction and how are they related. This is in the nature of fact finding. Examining and reexamining the same factors, rethinking, sometimes help uncover creative alternatives. Examining this problem by these methods was helpful. First, time is always a factor and can sometimes be considered as money, and the examination of the time factors involved in this settlement revealed some interesting considerations. Part of the settlement agreement was that the plaintiffs were not to be entitled to any of the money until time for the final appeals had run out. The drug companies did not want one or more plaintiffs causing them additional problems by taking an appeal. Another basic element in any of today's situations involving lawsuits, settlements, etc., is the tax considerations. Many times tax considerations alone will help you solve a particular negotiating problem. It gives different insights for each party and enables you to meet their different needs. One person's tax position may be completely opposite to another person's position, possibly enabling each to complement the other.

In the year 1969, U.S. corporations had to pay a 10 percent surtax. The drug companies had had a particularly good year, and any expenses that they could pay within the year 1969 would be beneficial to their tax position. The plaintiffs' lawyer approached the drug-company defendants with the following propositions: Would they deposit with a bank in the year 1969 at least $85 million of the settlement to be held for the account of the plaintiffs? The bank would hold it for thirteen months, which was the period necessary for the time to appeal to run out. At the same time, the plaintiffs' attorney had found a bank that was willing to take the $85 million for thirteen months and pay about $7 million interest. The drug companies agreed, the attorneys agreed, and finally the wholesalers and retailers agreed, knowing that they would get about $10 million at the end of thirteen months—the $3 million that had been allocated to them, plus approximately $7 million in interest.

No one is without creative alternatives, no matter what his circumstances. To prove the point, let us take some of the strategies and tactics used by groups that would seem to have few possible alternatives available to them. A poverty group in Chicago got Mayor Richard Daley to negotiate with them by threatening to disrupt his pride and joy, O'Hare Airport. Their threat was simple. They announced that would keep all rest-room stalls at O'Hare occupied until the Mayor talked with them, and talk the Mayor did. As a vivid reminder to the Health Department of its neglect of the Chicago slums, the same group piled dead rats on the steps of City Hall. Another community organization in Chicago brought home to an alderman the lack of garbage-collection service by dumping a truckload of refuse on his well-manicured lawn. The poor today realize that they do have power—body power. When used in concert as a creative alternative, it can change the status quo.

College students have also used legal (according to school standards) but compelling means of effecting change. In one university the rules prohibited students from dancing, smoking, or even having a can of beer. However, they creatively developed something they were permitted to do. The school administration magnanimously allowed them to chew gum. Several hundred students began to appear on campus, their mouths stuffed with gum. They did not seem to enjoy this sanctioned vice, however, and quickly discarded the gum on the campus sidewalks. The college soon came to a standstill. The administration surrendered: Students could do anything so long as they did not chew gum.

An alternative that is too little used today and is most effective is humor. Police departments have handled demonstrations with a minimum of violence by the use of humor. *The New York Times* reported on November 6, 1967:

> "Ladies and gentlemen, please move on or be prepared to get your bathrobes and towels ready. We are going to have to stage some unusual aquatics." The voice that boomed the message from the loudspeaker's car belonged to Werner Textor, a policeman. The crowd laughed and the people cheered. This took place during a student demonstration in the heart of West Berlin. By the time the water cannon was turned on a minute later against a sit-down demonstration in the middle of the street, most of the spectators and the protesting students had left. "There are always those without a sense of humor," Mr. Textor remarked of the few who remained to get drenched.

Negotiators who have the ability to use humor are never at a loss for a strategy. Although he frightened many people in the 1930's, Huey Long was a master of humor and he used it so effectively that he rarely failed to gain his end. One year the opening game of the Louisiana State University football team was marred by poor advance sales. To his horror, Long found that the circus was opening the same night. To prevent this unfair competition against his beloved team, Long searched the law books. There he found a Louisiana law, enacted but never enforced, providing for the compulsory dipping of animals to prevent the spread of ticks. He then called John Ringling North, the circus owner, and politely asked him to change his opening date. Mr. North would not. "Well," said Long, "Louisiana has a dip law. As I interpret it, your animals will have to be dipped. Did you ever dip a tiger? Or how about an elephant?" North did not open in Baton Rouge that day.

CHAPTER 11 APPLICATIONS

1. The following are illustrative words describing defensive and supportive climates.

DEFENSIVE VS. SUPPORTIVE CLIMATES

1. EVALUATION
   (a) Appraising
   (b) Accusing
   (c) Judgmental
   (d) Indoctrinating
   (e) Correcting
2. CONTROL
   (a) To change
   (b) To influence
   (c) To restrict
   (d) Persuade
   (e) Threaten
3. STRATEGY
   (a) Oneupmanship
   (b) Maneuvering
   (c) Gamesmanship
4. NEUTRALITY
   (a) Apathetic
   (b) Passive
   (c) Considered object, not person
5. SUPERIORITY
   (a) Does not desire relationship
   (b) Does not desire feedback
   (c) Does not desire help
   (d) Make dependent
6. CERTAINTY
   (a) Dogmatic
   (b) Teacher, not co-worker
   (c) Conformity

1. DESCRIPTION
   (a) Genuine requests for information
2. PROBLEM ORIENTATION
   (a) Continuing redefinition
   (b) Mutual problem
   (c) Cooperative quest
   (d) Common task
   (e) Plan with, not for
3. SPONTANEITY
   (a) Uncomplicated motivations
   (b) Straightforward
   (c) Free interaction
4. EMPATHY
   (a) Acceptance
   (b) Identify with problem
   (c) Share feeling
   (d) Opens his emotional reaction
   (e) Understanding
   (f) Confidence
5. EQUALITY
   (a) Mutual respect
   (b) Mutual trust
   (c) Permit growth and maturing
   (d) Mutuality
6. PROVISIONALISM
   (a) Willing to experiment
   (b) Willing to investigate
   (c) Creative
   (d) Innovate
   (e) Accept feedback

Can you add words to any of these subdivisions?

2. Using the list of supportive and defensive environments, with subdivisions under each, think of a current negotiation and think of how you could be completely supportive in it, checking off statements and actions that would indicate supportive character.

3. Is it possible, instead of using the theory of defensive driving, to view your own driving in an entirely different manner? Try driving in a supportive manner rather than defensively. See if the anxiety created by some former situations is still present. Can you think of other situations in which a supportive environment may be more appropriate than a defensive?

4. In the relationships that you will have within the next week, consider changes in relationship, changes in attitudes you may use in negotiating with a member of your family, with associates, and with a business opposer.

12

PURCHASING AND SELLING

Trades would not take place unless it were advantageous to the parties concerned. Of course, it is better to strike as good a bargain as one's bargaining position admits. The worst outcome is when, by overreaching greed, no bargain is struck, and a trade that could have been advantageous to both parties, does not come off at all.

—BENJAMIN FRANKLIN

We have a tendency to think of the purchase and the sale as two separate transactions. They even become the opposites of each other. However, when viewed objectively, to buy and to sell are the same transaction. They are merely seen from different viewpoints, that of the buyer and that of the seller.

Although many books have been written on selling, buying is a field that has been much neglected. There are, however, as many skills and requirements involved in buying as there are in selling. The purposes and goals of negotiation from a purchaser's viewpoint can be manifold. Negotiation can be considered a substitute for

196

mere price competition. The target of the negotiation can vary. It is not necessarily the seller's reasonable profit. It may be his production costs.

An investigation of most businesses reveals that there seems to be no purpose and no target in the buying concept of a purchasing agent. Many corporations feel that procuring is merely an administrative function, that other people have determined the products to buy and therefore the purchasing agent's job is rather perfunctory. The art of negotiation makes the difference between a paper-pushing clerk and a functioning, skillful purchasing agent.

His job is to keep the company running by supplying the goods and services that are needed at a realistic price. Like the negotiator, the purchasing agent is not born. He is a product of his experience. In most instances, however, the experiences have been limiting rather than broadening.

Before considering the purchasing agent's functions with people outside his organization, let us consider some of his internal responsibilities, beginning with internal communication. On a horizontal level he should be in touch with the other departments—engineering, sales, etc. He should extend vertically up to management to give and receive information and down to the personnel in his department to inform them and utilize their talents.

Vertically from above he should be informed about needs and should coordinate efforts. Horizontally he should find out about inventions, finances, scheduling, timing, and specifications. For example, his understanding of the specifications could permit him to suggest altering certain unnecessary features so that design, material, and method—changes on the producer's part—can produce savings. He must tell others within the company about new products that he comes in contact with; about substitution of materials and methods; trends of the market and cost; whether his firm should increase or decrease stocks; and new methods of production.

Externally, purchasing should be treated as the contact point of one organization with another. In selling, other organizations can be encouraged to present the purchasing agent with innovations, new products, and new uses for his company's products. The entire educational process that the selling organization possesses can be utilized. Sellers can teach the specifications, what the product should or should not do, what the capabilities are, and what the price range is. Some companies utilize or attempt to utilize this principle by requiring that they be supplied by more than one company, one seller bidding against another.

Many elements are vulnerable to a good purchasing negotiator. Some of the techniques purchasers use are: determining certain types of engineering available; learning through a study of wages and hours how one method of production would be more costly than others; finding out what the present state of development of the item involved is: determining whether there is a likelihood that methods of production might change in the near future; asking whether all the specifications of the item are important or whether some can be modified to get a better price; judging the reasonableness of the overhead in view of projected production; studying specifications or engineers' drawings to determine if information might be obtained that is of value to the buyer or seller. The purchasing agent, having knowledge of some of these factors, should not keep it to himself but should share it with the seller. In this way the seller can then assist the purchaser in formulating a better deal. At the same time, of course, the purchaser is helping the seller make a better deal.

One of the more direct ways the purchasing agent has of analyzing the cost of a product is by understanding the direct materials involved, the direct labor involved, the factory overhead, and administrative expenses. It is not necessary for a purchasing agent to be an expert in each of these fields, but he should know how to get such information. Some of the sources are the seller himself, a competitor of the seller, his own buying organization, engineering department, and other staff departments. It is also very helpful to do some research on similar types of products, similiar manufacturing processes, and published reports in any field concerning the project or product that one is interested in.

As a result of the above methods of analysis, the purchasing agent is only too familiar with the common errors that are made concerning the various items—for example, direct material costs. Some of these errors are: inflated estimates of what the future of the price may be, prices based on a better grade of material than is necessary, improper assessment of requirements, and small-quantity price for a large-quantity purchase. Scrap, which is too often neglected, is also an element of value that can be taken into consideration. Labor costs can be dissected into two basic factors: the number of hours that are spent and the hourly wage rate. As elementary as this may seem, these factors have a greater variation than the cost of material. The major object of these analyses should be to consider methods whereby both the purchaser and the seller can induce the other to control his costs and share the benefits with the company that each represents.

Because people choose the ways and methods to set the prices, negotiation is called for. It should be realized that a substantial amount of pricing is made as the result of inadequate information and just plain personal preference. This is a situation that a purchasing agent can take advantage of and utilize in his negotiation. There are many elements that the negotiating purchaser can bring out in discussion: the very fact that the price may be the result of administrative action based on individual preference and without regard to demand, extent of competition, and different competitive prices. The negotiator could point out the rate of return the purchasing company should expect, as well as the rate of return that is fair for the seller's company. A good purchasing agent knows how to comply with the law and yet apply it to his unique requirements to gain a concession. He is able to use the seller's house regulations concerning fair-traded prices or fixed prices.

Following an outline of different strategies discussed previously, we can see the different possible strategies the seller may use in setting price. We can understand how a knowledge of them would be useful to the purchasing agent's negotiations.

Forbearance: Seller waits until all his competitors have set their prices—waits until the last possible moment.

Surprise: He does it more by hunch. They are unrealistic prices. He intends to haggle with the various buyers over what each discount might be.

Fait accompli: He sets a price schedule, then waits to see what the reaction will be.

Bland withdrawal: He sends out a price list and waits for some response. At the first sign of opposition, he backs down and says, "No, that's not what I meant at all."

Apparent withdrawal: If the price receives criticism in a discussion, he leads the buyer to think that adjustments will be made and lulls him into a false sense of security. In the final analysis, he leaves the buyer without alternative sources and then keeps the price at the level that he first set.

Reversal: At the first sign of any pressure, he backs down and gives a new quotation. His prices tend to vary with the market. If he feels he can raise them, he reverses himself again.

Limits: He contends that his policy has been successful for a number of years and will keep his position the same within his prescribed limits.

Feinting: He puts up a smoke screen to deceive the purchaser into thinking he is going to get something that he is not. He makes the buyer believe that he has all the information when some of the important elements may be left out.

Participation: He will set his price only after he has discussed it with all his competition, despite the fact that this may be illegal.

Association: He gets all his competitors' price lists and then makes his. He then states that he has let his prices be set by competition.

Dissociation: Whatever price structure any of the competition has, his will be different. He will not abide by any industrywide standard practice. This can in instances lead to complete misunderstanding as to what his prices truly mean.

Crossroads: He creates a tie-in, bringing two or more elements of the price list together. The "best" price is supposed to be made when the purchaser meets both of his conditions.

Blanketing: The price list supposedly covers such a wide area that when a specific price is quoted the price that was originally set forth appears misleading.

Randomizing: He is a chartist who uses advanced mathematics and sets his price at a crossing point which may be far from reality.

Random sample: Able to sell at a certain profit ratio once, he believes that his established profit structure will last forever. If he changes it, it is only to keep his profit margin in line with his costs.

Salami: He cannot bring himself to have an established price. In his endeavor to vary it he will give each individual unit, segment, and section a separate price.

Bracketing: He sets the price above the mark; the buyer sets it below the mark; and the seller hopes that they can split the difference.

Management should remember what John Ruskin once said: "It is unwise to pay too much but it is worse to pay too little. When you pay too much you lose a little money. . . . When you pay too little, you sometimes lose everything, because the thing you bought was incapable of doing the thing it was bought to do. The common law of business balance prohibits paying a little and getting a lot—it can't be done. If you deal with the lowest bidder, it is well to add something for the risk you run. If you do that, you will have enough to pay for something better." A final bit of purchasing philosophy comes from an anecdote told about astronaut Gordon Cooper, who, on returning from a space shot, was asked if he was ever worried. "Only once. While concentrating on the panel I suddenly looked at all the dials and gadgets and it occurred to me that every one of those parts was supplied by the lowest bidder."

COMPONENTS OF BUYING/SELLING NEGOTIATION

There are certain components of a buying/selling negotiation that a purchasing agent will come in contact with. He must have the ability to understand and distinguish between them. In negotiating a contract at a fixed price, he must be able to provide for revising prices and other unexpected problems. He must also consider his job as getting acceptance for the internal changes that these contracts may lead to and the carrying out of the end product of his negotiation. How many purchasing agents are familiar with their stock in trade, the various forms of concessions they may make, such as tie-in sale aspects that may permit them to get a better price, and asked-for guarantees against price changes? Is the purchasing agent aware enough of various terms of payment to get the proper discount for cash, prepayments, quantity buying, and cumulative buying? Does he know what clauses will guarantee against known possibilities and unknown possibilities? Will he be aware of the long-term contract and when it will be useful to his organization? Has he considered changes of specifications to meet the seller's needs and not interfere with the type of product that he desires? Is his timing right? Is he aware that seasonal buying may bring him a price reduction?

What are some of the elements that a buyer and seller should consider when profit is considered as an item of cost? They should look at the input that is necessary for full performance, the management and technical effort necessary to acquire the materials and skills involved in the contract, the risks of the contract costs, rising or falling market, the performance record of an established producer, and, last, the possibility that the manufacturer is being asked to produce something unique or outside his usual field, something that has very little chance of future orders or rewards. If, however, subsequent contracts are expected and they are to be much larger than the original order, the buyer might as a matter of strategy request a lower price. The seller will be offered the carrot of being able to supply the larger subsequent contracts. This practice is known as "buying in."

Some ways to analyze proposals are to study the history of the price involved, the various industrial and governmental indices that are available, how the price was built up, how the price breaks down into its various elements, detailed cost estimates, contingency factors, value analysis, functional evaluation, and the vendor's cost analysis.

PRICE-COST NEGOTIATION

Let us take a typical example of a negotiation for cost contract as opposed to a negotiation for total price. There are advantages to be derived from cost negotiation. It requires the buyer to prepare more effectively and in greater detail; it requires the seller to examine each factor that has gone into his calculations and makes him careful about padding costs or misapplying certain costs; and finally, where both parties have made detailed cost analysis, they are more likely to make their own improvements in the advantages that can be gained from reducing technical requirements or using different materials. Of course, a seller may counter with the fact that he would like separate agreements for the separate cost items involved. He may require a contingency allowance for each cost element rather than a reasonable contingency applicable to all factors. The seller realizes that these separate agreements have a tendency to enlarge his profits. In this instance the whole does not equal the sum of the parts, since it is impossible to prevent at least some of the allowances from being duplicated. So the moves and countermoves might go in a cost negotiation, but the end result should be that all the knowledge gained should be shared and these things worked out for mutual advantages. What is happening is that by each side making a penetrating analysis of all the elements, creative alternatives are arrived at that can lead to improvements in terms of altered materials, revised buying practices, relaxed specifications, simplified manufacturing processes, and so forth. This is negotiation with action.

SELLING—THE REVERSE SIDE OF THE COIN

Analyzing what he is selling is a substantial part of the seller's job. Self-analysis in this area is vital. If his selling concept coincides with the buyer's objectives, the sale may be made long before he gives the buyer a price or starts talking about writing up the orders. A certain portion of the initial stage of every negotiation should be involved with comparing the seller's concepts and the buyer's objectives so they can be brought closer together.

A seller should know who makes the decisions in the purchasing company. He should recognize that the decisions are not necessarily made by the person who has the title and the responsibility. Decisions, after all, might be made by the chairman of the board's secretary. In addition to the decision-makers, he should get to know all of those who have an influence on the company's buying. Many times he can establish an alliance with these people. Examining the purchaser in depth will permit him to see some of these relationships and will also prevent him from creating unnecessary adversaries within the buyer's firm.

A salesman is a representative of his company. He must be able to convince the buyer that, as such, he can bring to bear all this company's resources in fulfillment of the buyer's needs. Too many salesmen fail to make the purchaser aware of the resources of the organization he is representing. Whether his company is large or small the salesman should make it clear to the buyer that he can get the job done, that he and other members of the sales staff are really an arm or branch of the buyer's organization, and that he is capable of marshaling the full resources of his company on behalf of the buyer. Several Union Carbide salesmen met to discuss negotiation with their higher officers. They were not told how to handle a price situation that concerned them but rather were shown how they could make available to their customers the full resources of their entire organization. This, they found, was more important to them and to their customers than any price considerations they thought they were forced to deal with. John Ruskin understood people and price when he said, "There is hardly anything in the world that some man cannot make a little worse and sell a little cheaper, and the people who consider price only are this man's lawful prey."

Many salesmen feel that their entire selling job involves price concessions. Price as a single item is unimportant. Price is one of the elements that goes to make up value. The value signifies the full-scale relationship of a particular product to a process, not the dollar cost alone. The product must fit into an entire process. Every element involved in the process is of equal importance; if any element does not stand up, the entire process fails. A salesman should learn the values that he represents: his knowledge of his company's objectives, of his product, and the present and future business potentials of his own and the buyer's company. He should have an interest in the ability of his customer to continue and improve his profits, and he must have the ability to demonstrate his capacity to meet objectives. All of these are meaningful in establishing a relationship with a buyer.

In the overall scheme the buyer's and seller's objectives are the same, and the seller's representative should establish a satisfactory arrangement in which the objectives of both can be achieved. What are some of the objectives that he has to work for? He has to show the buyer that he can have a better value with, possibly, less work involved, promotional values, greater profitability, or potential for growth. The product might also represent consolidation of supply or an additional source of supply. Service might be better so that past performance would be remembered and rewarded. He might point out that the selling company is not a competitor and would not become one, that purchasing the product might aid in breaking into a market or making a firm market to the buyer's advantage.

The seller should evaluate the tax advantages, credit advantages, research and development advantages, and information advantages to the buyer. He should review every possible need that he can envision on the part of the buyer. Then he should see how he is capable of filling these needs or what needs he can influence.

Not all sellers have the same problems. If you are a giant in the field, special rules apply to you. When a firm is controlling in the field, it is concerned about the antitrust laws. The giant is permitted under the law to meet a competitive price but not beat it. If a customer says he is buying a product at ten and a half cents, the large company is allowed to meet the ten-and-a-half-cent price. It is *not* allowed to offer ten and a quarter cents. If the customer misleads the company and says he is getting it for ten cents, the customer is guilty of an antitrust violation under the law. This law violation is not as widely known as selling below competition. The following are some of the tactics used by some salesmen of a dominant chemical manufacturer in order to obtain the prices offered to its customers by the competition.

First is bracketing. When the chemicals salesman sees a customer, he does not usually say directly, "What price are you paying?" Instead, he goes to the customer and says, "I know that you're too experienced to pay eleven cents a pound, and I know you couldn't buy it for ten cents." Suddenly he has bracketed in; he knows the area. "If I wanted to offer it to you at ten and three fourths, it would do me no good if you were paying ten and a fourth." By bracketing he has narrowed in on the target; he knows pretty well where the price falls. The salesman can use a series of questions which help disclose the price being paid without having to commit himself.

A second way for the salesman to handle the situation is to say to the customer, "Look, if you make me guess what the price that you are paying is—let's say ten and a half cents—and I meet it without absolutely knowing that your supplier is giving you that price, not only must I offer it to you at that price, the antitrust laws say I must offer it to all your competitors. However, if *you* tell *me* what your price is, and I can meet it, then I don't have to offer it to your competitors. For example, if you tell me what your price is— say ten and a half cents—I can meet it and meet it for this instance only and I do not have to make the same price available to all your competitors." This takes into account the fact that if the seller lowers the price just to meet competition he does not have to offer it to all of his other customers.

A third method is feinting. It can also work in this situation. The salesman says, "With your price in mind, we can make the regular quantities available." The ensuing conversation between seller and buyer takes place without a mention of price because the salesman convinces the buyer he knows the price and has taken it for granted.

Misstatement, a fourth way, works as follows: "I know that you're paying twelve and a half cents." The buyer interrupts, "What do you mean twelve and a half cents? I'm only paying ten and a half." "I meant ten and a half, sorry." An intentional misstatement has produced the wanted information. Or the misstatement might be, "I hear the price has gone up." "No, no, the price is still the same . . ."

A fifth way of getting the information is by asking the other person's opinion: "Look, I respect your ability to analyze the market. Now, what do you think the market for the product is today?" You are not asking him for the price he pays; you are asking for his evaluation of the marketing conditions. You will usually get a straightforward answer using this tactic, provided you have established a relationship marked by mutual respect.

There is not any one method that is "best" in all instances, certainly not in the buying-selling procedure. A salesman must use his imagination to sell his product. In the process he may have to sell the buyer on different methods of buying. A salesman must always be ready to sell his customers on changing the way they buy. As an illustration, some companies have decided that they get the best terms by requiring the sellers to submit bids. Competitive bidding is valuable, but it also has disadvantages.

Many large selling firms do not favor submitting bids. They find themselves at a disadvantage with respect to the smaller company. The smaller firms can make decisions more rapidly, make adjustments in their bids, and be more successful in obtaining the orders.

A salesman for a large firm found the following method useful in overcoming this problem. First he tried to change a bidding situation into one which becomes a negotiating situation. This was done by submitting, in answer to the bid, a price or terms that were ambiguous and indefinite. As an example, if the period in which delivery was to be made was for six months, the bid would specify delivery over a year. The buyer would then have to call the salesman to ask about the vague term. At that time the salesman would be in a position to initiate negotiations. Then he would be in a position to point out that the bidding method cannot take into account subsequent changing market conditions and that a negotiated price for shorter terms than even six months with price protection might serve the interest of the buying company more fully.

No matter whether you are a buyer or a seller, knowing and acquiring the skills of both is essential for involvement in the purchasing-selling process.

Let us now consider in the next chapters some specific buying and selling applications.

CHAPTER 12 APPLICATIONS

1. Use the Need Theory of negotiating, strategy, and questions to set up an advance outline of how you would approach a typical purchasing-selling situation.

2. Try to create a supportive climate in a selling situation, then in a purchasing one.

13

REAL ESTATE NEGOTIATIONS

It appears that in the usual purchase of real estate, the buyer feels that he can do a somewhat better job or sees the property in an entirely different light than the seller. There are instances, of course, where the seller has to convert his investment, perhaps liquidate it, but we are talking about the normal course of real estate transactions. The buyer feels a little more creative or better informed than the seller. These thoughts are especially true when there is land or property to be developed.

Here also as in other purchases there is a grave danger in asking the seller of real estate why he is selling. The danger is that you are likely to believe him and therefore not investigate the proposition as thoroughly as you should. The seller will give excellent reasons for selling a piece of property, in spite of the fact that it has continuing growth possibilities and that it is the finest piece of land for anyone to own. He will open up his desk drawer and show you electrocardiograms that the doctor has just sent him, revealing that he has a heart condition and must give up all work. In other words, he has been prepared for that question and will, instead of the truth, give the answer that he feels will somehow induce you to buy the property. Lying seldom has the long-term effect that the liar would hope to gain. One seller's strategy is to make a realistic use not only of the truth which people affirm but also the untruths which generally are widely and confidently believed, like the selling tactics used by real estate brokers when they try blockbusting.

Few people know how to use brokers in real estate. Brokers serve a vital function. They are your antenna out in the field, feeding you new information: new sources of financing, areas for development, and new methods of closing transactions. All of these are vital to any real estate organization. Brokers, as well as lawyers, should be informed of the function you want them to serve. A broker may conceive of his duties as including an attempt to negotiate for you. This should rarely be the case. An opportune time that such service of a broker should be utilized in this way is when you want to make use of the agent with limited-authority approach. In this case, you do not want to commit yourself to any final decision but prefer to have the broker bring the details to you. You in turn will have him submit your proposition without the necessity of a face-to-face meeting in which you run the risk of having to make or break a deal on the basis of an offer. If the broker acts as an intermediary, however, you have a second chance of going in ultimately as a principal and varying the terms.

If you use an agent, understand some of the inherent limitations in such a situation. The agent, broker, or attorney, as the case may be, tries not to let your expectations become fixed until the other side's position becomes clear. The agent tries to prevent your early freezing of position. If you do freeze, he will try to change your expectations. This is usually done by getting or revealing new information which is designed to alter your point of view—e.g., the agent says he can get property at a cheaper price. The agent understands that he does not usually earn his commission until the closing. Therefore, when the preliminary contract is signed, he will do his best to make you feel that the contract deal conforms to your needs and expectations. For example, he will say, "You have everything you need."

There are many instances where the agent will not reveal all aspects of the result unless forced to by the principal. The agent may calculate that everything will turn out all right. He hopefully rationalizes that things we worry about most are those that rarely happen.

CHAPTER 13 APPLICATIONS

1. Use the Need Theory of negotiating, strategy, and questions to set up an advance outline of how you would approach a typical real estate situation.
2. Think of at least ten ways in which a broker's service could be used advantageously.

14

DEALS AND NEGOTIATION

Deal men are a special group. Of necessity they must be optimistic. Most of their fees are contingent on success and are therefore higher than mere compensation for work. In the rare instances where they triumph, the clients immediately try to reduce the fee. The following are aspects of "wheeling and dealing" that should be considered before any formal negotiation begins.

Creating new ideas requires the greatest imaginative effort. With a truly new idea, be careful. You are a pioneer. As a pioneer you are going to get shot at. This is true today with the British. They fear being first again, as they were in television broadcasting, jet engines, and jet transports. They ran into difficulties and were overtaken by the Americans, who had learned by their mistakes. If you want to change the world, get involved with "good ideas." If, however, you want to make money, become involved with successful ideas. A successful idea is one that shows a present financial return. Nothing is wrong with the good or successful idea. The question is, What is the goal? Do not confuse the goals.

Before a broker gets into a proposition, no matter how good it seems, he should first make sure that one side of the deal is tied down. So many people blindly go in on the basis of a third party's say-so. That third party cannot commit the principal, and when he says, "If only we could find someone interested in X piece of property, everyone could make money," the broker runs off looking for a buyer. He has failed to get one side of the deal pinned down. It is like trying to hold a snake in the middle—at least get the head secure before fooling around with it. When the broker comes up with a buyer for X property he usually finds that it was never for sale in the first place.

Another type of unproductive venture that a deal man gets involved with is called a daisy chain. That is, someone comes to him and asks if he can obtain a particular product that is quite difficult to find. After investigating he discovers that the person who made the request does not use the product at all. He was told by a person who was told by a person who was told by a person that he could use it. Each one in turn adds a little percentage to the price and cost. This makes a daisy chain out of the deal. The deal man is unfortunately on the end of it. These are poor types of propositions to get involved with, because as each person is added to the daisy chain, the economic feasibility and the chance of success are decreased.

How can one interest people in investing in deals? Try to change the concept of the approach from one that would call for a speculation into one that is an investment. To some people, putting money into an idea is a speculation; to others, it is an investment. It is much easier to get a person to make an investment than a speculation. For example, when a new restaurant that is about to open needs additional capital, the most willing investors are people who will do business with the new venture. The laundry man, the milkman, the cigarette-machine man, etc., all will be willing to lend or advance money for the operation. They are making an investment for an account. Consider who will gain from the operation of the business. Ask them to share the risk and make an investment. This arrangement offers mutual satisfaction. A helpful guide for approaching people for an investment is to find someone who has been successful in a similar venture. The sooner he is asked after the prior success, the more likely he is to make a similar accommodation.

GETTING OUT OF A DEAL

It would seem that many of the same considerations that we use in getting into a deal would apply to getting out. Yet the one is almost completely different from the other. We could make excellent decisions about what we think would be worthwhile reasons for getting into a deal but they would be useless in setting forth alternatives of how to get out of the deal. Getting out seems to require as much creativity. Although the creative people who come up with propositions are usually there to put the propositions in operation, when a decision is made to get out of a deal, the same type of creative person is not usually around.

Many times we find ourselves so entangled in a deal that we feel like the little Dutch boy with his finger in the dike. If we should leave, the entire sea would inundate us. Even in such a situation there are people who will come along and ask, "What are you doing?" This is similar to the episode in *Tom Sawyer* where the children saw him whitewashing the fence and asked him, "What are you doing?" The more he told them to go away the more they were interested, until finally he had them painting the fence, doing his work. The more you refuse to let people in on what is happening, the more they want in. One way of withdrawing from the situation is to get someone else to put his finger in the dike. An alternative, in getting out of a deal, is to get someone who has a greater interest than you in making the deal successful. It then becomes his problem. With his sustained interest you can withdraw and rely on his pulling it through.

When we talk about alternatives for getting out, one is reminded of the story of the scientist who decided to test the intelligence of several monkeys. He figured out scientifically that there were four ways a monkey could get out of a cage, and each way was progressively more difficult. Therefore, a monkey's intelligence would be rated on what method he used to get out of the cage. On putting one monkey into the cage, the scientist discovered that there was a fifth way of getting out of the cage—the one the monkey used. The Chinese say, "Think three times before you take this first step," recognizing that it is harder to get out of a deal than into it.

CHAPTER 14 APPLICATIONS

1. Use the Need Theory of negotiating, strategy, and questions to set up an advance outline of how you would approach a typical deal.
2. Think of several additional unproductive ventures in which deal men may find themselves.
3. Make a list of reasons for getting into a deal. Now make a list of reasons for getting out of a deal. Do you see any similarity?

15

CORPORATE NEGOTIATIONS

An officer in charge of acquisition, reconfirming other purchasing experience, told me, "I never ask anyone why he wants to sell. The reason is, I might believe him." We all want to do as little work as is required. If we believe someone, we might fail to investigate as thoroughly as possible.

In the many seminars that have been given on mergers and acquisitions, the participants start off with the question, How can we tell the intent of a buyer making an overture for a merger or acquisition? Then the other question occurs: How can we tell the intent of a seller making an overture for a merger or acquisition?

A person who says he is interested in acquiring another company may be believed or doubted. What are some of the reasons that he might not be sincere? He might merely be looking for business secrets or even be interested in setting up a competitive company. There may be a group within the buyer's organization that has set up opposition to the management and is demanding certain changes. The management, in order to pacify these people, is on a course of alleged acquisition. Earnestness may also be questioned in the seller. It might be that the president of the alleged seller merely wants to know at this stage of his life what his business is worth. Or he might just like the challenge of entering into a merger negotiation. When there is a dissenting group within the organization, the same may be true for a seller. They may feel that the management or the president is not doing everything that he can. In order to prevent changes in management the president is supposedly looking for a buyer of the corporation. Or the seller may be attempting to discourage a take-over by an outside group.

One direct way for the buyer or seller to determine the seriousness of the approach on the merger or acquisition is to ask for detailed, difficult, and costly information. Require the other party to go to a great deal of work in order to satisfy your request. This will discourage window shopping.

At the proper time in the discussion ask that other people be brought into the negotiations: their lawyers, accountants, dissenting stockholder groups, public relations people. In the event that the person you are dealing with is reluctant, that reluctance would certainly give an indication of whether he is sincere in his buy or sell offer.

Project your plans into the future. See how the other side reacts to it. Is their philosophy the same? Is your emphasis and direction the same? Are you willing to risk funds for research and development? Would the other party find this difficult? These are subjects that will precipitate discussion or problems that would come up later in the negotiation. If these questions are delayed too long, you will waste a tremendous amount of time and energy. In line with that, if there are questions that will require ultimate resolution, with due and timely consideration, bring them out into the open. How are we going to utilize the real estate in the future? Whose salaries are going to be frozen? What relatives are we going to retain in the company's employ? Might there be emotional problems with the employees in a future merged or acquired company? Caution should be used in how these topics are brought up, but brought up they should be.

For some reason in negotiation discussion, there are sensitive areas that the parties are reluctant to go into. These are the areas that should be gone into immediately. Do not rely on abstracted or hearsay information. Consult the people involved immediately: the research and development people, the engineers within the plant, the managers, the marketing people, and the personnel people. Visit the plants and discuss any problems. Do not be satisfied with the cold figures contained in the balance sheets. They are only indications of what is going on. Some people might resolve the entire deal, having looked at nothing more than the financial figures and statements. They have never asked for or sought verification from the makers of these facts—namely, from the people involved. (Lawyers are later kept busy by these clients.) The person being acquired should not be shy, bashful, or reluctant to visit the company that is acquiring him, to see the people who are involved, to discuss with the former officers of other acquired companies whether they are satisfied. This is essential.

If you are a seller you must review your own critical information long before the buyer asks for it. You should review yourself, review the figures, talk to your own people. If you do not find your review satisfactory, bring about changes that would make your company more valuable to the buyer.

There is a recent movement within the accounting profession to establish standard methods to attempt to put a monetary value on the personnel involved in a selling company. It will be some time before this can be accomplished, but the least that one can do presently is to make his own form of evaluation of the personnel and the value that such personnel have to the organization. He should then consider if the resulting organization will be attractive enough to keep them.

When interviewing various personnel, ask yourself these questions: Is he a company or a noncompany man? Are his goals the same goals as the corporation? This will help you to deal with that individual, recognizing the fact that a deal that you may put together would be very advantageous for the company but it might cause the individual to leave because of his own particular economic needs—or even emotional needs.

DON'T SHOOT THE WORKS IN AN ACQUISITION

No matter how bright the prospect may be for a merger or acquisition, never risk your entire company. Do not bet the complete future of the firm on a payoff, no matter how good it may appear.

If a tempting situation cannot be passed by, and you must handle it, try dividing the great risk into scaled-down, smaller ones. As an executive of a corporation, you cannot afford to think of a single scale. You must see the broad picture and understand that your duties and obligations are manifold to stockholders, management, employees, their families, and general society. As Leonardo da Vinci said, "Do not undertake things if you see that you will suffer in case you do not succeed."

Remember, too, Agnes Allen's law: "Anything is easier to get into than out of." It is harder to get out of a deal than into it. It would be most appropriate, when you are considering getting into a deal, to have another group of your associates considering realistically what it would be like if you were already in the deal and wanted to get out of it. Before getting into a deal, try considering that you will do as well as but not necessarily better than the present owners. The people who have the business have lived with it, thought about the problems, and from the involved vantage point are probably doing pretty much the same thing that you might do in their position. Unless you have significant information that is unknown to the present seller, you will end up, most probably, doing about as well as he is with the operation. Keeping that in mind, if you then feel that a merger or acquisition is warranted, go further. If not, drop it.

SETTING PRICE

Although some people feel that it is up to the person who is selling to set the price, this is not necessarily the case. If someone approaches a firm on the basis of being interested in acquiring it, he may very well be forced into a position wherein he has to set a price or set a method that he would be willing to use in acquiring the company. This can, for example, be some multiple of earnings or profit. It is not always up to the seller to set the price, but when the seller does set the price in the negotiation, the buyer should not immediately attempt to knock it down. Let him finish. The price that he asks represents more to him at the initial stage of the negotiation than you can realize.

In addition to the obvious economic factors, the price has the owner's life tied up in it. This is especially true if it has been a corporation that the individual has built from the start. It has his ego and his esteem built into it. It is a symbolic representation of his life's work. Do not undercut it directly. When the seller has furnished the asking price, the buyer might then say, "I would very much appreciate it if you would tell me the various basic elements that make up the price. Could you also let me know what formulas you have used, shall we say for goodwill, and what formulas you have used for inventory?" In this way, without directly challenging the price, you put the burden on the seller to justify his position.

As expectations rise and fall during a negotiation, so can a price and the things directly related to the economic aspects of the merger or acquisition. One error that is sometimes made is that the buyer by some action makes the seller feel that he has not asked a high enough price for the corporation. The seller might feel that way if the buyer immediately accepts the first asking price. If this ever happens, it can be a very costly mistake. The seller does not feel that he can then raise the asking price. He nonetheless thinks he made an error. He might try to kill the negotiation and then possibly look for another person to deal with, or do some other things that will add to the price and make the deal more costly. Try to let the seller work a little for what he is offering. Let him do a little selling. Let him do as much persuading and convincing as you can reasonably allow him.

In many negotiations the price that is initially asked might be put aside at that particular time. It is left open and the negotiations continue. Other points are then raised that reflect on the price and might cause the seller himself to reduce the price in order to compensate for the other demands: a guarantee of accounts receivable, the deterioration of certain of their properties, employment agreements, etc.

SUCCESS CAN KILL YOU

Did you ever realize that even success can kill you? A U.S. law firm had been retained by a British company which represented that they had control of a self-lighting cigarette. It was being made ready to be introduced into the American market. No matches were required; you merely rubbed a red dot on the tip of the cigarette against the bottom of the package, and it lighted. The product appeared to the law firm to have great appeal and public acceptance, yet on investigation it was found that it had failed in the English market. Success had ruined its sale.

In its campaign to start selling the self-lighting cigarette in England, the company had considered every potential problem except for great success. A major tobacco distributor was selected and he was given full responsibility for handling sales. As with other brands that he had introduced, he started an advertising campaign using television and other media. He covered the entire British Isles. The strategy was that everything would break in one day. It did, and as a result of the tremendous campaign that was launched, the shopkeepers sold out their entire stock in one day and immediately began to clamor for more. Although all the principals of the manufacturing film agreed that the cigarette was unique and should interest the public, no one had anticipated the phenomenal success.

The pipelines of distribution were quickly emptied. Only a small percentage of the demand could be met. The factories went into overtime production, but to no avail. Customers continued coming to the shops asking for another pack, but it took more than a month to get new shipments to the shopkeepers. By that time the demand had fully dissipated. People had tried the cigarette, found it to be a novelty, and asked for more, but when they could not get them, they went back to their old brand and forgot about the innovation. The distributor had spent the entire advertising budget in the first shot and it could not be started again. Hindsight permits us to say that a more realistic approach would have been to cover only a small section of the entire country and to promote the cigarette properly, keeping the pipelines of supply filled. Remember, when moving into unfamiliar territory, degrees of success should also be considered.

BLOCKING A TAKE-OVER

Along with mergers and acquisitions, some consideration should be given to blocking a take-over. Even the best management should have a plan to prevent one from taking place. Some basic advice in this situation would be: Do not make your company appear that attractive for a take-over. Make sure that its shares do not become undervalued by failing to maintain proper public relations. Let the stock market price reflect the true value within the industry. Have an early-warning system set up. Information can be obtained from inside connections with newspapers, investment bankers, and other people who keep their eyes and ears attuned for rumors. Advance notice is an important element so that you can immediately start fighting back. Have a plan set up to go into split-second action in the event that a take-over is brought to light. This should include an entire strategy with minutely developed tactics. The plan should have the implementations down to the notes and telegrams that one would send to the shareholders advising them of the financial status of the possible raider. Do not let a lifetime of devotion be dissipated through failure to heed early-warning signals or to consider adequate defense plans.

CHAPTER 15 APPLICATIONS

1. Use the Need Theory of negotiating, strategy, and questions to set up an advance outline of how you would approach a corporate negotiation.

2. With reference to a merger can you give any additional reasons why a corporate purchaser or seller might not be acting in good faith?

16

LABOR RELATIONS AND
CREATIVE ALTERNATIVES

A keen observer once said of Einstein that part of his genius was his inability to understand the obvious. The Japanese on the other hand were able to put the obvious to good use when they began to fight water with water. They came up with a system that uses plastic bags filled with water and piled up into dikes on the banks of an overflowing river.

Creative alternatives show up in rather strange but obvious ways. Here is a situation in which a union, very much aware of the attitudes of its potential members, used their attitudes to ensure that the union would win as the bargaining agent for the Puerto Rican Consolidated Cigar Company. The plant in Puerto Rico was unorganized. The union petitioned for an election.

Prior to the election, the union thoroughly propagandized the workers by using witchcraft. Witch doctors stated that anyone who voted against the union would have illness strike the family. Each member of the union was given this message personally. The sign that the witch doctors said would be shown them is that it would rain on the election day. That election day it poured for hours befor the election. Consolidated Cigar, on losing, felt that an unfair advantage was taken of it and brought an action before the National Labor Relations Board. Unfortunately the Puerto Rican government found this matter rather embarrassing and wanted it disposed of quickly, so when the N.L.R.B. said that the atmosphere of the election was acceptable, this ended the matter.

CREATIVE ALTERNATIVES

Creative alternatives can be used throughout a management-union negotiation. They can be different combinations of new and fresh or old and obvious approaches. The processes themselves can be constructively designed to lead to the improvement of conditions. Let us consider some of these creative methods:

One: Use continuous bargaining both around the clock and yearly; allow crises to be only minicrises by keeping the bargaining open and going.

Two: Use subdivisions of a negotiating committee to divide crises. Send out a subcommittee for discussion of the points on which there may be disagreement.

Three: When you feel that there might be a crisis, have a precrisis mediation that starts from the beginning and goes along with the negotiation right to the finish.

Four: As mentioned in the chapter on strategy and tactics, under participation, coalition bargaining is a new method that became known as a result of a San Francisco newspaper strike. The publisher and all the unions meet together, at the same time. Each labor contract is discussed separately. However, all unions and the employer are present during each negotiation. The unions retain separate autonomy and the employer does not have to deal with more than one at a time. You can see that what is said by the employer must be consistent and presented to all the unions.

Five: In the discussion of a contract, it could be decided that the noneconomic aspects will be negotiated individually, and, if not resolved, they could be turned over to compulsory arbitration.

Six: In order to stimulate early ratification, the parties can agree that the matters will not have retroactivity. This encourages early action because if the union ratifies late, the contract is retroactive only to the date of the ratification.

Seven: In the hotel industry in New York, a contract is entered into for a long period, perhaps three or four years. Wages and hours are the only part of that contract that can be reopened, and this must be before an impartial chairman. Although the wages and hours can be reconsidered during the life of the contract, many of the side issues that would cause problems for the industry are eliminated. This is a valuable approach to industries dealing with perishable products. Examples of perishable products are airline seats, theater seats, and hotel rooms. Once an airplane takes off with an empty seat, once a show begins with an empty seat, once a hotel lets a day pass without a room being occupied, that is the end of the product. People in perishable-product industries should realize this, both management and union.

Eight: In order to encourage early agreement, there is a method referred to as preactivity, a sort of retroactivity in reverse. When a point of dispute between an employer and employee is agreed to, on the date of that ratification, the new term goes into effect and this can be much in advance of all the other terms.

Nine: When the negotiation is centralized and occurs on a high level and the individual local unions are not bound as to how the package or the amounts in the packages are to be distributed, they are allowed individual choices. As an example, the Southern members might prefer Confederate Memorial Day rather than Lincoln's Birthday as a holiday. This encourages self-determination, with employee involvement as the result.

Compare creative negotiation (with various alternatives) to the "one" type of negotiation that epitomized General Electric. GE allegedly adopted an approach of "take it or leave it," which soon became known as Boulwarism. At the same time it adopted Boulwarism, GE was alleged to have continued to communicate with the employees in a program that was designed to undercut the union. GE's bargaining policy was simple. At the start of the talks it would make one offer that considered all the factors that would go into the final settlement. It might be willing to modify the terms in negotiation but not go beyond them. Although in 1964 the National Labor Relations Board held that GE failed to bargain in good faith in 1960 negotiations, by continuing this method over and over again GE encouraged thirteen unions to band together in the strike of 1969–70.

Boulwarism, the GE bargaining pattern, is named after Lemuel R. Boulware, former chief of labor relations for the company. It is supposedly founded on the concept that management weighs all the equity and then makes an early offer that it considers fair to the employees, the stockholders, and the company. The important fact is not that the matter of Boulwarism was contested in the Supreme Court of the United States or that GE's 1963 Boulwarism in bargaining was disputed by the unions. What is important is that GE's repetition of one method in a continuous bargaining situation does not utilize the many possible creative alternatives, the creativity of possible solutions in which both sides are successful and feel that they have each gained something from the negotiations.

LABOR RELATIONS AND COMMUNICATION

One obligation of a manager is to maintain successful and open communication with employees. He uses many other people to help him accomplish this: his foremen and anyone else who comes in contact with the employees. This might be considered in line with the strategy of participation. In many instances the employees have not been made aware of who is paying for the various benefits that they receive through welfare funds, retirement plans, insurance, etc. Some of these may come from the union, others through the government, but most of them are paid for by the employer. A consulting company has been formed which offers the employers the following services: the company will interview each employee and make a computerized estate-planning program for him to have for his personal use. These people are experts in the fields of mutual funds, estate planning, and health and life insurance. The employee discusses with the estate planner his own investments, his savings, his house, aside from the benefits that flow from his job. He is then able to plan his entire economic future. The employee can be made to see who is paying for the bulk of his job benefits. Taking a broad economic view facilitates job satisfaction and makes the employees less prone to job changing.

An entirely different type of communication, which may be necessary in the course of labor-management negotiations, involves preparation for a possible strike. Here, the company can do certain things that are direct indications to the union of building strength in opposition to the strike. They might prepare themselves to operate the plant with other personnel or management personnel, start to build inventories, make preparations for the transfer of production, try to secure financial resources that would enable them to withstand a strike. The union, on the other hand, in preparation for a strike may order signs, cause intentional leaks to the press of the difficulties that are going on, become more violent in their emotions, and also make arrangements for strike funds from their national union or other source.

SHIFTING LEVELS IN LABOR RELATIONS

In labor negotiations it is easy for one side or the other to shift levels if the various elements of the different levels are recognized. For example, let us take a company: Its top-level management is perhaps concerned with principles and money, the central management with policies and precedents, and the plant level with convenience in administration. Let us next consider the union: The rank and file is more concerned with efforts to obtain higher wages than the union leadership is. The employment issues, work rules, and disciplinary action are also concerns of the rank and file. The union leadership on the intermediate level is concerned with parity among the members, even in different plants in separate fields. They are concerned with the institutional character, the precedent, the policy, the public image, and the size of the membership. The national union leadership, on the other hand, may be concerned with the national wage pattern. Recognizing this in the negotiation would permit you at certain times to shift levels and apply the pressure to the area that is most appropriate.

Further, there is a difference in the interests of different people in the event of a strike. First, the top union officials may be open to criticism in the event of the failure of the strike. They may be less willing to gamble on it. Second, whoever is paying for the strike may not be inclined to have one. There are levels in information. Various people in control of a strike can look at the situation only in terms of the information that has been made available to them, on the basis of their experience and the novelty of the situation.

The following are specific labor relations examples of shifting levels. Instead of striking a restaurant, some union people decided that they would come into the restaurant just before lunch hour, order coffee, and sit. Another way of shifting levels would be to go outside the labor-management scope. Instead of striking, bring an action before the National Labor Relations Board or in the courts. A third way is one in which the union circulates a newspaper to the management personnel, to influence them.

EVOLVING STAGES IN LABOR RELATIONS

I. FORMATION STAGE

The management's reactions during the organizing stage can be described as anxious and puzzled. Management is not inclined to permit the union to participate in the management area nor in the distributions of any other rewards of the business. Management finds it difficult to believe that the workers, for whom they have done so much, are now turning against them. Some management groups will do only the legal minimum—that is, sitting down to negotiate, just listening to the union leaders, then making arbitrary decisions, and expecting that those decisions will be acted on by the union.

The union's reactions during this stage are just as childish. Some of the union's activities are merely engaged in to create the maximum amount of harm to the business organization without a reciprocal gain for the individual members or the union.

II. DEVELOPING STAGE

During this stage the disagreements are classified. Everyone is looking for the cause of the problems. But the union and management have more or less learned that they are going to have to deal with each other and the contract becomes the all-important document that sometimes may run for hundreds of pages. Management tries to strengthen its rights and the various clauses are used to contain the union. The union tries to widen the scope of its bargaining power. Both try to limit the freedom of action of the other to deal with problems of the business.

At this stage many people feel that solutions to management-labor problems lie in a literal interpretation of contracts. They do not consider the fact that the relationship of the parties is always superior to the agreement. Unfortunately, however, when problems concerning rights of the parties arise in this stage of development, the words written on paper are more important than the continuing relationship. The spirit of the agreement should be controlling. When a satisfactory relationship has been established, the written contract is merely incidental. The written contract is only there to prevent memories from failing and other confusions from occurring. I have seen an identical contract existing in twenty shops. Nineteen of the employers were able to live with it; the twentieth was having daily contract interpretation problems.

Labor relations probably runs ahead of diplomacy in attempting to continue negotiations past the formalized conclusions of the signing of a contract. Just how is this done? Even though labor lawyers have come up with a large vocabulary of specific language covering labor disputes and this language is used in the contracts, the way the parties use it subsequently allows them to continue the negotiation. Sometimes the contracts are concluded with ambiguity intentionally written in to permit discussion of a problem after a contract has been signed. If the language of the contract is unambiguous, but the action of the parties leads to an ambiguity, arbitrators and mediators will go outside the terms of the contract.

With this pattern being used in labor negotiations, it is not difficult to see how ambiguities of all types, which rest in the very nature of our language, are used to bring about results that were unanticipated when the contract was signed. When two parties are contending that a particular paragraph has different meanings, you might ask them to read the paragraph aloud to each other. You will notice that the intonations vary with the meaning that each one desires.

III. UNIFYING STAGE

The question now becomes how management and labor can make this structure and relationship work. Specific terms do not become the important items; the general nature of the relationship now is important. It shifts from a test of power to one of recognized areas in which they can accommodate and cooperate with each other. They begin to think in terms of relations, of a balance between the various determinants, and they choose to act on whichever one is within their reach and likely to have a better influence on the situation.

Even in the final stage there are vestiges of the other stages. Understanding these relationships and the different stages might permit the parties to adopt suitable negotiation strategies for each stage. As an example, there are several types of management responses. A hostile response will lead to perpetual conflict. The appeasement response gives away too much. A third is to be firm but fair, recognizing the union's concern with satisfying the employees' needs through collective bargaining and also the management's needs. Let us hope that in the future, management and labor will not only be concerned with the problems but that they will be just as concerned with the objectives that can be jointly achieved.

CHAPTER 16 APPLICATIONS

1. Use the Need Theory of negotiating, strategy, and questions to set up an advance outline of how you would approach a labor-management negotiation.

2. Think of additional creative alternatives in a management-union negotiation.

3. In any labor relations with which you are familiar, identify the evolving stage, with reasons.

17

LAW, LAWSUITS, AND EFFECTIVE NEGOTIATION

The lawsuit is one of the negotiating tools of a lawyer. It should not be used frivolously, but it can be used to induce the other side to negotiate. There are several stages in the litigation to recognize as opportunities to induce negotiation: the threat of a lawsuit, the commencement of a lawsuit, the preparation for trial, and the course of the trial. Even when the jury is out it is not too late to negotiate. In some matrimonial actions the parties refuse to start to negotiate until the trial is over and a decision has been handed down by the court. Over the course of these events, it is important to avoid intentionally arousing undue emotional reactions. Emotional actions have a tendency to induce retaliatory emotional reactions.

There is usually an excellent opportunity preceding a lawsuit for a discussion of settlement. However, if the defendant, the defendant's attorney, or his insurance company has a reputation for being difficult to negotiate with, an attorney may bypass this opening. This tactic, he feels, will indicate to the opposer his seriousness.

The opposer will then start to examine the attorney's reputation for conducting lawsuits, his ability to investigate, and continue into all the factors that make a case. The attorney for the plaintiff at the same time will be investigating the reputation of the defendant and his attorney and the witnesses for both sides. The best preparation for being able to negotiate to settle is to have the case ready for trial.

The lawsuit is only a segment of our behavioral process. Considering this, there are certain things to bear in mind. For example, everything is constantly changing so that one can never come up with the best answer or the only answer. Time itself will change the answers, the course of the lawsuit, and the expectations that one may have. You should reevaluate continually, look for new information, and keep rethinking the problem. Recognize that your perception of the problem comes from one viewpoint, that each and every person involved will consider the problem from a different point of view that is not objective. It is taken from a different angle and will have a different significance to each participant. In addition, we perceive selectively. An example of this was a broker who brought an action for a real estate commission. He stated that a deal was made and that he was entitled to his commission. On examination of everyone else present at the meeting, it appeared that the broker had selectively perceived only those factors that were of interest to him, mainly those things that indicated that a deal had been made. He excluded from his perceptions anything that was not in conformity with his preconceived idea that the deal was going through. If you do not think that you perceive selectively, try to recall where each letter and number appears on the telephone dial.

REMEMBER: MEANINGS AND VALUES ARE NOT STANDARD

The meanings and values involved in a lawsuit are different. One attorney's value may be completely different from the value of the other attorney. His concept of a good settlement may be far beyond what the other attorney might consider. The case may have great importance to the plaintiff and little or no importance to the defendant.

Everyone, being human, will make his own evaluations and assumptions. The assumptions are the foundations on which we build our problems. Try as best you can to state consciously the assumptions that you are making in reference to the problem. Before starting a lawsuit, are you assuming that the opposer cannot afford to go to trial? Are you assuming that the publicity involved will be detrimental to him? Or to yourself? What assumptions are you making? Do they have a foundation in reality? One way of answering these questions is to attempt to check your assumptions against the real outside world. This can be done by actions. Reexamine to what extent your assumptions check against your perceptions, the things that you can see, learn, smell, taste, and feel. Can the assumptions be worked with and relied on? If not, restate your assumptions, changing them according to the facts and your experiences. Our assumptions are somewhat like the scientist's hypotheses. They are useful until they prove themselves false to fact. You must be as ready to change your assumptions as a scientist is to change his hypotheses.

SHIFTING LEVELS

As we have discussed under strategy and tactics, we tend to divide the world into levels. A problem can have entirely different appearances, almost like the faces of Janus, on different levels. At one level it will smile and be resolved, and on another it will frown and be unresolvable. Look at it on a different level. Many times, in negotiating with government officials on a local level, attorneys have merely been battering their heads against a wall. However, when they shifted the problem to the state level and spoke to people who possibly had a broader view and were more skillful in their approach to negotiations, the attorneys were able to resolve the difficulty in a short time. We can change a legal problem by shifting levels to the more general or the more particular.

You may feel that the particular lawsuit cannot be negotiated. It may be that you have placed it in a context that made it less resolvable. Try to place it in an entirely different relationship from the one you would consider its normal context. To cite an example, a member of management of a very large company explained that the management was not interested in enforcing most of the legal implications of its contracts. In the event that there was difficulty with a good customer, it would resolve that problem without regard to legal rights or responsibilities. An attorney instituted suit against this company for a large amount for damages resulting from alleged material defects. When he changed the context of the approach from one of pure litigation to contacting the customer relations department, the problem took on a new significance. As a business matter it was immediately resolved.

Many times, when a matter does not lend itself to resolution, it is because we attempt to resolve it in one fell swoop. If, however, we analyze the problem and look at the elements involved, some of the elements may be resolved one at a time, and those that are unresolved may turn out to be of no importance. This can lead to the resolution of the entire legal problem.

Many people on consulting attorneys take the almost absolute position that their approach or their view of the situation is right. Many of these clients waste a substantial amount of time with their attorney, attempting to convince him that they are right, feeling that if they are able to convince the attorney, he will have the necessary incentive to defend or prosecute their suits properly. They are projecting, projecting their own viewpoint, which may be very limited, on everything they see. This is a normal human psychological limitation, but realizing this limitation can open the mind and expand one's life-style. People begin to extend their horizons when they recognize that they are tending to project their viewpoint onto everything they come into contact with. This can be considered an example of the self-fulfilling prophecy.

The businessman who justifies everything that he does with the statement "Business is business" and expects in return that which he has been prepared to give projects all his expectation into his interpretations of the situation. He is prejudging the world through his own prejudiced eyes.

INVESTIGATION

Investigation, gathering the facts, is a very important aspect of handling a lawsuit. What information is available? It is best to come as close to the experience level as possible, not what one person thinks about what occurred but what was actually seen and heard or experienced by the participant. One can get witnesses who are farther and farther away from the actual experiences and at this distance some of them could not be used as witnesses because they would violate the rules of legal evidence. In investigating, go to the source, come as close to the experience as possible. Instead of relying on what an associate may say the witness said, speak to the witness. Instead of relying on diagrams and photographs of the scene of the occurrence, visit the scene. Each of us must resolve the question of how much information he needs to work toward a solution. Remember, a fact may merely mark the position where we stopped the investigation. What data would be extraneous and of no importance? This is viewed through the filters of one's assumptions, prejudices, and previous experiences. Recognizing these limitations may permit a person to open his mind further and more fully to information to which he may be exposed, and also to see it from different points of view and with a fuller appreciation.

A problem tends to take on a certain shape or structure within one's concepts. It can be of great assistance to be able to relate a problem to an entirely different structural interpretation. As examples, a chemical problem when reduced to a formula may lend itself to different solutions, a biological problem when converted into mathematical terms may lend itself to a different formulation. Therefore, diagram the problem in an entirely different way. This may give new insights.

Any lawsuit, as a life experience, is unique. It will never be duplicated. If you recognize this, every aspect of the case can be viewed as unique. One may know the law involved in the situation. However, research should be done specifically for this problem. Bear in mind: What are you looking for? Are you looking for a legal answer? Are you looking for a solution? Are you looking for just one solution? Perhaps there are many solutions. Try one, try two, try more, so that you may use the one that is appropriate. What you may once have conceived to be the "best" solution, you may, merely with the passage of time, be forced to discard and rely instead on another solution that you may once have been ready to ignore.

CHAPTER 17 APPLICATIONS

1. Use the Need Theory of negotiating, strategy, and questions to set up an advance outline of how you would approach a lawsuit situation.

2. Consider when a lawsuit is a necessity as opposed to a negotiating device.

18

SUCCESS

In conclusion, our study of the art of negotiation has included an examination of the philosophy and psychology of negotiating, and the preparation that is necessary beforehand. We have considered human behavior, both in its relation to negotiation and in its connection with fundamental human needs. We have evolved the Need Theory of negotiation, the variety of application to various types of needs, the methods for recognizing needs, asking questions, supportive climate, and finally the proper planning of strategy.

Negotiation is a tool of human behavior, a tool anyone can use effectively. I have tried to avoid shaping it into a specialized tool that would be suitable for use only by professionals. I have sought to give the realm of negotiation new forms that are allied to the forms of other types of human activities.

The successful negotiator must combine the alertness and speed of an expert swordsman with an artist's sensitivity. He must watch his adversary across the bargaining table with the keen eye of a fencer, ever ready to spot any loophole in the defense, any shift in strategy. He is prepared to thrust at the slightest opportunity. On the other hand, he must also be the sensitive artist perceptive of the slightest variation in the color of his opponent's mood or motivation. At the correct moment he must be able to select from his palette of many colors exactly the right combination of shades and tints that will lead to mastery. Success in negotiation, aside from adequate training, is essentially a matter of sensitivity and correct timing.

Finally, the mature negotiator will have an understanding of the cooperative pattern. He will try to achieve agreement and will remember that in a successful negotiation everyone wins.

And if this is the case, why shoot it out, when we can still talk it out?

CHAPTER 18 APPLICATIONS

1. What do you consider your present short-term goals of negotiating and your long-term goals of life?

2. Is there anything useful in the cooperative human process of negotiation that can assist you in achieving these goals?

APPENDIX: LIFE ILLUSTRATIONS

THESE ILLUSTRATIONS REFER TO CHART IV ON PAGE 101

The following life illustrations, 126 in number, offer you a handbook for future use in seeing alternatives. In a future negotiation it would be advisable to look at the matrix (see page 101) carefully from the number I to the number VII needs and the number 1 to the number 6 varieties of application from the A through C levels of approach in order to stimulate thinking of a possible creative alternative. After you have done that, verify it against the life illustration to see if it is precisely what you anticipated and whether still other alternatives may occur to you.

In a number of cases you may find examples that bear directly on negotiations you have conducted, are conducting, or will conduct in the future.

You can utilize these applications from the point of view of negotiator and/or opposer. Because you may find yourself on either side in the following negotiation illustrations, I have used the word

"opposer" to designate the opposite party rather than the word "opponent," which may carry an adverse connotation.
' But let us not forget the underlying philosophy of negotiating success—everyone wins.

I. HOMEOSTATIC NEEDS

I. NEGOTIATOR WORKS FOR OPPOSER'S HOMEOSTATIC NEEDS

Interpersonal. The drama of a would-be suicide (the opposer) who is persuaded to preserve his own life is an example of an individual (the negotiator) working for another person's homeostatic need. The object of the negotiation is to save a human life, and the negotiator will run the gamut of techniques in an effort to persuade the other person that his life is worth retaining.

Interorganizational. The periodic New York City newspaper strikes in the 1960's were an example of rivals working together. The members of the Publishers Association suspended publication of their newspapers when any member was struck. In 1965 *The New York Times* (the opposer) was struck, and six other daily newspapers (the negotiators) suspended publication. The *Times,* which carried more advertising than any of the others, was the chief economic rival of the other members. By closing shop along with the *Times,* however, the other papers brought great economic pressures to bear on union leaders and others affected by the strike. The financial pressures they endured themselves were also enormous, and several papers were later forced to withdraw from the Association and finally to merge rather than risk business failure. Of course, as we have noted in Chapter 2, the union's excesses resulted in the ultimate shutdown of the papers.

International. Nations frequently use the gambit of encouraging a newly emerged nation to prove its viability and then extending diplomatic recognition. An example of the use of this gambit took place during the American Revolution. In 1763, at the close of the Seven Years War, France had lost back most of its colonial empire to Great Britain. Therefore the revolt of the British American colonies in 1775 seemed to the French a heaven-sent opportunity for weakening England.

Pierre de Beaumarchais, whose comedies *The Barber of Seville* and *The Marriage of Figaro* still live as operas, organized a dummy corporation with the secret assistance of the French government. The company funneled French money and supplies into the American colonies. However, France (the negotiator) was not being altruistic in all this. Her strategy was to keep a steady pressure on the colonies (the opposer) to make a complete break with England. Many colonists were reluctant to make such a move in spite of the fact that the patriot cause seemed hopeless without official French aid. However, the Declaration of Independence was finally adopted in 1776, more than a year after the Revolution had begun. Still France held back from overt aid until the colonists proved they had a chance of winning the war. Happily for the patriot cause, John Burgoyne, a boring playwright and a worse general, provided the opportunity in 1777, when he invaded New York from Canada. Led into a trap at Saratoga, Burgoyne and his army surrendered.

Proving that they were able to maintain themselves successfully, the colonists found the benefits enormous. Within a few months France, Spain, and the Netherlands recognized the United States. Not only could the new nation obtain money and supplies from them, but the French Navy was a constant threat to the British Isles. The British Navy had to split its fleet: one part blockaded France while the rest was employed in America. The final victory at Yorktown was possible only because the French fleet was put at Washington's disposal. Washington's army pinned the British forces against the coast and the French fleet prevented their rescue by sea.

2. NEGOTIATOR LETS THE OPPOSER WORK FOR HIS HOMEOSTATIC NEEDS

Interpersonal. Occasionally guards negotiate with a prisoner. Although his freedom of action is controlled and his area to negotiate limited, he can be made to work for his homeostatic needs. Nevertheless, some guards (the negotiators) can motivate him (the opposer) by offering to increase his diet. The prisoner has been negotiated into a position of working for his basic need to survive.

Interorganizational. Some giant organizations (the negotiator) have used this gambit with success. The owner of a small gasoline station (the opposer) might operate with such a low overhead that he can afford to cut prices to increase his sales. A large company persuades him against taking this action. Although the large company wants high gasoline prices in the long run, it can cut prices in the short run so drastically that the very existence of the small company is in jeopardy.

International. At the beginning of the twentieth century, 562 native states still existed within British India. These states based their independence on treaties their rulers had made with the British during the eighteenth and nineteenth centuries. Within their own domains the native princes ruled as absolute monarchs. Yet many of the states were small and most of the princes owed their thrones to the protection of the British Army. In their circumstances the princes (the opposers) were quite willing to work for their thrones, for their homeostatic need, by offering Britain (the negotiator) economic support and military loyalty even at the expense of their own people.

3. NEGOTIATOR WORKS FOR THE OPPOSER'S AND HIS OWN
HOMEOSTATIC NEEDS

Interpersonal. The extraordinary success of the fight against polio as opposed to other diseases is an example of this gambit. Franklin D. Roosevelt was crippled by the disease in 1921. When he became president twelve years later, he put his efforts into establishing the National Foundation for Infantile Paralysis. His appeals to the nation for funds met with great success, partly because of the openhandedness so typical of many Americans, but also because of the fear of this dread disease. Thus Roosevelt (the negotiator) worked to establish the Foundation for his own need and that of others (the opposers) to conquer polio and end the threat of physical impairment or even death.

Interorganizational. The 1961 conviction of twenty-nine major electrical manufacturers for price fixing brought to light a hitherto successful, albeit illegal, use of this negotiating gambit. It was to the advantage of the companies and officials involved to keep prices artificially high. To protect profits, the lifeblood of industry, they (negotiator and opposers) secretly agreed to fix prices on their products and to rig bids so that each company would receive its "fair" share of business.

International. National survival is a basic homeostatic need. In the nuclear age, nations at last have the power to annihilate their opponents in a single strike. Yet this awesome power has not and probably will not be put to use by either the United States or the Soviet Union. No treaty between the two nations can guarantee that nuclear weapons would not be used. However, by tacit agreement both (negotiator and opposer) have accepted the deterrent power of nuclear weapons. If one nation should use them, it could expect swift and devastating retaliation. Sir Winston Churchill, in his last major speech as Prime Minister, summed up the grim reality of the situation: "It may well be that, by a process of sublime irony, we shall reach a stage in this story where safety will be the sturdy child of terror and survival the twin brother of annihilation."

4. NEGOTIATOR WORKS AGAINST HIS HOMEOSTATIC NEEDS

Interpersonal. The variety of application may seem paradoxical, but there are many instances where this type of gambit has forced the issue and brought the negotiation to a successful conclusion. An article in the October 2, 1964, issue of *The New York Times* provides an example:

> *A special mission to Saigon last summer taught Herbert Schmertz how hazardous the life of a lawyer-labor arbitrator can be. Shortly after he checked out of his hotel, a bomb blew up on the floor where he had been staying. "I was sent by the government to study labor relations in the port of Saigon and found myself in a hotel whose staff was on strike," he explained. "When one employee threatened to disembowel himself in the lobby, it was too much. I got out, and I just made it in time. The prefect of Saigon later settled the strike by threatening to arrest the hotel manager. It was efficient but it's not the way we mediate in America."*

The lawyer arbitrator was wrong. It *is* one of the ways Americans negotiate. However, he failed to see the structure into which these techniques fit. He failed to realize that the child who holds his breath to force his mother to give in to his desires, or the insane person who threatens to slash his wrists if the guard will not give him a cigarette, is using the identical method. In each case the individual (the negotiator) works against his physiological need to gain his objective. Undoubtedly these acts are considered by some to be irrational, but they are not. They are a well-thought-out and effective means of achieving the desired goals. Only those who cannot rationalize the other person's premises for these acts consider them irrational.

Interorganizational. For a business organization (the negotiator) to deliberately work against its need to increase its income would also seem at first glance to be an irrational act. It would be much like the story of the merchant who does a land-office business by selling below cost. His explanation: "I may lose a little on each piece, but I make it up in the volume." Yet many large retail corporations (the negotiators) have found it to their advantage to sell loss leaders or bait merchandise. These are items sold at little or no profit to lure customers (the opposers) into the store. Their individual profits on the loss leaders may be nil, but they hope the gross profit from all sales will be higher.

International. Anschluss, the union of Austria with Germany in 1938, provides a vivid example of negotiators (the Austrian government) working against their homeostatic need for survival. After World War I the great Austro-Hungarian Empire was divided and Austria became a minor power deprived of the economic resources it needed to survive. Although the Treaty of Versailles had forbidden union between Germany and Austria, sentiment for it grew every time Austria went through one of its periodic financial crises. Adolf Hitler's rise to power brought the threat of *Anschluss* nearer. For a time the National Socialist (Nazi) Party was banned in Austria because of its strident support of *Anschluss.* However, Chancellor Kurt von Schuschnigg (the opposer) was forced to legalize the Nazi Party and in 1938 to appoint three Nazis to high government offices. Now thoroughly alarmed by German threats, Schuschnigg called for a plebiscite on *Anschluss* and made a belated effort to unify his bitterly divided nation. Hitler's response was a demand that the plebiscite be called off, and German troops were massed at the Austrian border. Schuschnigg resigned. German troops occupied the country without resistance from the Austrian people, who then voted overwhelmingly for *Anschluss.* The Austrians (the negotiators) had traded their national identity for possible individual advantages.

5. NEGOTIATOR WORKS AGAINST THE OPPOSER'S HOMEOSTATIC NEEDS

Interpersonal. A simple example is the case of a woman (negotiator) on a sinking ship. She wants to get into the lifeboat, but there is a man (opposer) ahead of her. She negotiates for her own life by using a culturally accepted formula as a gambit. She states a law of the sea—"Women and children first." She works against the most basic need of the man—preservation of his life—in her attempt to have him step aside at his own mortal risk.

Interorganizational. In 1964 a federal panel headed by U.S. Surgeon General Luther Terry reported that smoking was definitely harmful to health. Most damning was medical evidence indicating that cigarettes, in particular, increased one's susceptibility to lung cancer. Although some measures were taken to control cigarette advertisements, smoking is still allowed to be advertised in magazines and newspapers. When a cigarette advertiser (negotiator) shows a beautiful girl and an adoring swain enjoying a good smoke, the advertiser is working directly against the homeostatic survival needs of the public (the opposer).

International. Control of territory is one of the basic homeostatic needs of a state. The purchase of Florida in 1819 by the United States (the negotiator) from Spain (the opposer) illustrates the use of this gambit, not only of working against one's opponent's need but brazenly using the gambit as an argument to *justify* the giving up of territory. The negotiations began as a result of an invasion of Spanish-owned Florida by General Andrew Jackson. A band of Indians and runaway slaves living near Pensacola had been making raids along the Georgia border. Jackson had orders to drive them out of the United States; he did so and then swept into Spanish territory and captured Pensacola and St. Marks.

James Monroe's cabinet, with the exception of John Quincy Adams (the negotiator), voted to apologize to Spain (the opposer) and reprimand Jackson. Adams, then Secretary of State, condemned both proposals and won Monroe's support. In a tough ultimatum Adams told Spain (the opposer) that if it could not police Florida, it should cede the territory to the United States. Spain, which was embroiled with its own rebellious South American colonies, could offer neither armed resistance nor effective argument against

Adam's gambit. After long negotiation, Florida was ceded to the United States for $5 million, and even that sum did not go to the Spanish government. It was used to pay outstanding debts owed by Spaniards to U.S. citizens.

6. NEGOTIATOR WORKS AGAINST THE OPPOSER'S AND HIS OWN HOMEOSTATIC NEEDS

Interpersonal. A negotiated, joint (negotiator and opposer) suicide pact is an illustration of this type of gambit that carries finality.

Interorganizational. When a strike is called, each side (negotiator and opposer) from that time on gives up its homeostatic need. The supplies to the factories are cut off and the wages to the employees are stopped. The fact that a strike affects the homeostatic needs of both sides makes it a very strong negotiating gambit.

Of course, in some union-industry disputes the participants are the last to feel the economic strain. Industry merely pays less in taxes or receives a tax refund. Employees are able to receive unemployment insurance plus compensation from union funds.

International. The U.S. Embargo of 1807 provides a unique example. The French Revolutionary Wars, and the Napoleonic Wars that followed, brought the United States to the brink of war with either Great Britain or France on a number of occasions. The national feeling varied as first one nation and then the other committed new outrages against American merchant shipping. Britain was trying to shut off all neutral trade with France. Napoleon, under his Continental System, seized any ship that was trading with Great Britain. Numerous American ships were seized by both sides.

President Thomas Jefferson (the negotiator) tried a bold new approach—bold because U.S. revenue relied for the most part on import duties, new because no Western nation had ever tried to shut off all commerce with all European nations (the opposers). The Embargo of 1807 did just that. No European ships were allowed to enter or leave American seaports. When it became apparent that trade continued with Britain through Canada, which was then its colony, Jefferson put an end to shipping on the American inland waterways as well.

Jefferson hoped that by depriving England and France of U.S. agricultural products and other trade he would work against their homeostatic need for food and clothing and force them into making concessions to the United States. He was also willing to sacrifice an even more basic national homeostatic need: sources of revenue. The gambit was disastrous to the United States. The American maritime fleet did not recover for many years. Shipbuilders and farmers suffered from the cutoff of international trade. And in two years U.S. revenues dropped to from $16 million in 1807 to $7 million in 1809. Jefferson had worked against his own country's need with a vengeance. Unfortunately he underestimated the homeostatic need for national survival that dominated British and French thinking. This was more important to both nations than commerce with the United States. In 1809, shortly before his second term ended, Jefferson reluctantly admitted the Embargo was a failure and obtained congressional repeal of the act.

II. SAFETY AND SECURITY NEEDS

1. NEGOTIATOR WORKS FOR THE OPPOSER'S SAFETY AND SECURITY NEEDS

Interpersonal. The efforts that parents (the negotiators) may use to try to promote "desirable" marriages for their children (the opposers) is an example of this gambit. The appeal is directed toward the child's need for the security that the parents say wealth and social position will provide. At the parent's age this need seems more basic than the child's romantic aspirations.

Dr. Samuel Johnson's statement on this subject was considerably more blunt than anything today's wise parent would be likely to say: "Were I a man of rank, I would not let my daughter starve who had made a mean marriage, but having voluntarily degraded herself from the station she was originally entitled to hold, I would support her only in that which she herself had chosen. . . ." Note that Johnson's unforgiving attitude adds further force to this gambit.

Interorganizational. It is common for a modern corporation to work for the security of its employees. The corporation (negotiator) may do this by financing pension plans, by sharing its profits, or by giving large deferred bonuses to its employees (the opposers). The corporation may use its employees' need for economic security to encourage loyalty to the firm and better work. This negotiating gambit has become increasingly important in recent years in settling labor disputes, in obtaining new union contracts, and also in preventing unionization of an unorganized segment of the corporation.

International. On April 7, 1965, President Lyndon Johnson (the negotiator) offered to enter unconditional peace talks with North Vietnam, Communist China, and the Soviet Union to end the war in Vietnam. To persuade the Communist countries (the opposers) to agree, he used a negotiating gambit that was in marked contrast to the usual tactics of war. He urged all the countries in Southeast Asia, including North Vietnam, to undertake a massive cooperative development program. This program would be initiated by the United Nations and financed by all industrialized countries. He himself would ask Congress to appropriate $1 billion to the project as soon as it was under way. Although U.N. Secretary General U Thant praised Johnson's gambit as "positive, forward-looking, and generous," the Communist countries felt quite differently. "Stinks of poison gas," said Communist China, and within a week all three countries involved had rejected Johnson's efforts to work for his opposer's needs.

2. NEGOTIATOR LETS THE OPPOSER WORK FOR HIS SAFETY AND SECURITY NEEDS

Interpersonal. Captain John Smith (the negotiator), who led the English settlement at Jamestown in 1608, understood how to make the colonists work for their needs. In the colony's earliest days, the settlers (opposers) did not have the right to own land and property. Many were unwilling to spend long hours tilling fields they did not own—even though food was extremely scarce. John Smith countered their laziness by taking charge of all the food produced in the colony. He then issued a very simple order. All those who were well enough to work must work to get food. His maneuver worked and so did all the colonists.

Interorganizational. A truly remarkable example of forcing opposers to work for their security needs was made by a client of mine. He was a wealthy Chicago philanthropist who had generously contributed his time and money to the field of heart research. He (the negotiator) was requested to testify before a Senate committee (the opposers) that was investigating the possibility of establishing a National Heart Foundation. The cause was one that he held dear and he consulted with the best experts to prepare his address. Private heart organizations worked with him, furnishing concise, well-documented appeals for presentation to the senators. Armed with this prepared speech, my client took his place in the hearing room, only to discover that he would be the sixth person to be called to testify. The five speakers who preceded him were outstanding professionals—medical men, scientists, and public reltions men. These men had spent their lives at this work. The committee put them through their paces and at one point asked the witness before them, "Who wrote your speech for you?"

When my client was called, he stood before the senators and said, "Gentlemen, I had prepared a speech but I have discarded it. For how could I compete with the eminent men who have already spoken? They have given you all the facts and figures, but I am here to appeal to you on your own behalf. Hard-working men such as you are the victims of heart disease. You are men in the prime of your lives, at the top of your careers; you are just the ones most susceptible to heart attack. People who have achieved outstanding positions in their community are the ones most subject to heart disease."

He continued in this vein for forty-five minutes; they would not let him stop. He was making each senator work for his "need," his need of safety. The National Heart Foundation was thereafter created by the government, and my client was its first governor.

International. The deals that Iraq (the negotiator) made with foreign oil companies (the opposers) operating within Iraq illustrate an international negotiation in which the opposers were forced to work for their needs. In 1951 the ownership of the Iraq Petroleum Company was typical of the ownership of all the large oil companies in the country. Ninety-five percent of the shares in the company were held by foreign interests—American, Dutch, French, and British. In negotiating a new deal with this foreign-held company, Iraq forced the company to work for its need to extract Iraq oil. The company agreed to give 50 percent of its profits to Iraq. It also promised to work harder and to increase its oil production, further increasing the Iraqi government's oil revenue. The other foreign-held companies were soon forced to make the same concessions.

3. NEGOTIATOR WORKS FOR THE OPPOSER'S AND HIS OWN
SAFETY AND SECURITY NEEDS

Interpersonal. Frontier days in the American West furnish a good example of people working for their need for safety and security and for their opposer's need as well. Invariably, as communities were founded and families moved in, the settlers (negotiators and opposers) demanded "law and order." Although their demands would mean giving up the absolute freedom the frontier afforded, the need for safety made the sacrifice worthwhile to most people in the community.

Interorganizational. The "common enemy" gambit has often persuaded opposing organizations to work together for their own security. The threat of an outside force, either real or imaginary, makes their differences seem less important. Political parties, especially in Europe, are very dependent on this negotiating gambit. For example, in 1964 the Italian Christian Democrats (the negotiators) made a dramatic opening to the left and allied with the left-wing Socialists, the Democratic Socialists, and the Republicans (the opposers). This alliance was prompted by the power of the Communist Party in Italy, one of the strongest Communist parties outside the Soviet bloc.

International. The International Monetary Fund, set up at the U.N. Monetary and Financial Conference at Bretton Woods in 1944, works to stabilize the currencies of all member countries. Each nation (negotiator and opposer) that joins the IMF agrees to contribute to a foreign exchange reserve. The Fund can then draw on this reserve to help any member during a temporary balance-of-payments crisis. Many of the members of the Fund compete with each other for markets in international trade. Yet it is to their advantage to help their competitors indirectly through the International Monetary Fund. By supporting a weak currency, even the currency of a competitor, they help prevent an international financial crisis and protect their own economic security.

4. NEGOTIATOR WORKS AGAINST HIS SAFETY AND SECURITY NEEDS

Interpersonal. Playwright Arthur Miller (negotiator) worked against his own need for security in a drama that was only too real. Called to testify before the House Un-American Activities

Committee (opposers) in 1956, the Pulitzer Prize playwright was willing to answer all questions relating to his own political experience and affiliations. Never a member of the Communist Party himself, he could expect to emerge from the investigation safe and sound. However, the Committee wanted information not just about Miller's own experience, but concerning his friends and associates as well. This he refused to divulge. To protect others, he jeopardized his own security. His negotiating gambit failed. A federal district court convicted him of contempt of Congress the next year.

Interorganizational. A military maneuver in common use during the early Middle Ages furnishes an example of working against the need for safety. The defenders of a fort (the negotiators), under attack by a besieging army (the opposers), made it a practice to sally forth and give battle to the attackers. As they crossed the moat they burned the bridge behind them. By thus cutting off their only means of retreat, they served notice on their enemy that they never intended to reenter the fort again unless they were victorious. Their purpose was to inspire fear in the hearts of the besieging army. The defenders gave up their need for safety and apparently committed an irrational act, but it often proved to be an effective means of negotiation. This is the origin of the expression "burning your bridges behind you."

International. In 1936 General Francisco Franco led a revolt against the Republican government of Spain. Supported by the Spanish clergy, nobility, and army, he won control of vast parts of western and northern Spain in a matter of months. Germany and Italy came to his aid. France and Britain decided not to intervene. Only Russia officially helped the Republicans. However, thousands of individuals from all over the world came to Spain and fought on the side of those loyal to the Republican cause. The International Brigade made up of these volunteers was a key to the successful defense of Madrid and of Spain. In 1937 Franco continued his conquest of the north, and in 1938 he drove south to the Mediterranean at Vinaroz to split Republican Spain. Again aided by the International Brigade, the Loyalists mounted a desperate counteroffensive and succeeded in recapturing the southern bank of the Ebro River. The Republican government (the negotiator) tried to use this victory to persuade Franco (the opposed) to negotiate peace terms. To prove his goodwill, Don

Juan Negrin, Premier of Spain, worked against the security of his government. He sent the International Brigade home. Negrin's maneuver failed, Franco continued his offensive, and the Republican government fell.

It is possible for a nation to achieve more successful results by using the negotiation gambit of giving up its own safety. In 1940, early in World War II, the Germans invaded Denmark. For a time no move was made against the Danish Jews. Then one day in 1943, after the Danish underground had intensified its sabotage against the Nazis, the Germans decreed that all Jews in Denmark must wear a yellow arm band with a star of David. Similar decrees had marked Jews for deportation to concentration camps, country after country, all across Europe. That night the Danish underground relayed a message throughout Denmark. King Christian X had announced that each Dane was the same as every other Dane and he himself would wear the first star of David. He expected all Danes to follow his example. The next day in Copenhagen almost everyone wore the star of David. King Christian's negotiating gambit worked, the Germans rescinded their order, and the Danish Jews survived.

5. NEGOTIATOR WORKS AGAINST THE OPPOSER'S SAFETY AND SECURTY NEEDS

Interpersonal. If properly used, the "dare" can prove a very effective negotiating technique. Children appear to use it instinctively. The negotiator works against an opposer's need for safety and security by goading him into a dangerous act, or one that at least seems to threaten his need for safety and security.

Interorganizational. Nowadays armies have psychologists to help soldiers face the peril of war. They (the negotiators) explain to the soldiers (the opposers) that it is perfectly normal to be afraid and that the real problem is to learn not to be afraid of being afraid. In this fashion the psychologists persuade the soldiers to overcome their fear, to bear arms willingly, and to work against their need for safety. Abraham Lincoln (the negotiator) used this gambit to rally the North behind him at the outbreak of the Civil War. South Carolina had demanded the surrender of Fort Sumter, which guarded Charleston harbor. Lincoln refused to surrender the fort, saying it would violate the oath he had taken as President to protect federal property. He also stated that he would send un-armed supply ships to the fort but that they were to turn back if South Carolina offered resistance. The fiery Confederate general P. G. T. Beauregard (the opposer) did not wait for the confronta-tion. He fired on the fort and forced its surrender. Thus he gave Lincoln the priceless advantage of appearing as the defender of the Union rather than the aggressor against Southern liberties, as the South had portrayed him.

International. In 1917 Germany (the negotiator) effectively worked against the security of one of its opposers, Russia, in World War I. As Winston Churchill described it:

> *In the middle of April the Germans took a sombre decision. Ludendorff refers to it with bated breath. Full allowance must be made for the desperate stakes to which the German leaders were already committed. They were in the mood which had opened unlimited submarine warfare with the certainty of bringing the United States into the war against them. Upon the western front they had from the beginning used the most terrible means of offense at their disposal. They had employed poison gas on the largest scale and had invented the "Flam-menwerfer" (flame-thrower). Nevertheless, it was with a sense of awe that they turned upon Russia the most grisly of all weapons. They transported Lenin in a sealed truck like a plague bacillus from Switzerland into Russia.*

Lenin was living in exile in Switzerland when a revolt in Russia forced Czar Nicholas II to abdicate his throne in March 1917. Lenin's desire to end Russian participation in an "imperialist war" and to begin an internal "class war" was well known to the Germans. By allowing Lenin to return to Russia, the Germans worked against their opposer's need for a stable government. As expected, once in Russia, Lenin increased the power and influence of the Bolsheviks and overthrew the provisional government in a second revolution. Russia's war effort suffered as a result of its in-ternal problem. In addition, in 1918, as chairman of the Council of People's Commissars, Lenin sued for an early peace with Ger-many.

6. NEGOTIATOR WORKS AGAINST THE OPPOSER'S AND HIS OWN
SAFETY AND SECURITY NEEDS

Interpersonal. In the game of Russian roulette each individual
(negotiator and opposer) negotiates against the safety need of both
parties. This gruesome game is reputed to have settled many a
negotiation impasse in days of old. It is played by placing only one
bullet in the chamber of a six-shooter, spinning the barrel, and
then passing the revolver to each player in turn. Each player takes
the gun, holds it to his head, and pulls the trigger. Chance gives
the winner life.

Teen-agers have devised their own form of Russian roulette
in their game called "chicken." Starting some distance apart,
two cars are driven toward each other, each car straddling the
center white line of the road and going as fast as the courage or
foolhardiness of the drivers will allow. The first driver to veer off
the white line to escape collision is taunted as being "chicken," or
coward.

Interorganizational. The crusade for civil rights in the South has
seen many examples of organizations and groups (the negotiators)
working against their needs and those of their opposers. Sometimes the economic security of only a few people is affected when a
baseball park closes to avoid integration. Other times the loss of
economic security affects many when schools close and children
are not educated for future jobs and responsibilities. And in still
other cases a whole community, Klansmen as well as members of
CORE, lose economic security when riots against integration can-
cel plans for financial investment in the area.

International. A motion picture, *Dr. Strangelove*, suggests a fictional example of a nation working against its need for security and
the need of its opposers. In the film one nation (the negotiator)
had invented a "Doomsday" machine capable of incalculable destruction. The nation could conceivably use its superinvention to
negotiate with the rest of the world (the opposer) by threatening
to destroy itself and the entire world in the event of an attack. In
this way it would be negotiating against its own safety and the
safety of all its opposers.

Before the United States and the Soviet Union agreed to ban

testing nuclear weapons aboveground, increased radioactivity in the air presented a very real threat to the safety of all. SANE, an organization dedicated to working *for* the world's security, described the situation in an advertisement that read as follows: "We now have enough atom bombs to kill every Russian 360 times. The Russians only have enough atom bombs to kill every American 150 times. We're ahead. Aren't we?"

III.   LOVE AND BELONGING NEEDS

I. NEGOTIATOR WORKS FOR THE OPPOSER'S LOVE AND BELONGING NEEDS

Interpersonal. One day, while commuting to New York City, I had a conversation with a neighbor. Our discussion serves as a good example of working for the opposer's need for love and belonging. He asked what I was working on. I explained that I was writing a book on the art of negotiating.

"Oh, I negotiate all the time in my business," exclaimed my fellow traveler. "I buy up distressed lots of textiles and, in my opinion, there's *only one way* to negotiate." He explained his method.

"I have to get the merchandise at the lowest possible price, so I have found that the *best* way is to knock the quality and run it down. I often let the goods fall on the floor and then step on it accidently. After downgrading the merchandise, I make some ridiculous offer. Then we usually haggle a bit and close the deal."

I listened attentively and then said, "I disagree with your use of the phrase 'only one way.' Might I suggest at least one alternative approach, just the reverse of what you do? Your method, while useful, might create an antagonistic feeling, especially when you knock down fabrics that a man has spent his time, talent, and money to design and produce. People feel paternal toward things that are theirs. We speak with pride of *my* house, *my* car. How would you feel if somebody started knocking your house or your car? Now suppose you are the seller, showing me a fabric. As another gambit, I might say, 'The pattern is lovely but I think your design is ahead of the current market. Of course, if you hold the goods for about ten years, I think the taste of the general public will catch up with your ideas.' Without knocking the merchandise I have put it into an unfavorable position. The seller is certainly made more anxious to sell now when faced with the prospect of waiting ten years for the goods to become marketable. He knows it is not marketable or he would be offering the goods to the regular trade. I (the negotiator) have worked on his (the opposer's) need for love and belonging to reach agreement. Belonging can apply to things as well as to people. When we have concluded the deal, the seller will also be more likely to ship me some of the material in the best condition rather than the worst lot."

This attachment to things that are ours is very deep-seated and is well summed up by Shakespeare in the phrase "a poor thing, but mine own."

Interorganizational. "If you can't beat 'em, join 'em" is an old adage. It has proved a useful gambit for the negotiator to work for his opposer's need to belong by joining the opposer's forces. The epic battle among the railroad kings at the turn of the century provides a multiple illustration of the point. Three great financiers were involved: J. P. Morgan, who was financing a reorganization of the Northern Pacific; James J. Hill, who held a controlling interest in the Great Northern; and Edward H. Harriman, who controlled the Union Pacific. All three wanted control of the Chicago, Burlington, and Quincy. It would give Morgan and Hill entrance into Chicago and St. Louis, but it would give Harriman access to the Northeast.

Hill and Morgan—working against Harriman—combined to buy a controlling interest in the C. B. & Q. Then they split control of the road between their two companies. But Harriman was not a man to be thwarted. He turned around and bought enough of Northern Pacific's common and preferred stock to give him control of that railroad and also of its 50 percent interest in the C. B. & Q. Hill and his friends postponed the annual meeting of the Northern Pacific in order to retire the preferred stock and destroy Harriman's majority before he could elect a new board. All these maneuvers brought on the panic of May 9, 1901, when those who had sold short could not buy Northern Pacific stock even at $1000 a share. The three rivals had had enough. They combined to form a holding company, the Northern Securities Company, to act as trustee for the Northern Pacific, the Great Northern, and the C. B. & Q. Harriman was given minority representation on its board.

That is not the end of the story. Later we shall see how Morgan attempted to use the gambit once more, this time with the President of the United States. Theodore Roosevelt was a match for the financier, he turned the gambit around and used it against Morgan.

International. Harry S Truman's Point Four Program is an example of one nation working for the need of underdeveloped nations to belong. Truman (the negotiator) proposed the program in his 1949 inaugural address. He offered to share American technical skills, knowledge, and equipment with underdeveloped nations (the opposers) to improve their industries, agriculture, health, and education. The program also encouraged Americans to invest private funds in these countries. Point Four worked for the belonging need of the participating nations: by assisting their development, it gave them entrée to the ranks of the modern industrial nations.

2. NEGOTIATOR LETS THE OPPOSER WORK FOR HIS LOVE AND BELONGING NEEDS

Interpersonal. Just as a sentry on guard duty forces an unknown person to identify himself, so you, as a negotiator, can make other people identify themselves to you. If you listen carefully to what people say, you will find that "between the lines" of their conversation they are explaining their various needs for love and belonging. They tell you how nice they are, how their goals and aims are the same as yours. To use this as a gambit of negotiation, you (the negotiator) permit them (the opposer) to fulfill their need for love and belonging through you. Listen carefully to what they say and then act so that they fulfill their needs.

Another example of this gambit is the social club (negotiator) that enforces various types of restrictions on membership. It forces any prospective member (opposer) to work hard for his need to belong. It is, therefore, not odd that clubs with easier membership requirements sometimes find it more difficult to fill their roster than do clubs with stiffer demands.

Interorganizational. The New York Stock Exchange (the negotiator) uses this gambit very effectively. Before a corporation (the opposer) will be listed on the Big Board, it must file an extremely detailed statement of the company's affairs. Thereafter, it must make regular reports to the Exchange on its earnings and general financial situation. There are a number of reasons why a corporation might not wish to reveal this information, but the need for belonging outweighs them in many cases and a listing is eagerly sought, because when the Exchange lists a stock, it in effect endorses the company's status.

International. After World War II, the United States and its Allies (the negotiators) forced Japan (the opposer) to work for its need to belong to the family of nations. Although the Japanese government continued to function throughout the occupation, it was denied full sovereignty until it enacted a broad program of political, economic, and social reforms. After seven years, during which the reforms became firmly embedded in Japanese life, the Allies granted Japan full sovereignty.

3. NEGOTIATOR WORKS FOR THE OPPOSER'S AND HIS OWN
LOVE AND BELONGING NEEDS

Interpersonal. A real estate broker I know, in his capacity as agent in name and fact, uses this gambit effectively. He puts the gambit into operation by telling the prospective buyer that the seller feels that he is just the type of person to whom he would like to sell his home. Then the broker works on the seller, telling him all the nice things the buyer said in response to the seller's compliment. Naturally, when he brings the two together they are extremely cordial. The broker's negotiating tactics have created a feeling of belonging between seller (negotiator) and buyer (opposer). Usually the final closing of the deal goes quickly and smoothly.

Interorganizational. In the business community it is common practice to join associations in which competitors (negotiator and opposer) can work together toward a common goal. This might be done to secure legislation that will favor the industry as a whole —or to fight against unfavorable legislation. The goal may also be to share common experiences and problems encountered in the industry.

At future labor conventions it might well be a good idea to provide for displays, parades, floats, all graphically demonstrating what the workers and the industries produce together. The higher level of achievement, of belonging, is lost to union and management when there are protracted struggles for the more basic needs. Cooperative long-term possibilities are perverted by the immediate goals that both labor and management strive for.

International. Great Britain (negotiator), in setting up the Commonwealth of Nations, worked for its own belonging need and that of its former colonies (opposers). Although the Commonwealth ties are rather tenuous, there are definite advantages to be derived by all member nations. This was underlined by the extreme reluctance shown by South Africa to withdraw from the Commonwealth in 1961. The fact that it did withdraw again illustrates that an appeal to the more basic need will usually carry the day.

South Africa became a republic in 1960. It applied for readmission to the Commonwealth, which required the approval of the other members. South Africa had aroused great resentment because of its repressive racial policies directed against Indians as well as Africans. The basic argument for this policy was that it would save the white minority government from being taken over by Africans and Asians. In the face of vehement criticism from the Asian Commonwealth members, South Africa withdrew its application for readmission. Its need for security had proved stronger than its belonging need.

4. NEGOTIATOR WORKS AGAINST HIS LOVE AND BELONGING NEEDS

Interpersonal. Children (the negotiators) often negotiate in their endless fights with grown-ups (the opposers) by using the gambit of giving up their need for love and belonging. There is the story of the child who decided he wasn't being treated properly at home and therefore was going to run away. He packed his things and left a note behind: "I am running away from home. I will never come back. In the case of an air raid, I can be found in the attic." The boy was willing to give up his need for belonging, but was not so annoyed that he would give up his security need.

Interorganizational. The Protestant Reformation in Germany provides numerous examples of working against one's need for belonging. It might properly be used as an example on the personal, organizational, and international level. However, since Germany was divided into many principalities and free cities united only by their allegiance to the Church and their loose ties with the Holy Roman Empire, perhaps this example best exemplifies the interorganizational level of approach.

For 1500 years a common faith and the Catholic Church had been almost the only unifying force in Europe. It is difficult today to realize the agonizing choice that faced Martin Luther and his followers (negotiators): to remain in the Church (opposer), which seemed to them venal and corrupt, or to give up their membership in a religious community that embraced most of Europe. There were political and economic, as well as spiritual, reasons that brought half the inhabitants of Germany over to Protestantism, but in any event the choice was a bitter one to make.

International. When France and Germany entered the Common Market, agreement was soon reached concerning free trade in industrial goods. But the treaty provisions in agriculture were vague, far vaguer than the detailed schedule for industrial free trade. Germany wanted to maintain the unsettled state of the agricultural schedules because it benefited the German farmers. On the other hand, during four years of discussion and debate, the French pressed for a common policy on farm products similar in detail and precision to the policy on industrial products; this was what the French farmers needed and wanted. Tired of the stalling tactics of the Germans, the French issued a threat: if Germany did not go through with the original understanding on farm prices by a certain date, France would withdraw from the Common Market. Thus the French (negotiators) were working against their need for belonging in order to negotiate the Germans (opposers) into a satisfactory agreement on the farm schedules.

5. NEGOTIATOR WORKS AGAINST THE OPPOSER'S LOVE AND BELONGING NEEDS

Interpersonal. Earlier in this chapter I gave an example of working for the opposer's need for belonging, in my conversation with my commuting friend. It is sometimes advantageous to take the negative approach and work against the opposer's need for love and belonging. When negotiating to buy an article, you (the negotiator) devalue it by finding fault with the quality. This gambit is used in purchasing used clothes; the buyer often points out rips, tears, or stains, or holds the seat of the pants up to the light so the seller (opposer) and he can see the almost inevitable worn-out places.

Negotiating the purchase of a house, the potential buyer often calls attention to defective plumbing, a bad roof, or other faults.

Some people feel that this will make the owner give up his need for belonging—at least in reference to the article for sale.

Interorganizational. The boycott by the Arab nations (the negotiators) of U.S. companies (opposers) dealing with Israel is an example of this gambit on the interorganizational level. It has a double impact that few realize. If the American company continues to trade with Israel, it gives up its Arab market. However, if it complies with the Arab demand to prove it has not traded with Israel, the company is demonstrating weakness: it is giving up, to a degree, its sense of belonging to a powerful and independent nation (the United States).

International. Working against the opposer's need for belonging and love has been given various names, such as the phrase "sent to Coventry." On the international level, this had been done to Red China, which was kept out of the United Nations. The more Red China (the opposer) tried to work its way in, the more the United States (negotiator) had negotiated to keep it out. The United States' position was that Communist China must earn its place in the family of nations by proper actions before it could be admitted. The United States was working here against China's desire to belong (not to the U.N., but to the civilized world). China, however, had taken the understandable position of claiming no interest in a U.N. seat, even if one was offered.

6. NEGOTIATOR WORKS AGAINST THE OPPOSER'S AND HIS OWN LOVE AND BELONGING NEEDS

Interpersonal. In the last scene of Shakespeare's *Romeo and Juliet*, the Prince (agent) brings about peace between the Capulets (negotiators) and the Montagues (opposers). With both Romeo and Juliet dead, the Prince wants both families to work against their individual needs to belong. He tells them:

> *See, what a scourge is laid up on your hate,*
> *That Heaven finds means to kill your joys with love,*
> *And I for winking at your discords too*
> *Have lost a brace of kinsmen. All are punish'd.*

The Prince recognizes that each party gave up its need for love in losing a member of its family, and he uses this fact to make them acknowledge their folly and agree to negotiate peace.

Interorganizational. Hill and Morgan's Northern Securities Company has already been used as an example of working for the opponent's belonging need. Subsequent developments show that it is a good example of working *against* the belonging need. In 1902 President Theodore Roosevelt (the negotiator) ordered his Attorney General to enter a suit to dissolve the holding company, Northern Securities Company. J. P. Morgan (the opposer) and other major contributors to the President's Republican Party hurried to Washington to talk Roosevelt out of it. Morgan suggested to Roosevelt the time-honored solution of working together: "If we have done anything wrong, send your man to my man and they can fix it up."

As Roosevelt observed later, "That is a most illuminating illustration of the Wall Street point of view. Mr. Morgan could not help regarding me as a big rival operator, who either intended to ruin all his interests, or else could be induced to come to an agreement to ruin none."

This attitude did not suit the superpatriot Roosevelt. Duty to country came before any need for Wall Street support in the forthcoming 1904 election. Therefore he worked against his and Morgan's belonging need in order to protect "the interests of the people against monopoly and privilege. . . ." The gambit worked. The Supreme Court ordered the breaking up of the Northern Securities Company, and although Wall Street tried to prevent his nomination in 1904, Roosevelt won the nomination and was re-elected by the American people whose interests he had defended.

International. From the time of the creation of Malaysia in 1963, Indonesia had attempted to destroy the federation, using diplomatic pressure and guerrilla warfare. The United States attempted to force Indonesia into line by threatening to withdraw its aid to the Asian country. By 1964 aid had virtually ceased, and Indonesia (the negotiator) declared it did not want aid from countries (opposers) that did not support its Malaysian policy. In 1965 Indonesia also worked against its own and its opposer's need to belong when it withdrew from the United Nations, which had just elected Malaysia to the Security Council.

IV. ESTEEM NEEDS

I. NEGOTIATOR WORKS FOR THE OPPOSER'S ESTEEM NEEDS

Interpersonal. Sometimes you (negotiator) will find it advantageous to work for your opposer's need of esteem by becoming sincerely interested and involved with him. Dale Carnegie, in *How to Win Friends and Influence People,* describes many applications of this principle. Some of the methods he advocates are: become genuinely interested in people, smile, always remember that a man's name is the most important sound to him, encourage others to talk about themselves, talk in terms of the other fellow's interests, and strive to make the other person feel important. All these forms of conversing with your opposer feed his basic need for esteem, and when properly applied they are valuable assets in the art of negotiation.

Interorganizational. Modern corporations constantly work to obtain public esteem and goodwill. One corporation may use another corporation's need for public esteem to serve its own advantage. For example, a few years ago the Xerox Corporation wanted to extend its operations into England and other European countries. It therefore joined J. Arthur Rank, Ltd., a well-known English firm, and formed a new company, Rank-Xerox, to promote its products in Europe. By working for Xerox's (opposer's) need for public esteem in Europe, J. Arthur Rank (negotiator) gained the right to profit from the industrial processes Xerox had developed.

International. Nations traditionally indicate their acceptance of a change in leadership in another country by formally recognizing the new government. For some time following the Russian Revolution of 1917, no nation recognized the U.S.S.R. The United States based its refusal to recognize Russia on several factors: the U.S.S.R. refused to assume the financial obligations incurred by the czarist government, refused to recognize claims of American citizens for losses incurred during the revolution, and refused to end subversive activities against the governments of other countries. By 1933 the desire to increase American trade with the U.S.S.R. superseded these objections. Ignoring most American claims against the Soviet Union, Franklin D. Roosevelt (negotiator) worked for Russia's (opposer's) need for esteem and formally extended diplomatic recognition on November 16, 1933.

2. NEGOTIATOR LETS THE OPPOSER WORK FOR HIS ESTEEM NEEDS

Interpersonal. An opposer commonly works for his need for esteem during negotiations prior to a divorce. For example, a model husband (negotiator) may allow his errant wife (opposer) to sue him for a divorce. Thus he is protecting her reputation and in return she is forced to work for her need for public esteem by offering him a better property settlement, better custody arrangements, or, at the very least, peace and quiet.

Interorganizational. An employer (negotiator) can profitably encourage his employees (opposers) to work for their need for esteem. The employer sets up an award to honor the individual or division with the best record for attendance or production or any other kind of behavior he wants to encourage. The employees then exert themselves to win the recognition the award conveys. Perhaps the most famous employer to use this negotiating gambit is the Soviet Union. Production problems in 1935 led Stalin to call for all Soviet workers to produce more. One coal miner named Stakhanov surprised even Stalin by exceeding his quota several times over. Stalin, therefore, proclaimed 1936 as "Stakhanov year." All workers who succeeded in becoming Stakhanovites received not only awards but special privileges and bonuses as well.

International. The United States recognized the Soviet Union in 1933 with a few strings attached, but it had used a far different negotiating gambit in dealing with Mexico in 1913. Until that time the United States had usually recognized established governments as a matter of course, no matter how these governments came into power. However, in 1913 Victoriano Huerta organized a bloody coup against the government of Francisco Madero, the first Mexican government in many years that had sought to bring prosperity to the masses and political liberties to all Mexicans. Madero himself lost his life while in Huerta's custody. Although many countries established diplomatic relations with the Huerta government (opposer) at once, U.S. President Woodrow Wilson (negotiator) refused to recognize "government by murder." He went even further and insisted that the price for U.S. esteem was Huerta's resignation. Wilson's decision cost American investors in Mexico tens of thousands of dollars every day. The German Kaiser remarked, "Morality is all right, but what about dividends?" Dividends notwithstanding, Wilson persisted in his policy, eventually supplying arms to Huerta's enemies and finally sending in American troops. No longer able to resist U.S. pressure, Huerta went into voluntary exile.

3. NEGOTIATOR WORKS FOR THE OPPOSER'S AND HIS OWN ESTEEM NEEDS

Interpersonal. Sometimes all that is necessary to effect a successful negotiation between the negotiator and opposer is a gambit that will allow both parties to work for their need for esteem and to save face. One of the most common face-saving gambits is for each side to talk separately with a third, neutral party. By granting concessions to such a moderator rather than directly to each other, each party works for his need for esteem.

Interorganizational. Competing corporations sometimes work for each other's need for esteem by forming an industrial association. The association works to enhance the reputation of the entire industry, often with the help of a public relations firm hired jointly by all the firms through the association. "Together great things can be accomplished" could be the title of this gambit, which is used by competitors (negotiators and opposers) in industries ranging from ribbon to steel.

International. One of the most famous and enduring examples of nations working together to build mutual esteem is the Olympic Games. The range of contests is wide so as to touch the skills of many nations. Small nations can hope to win esteem in competitions against large ones. For example, in the 1964 Olympics, New Zealand, Ethiopia, Finland, Rumania, Switzerland, and Norway were among those winning athletic events.

4. NEGOTIATOR WORKS AGAINST HIS ESTEEM NEEDS

Interpersonal. To work against your own need for esteem would seem to be an inconceivable method of negotiating. Nevertheless, this is exactly the technique that is used by a lawyer (negotiator) who is about to be held in contempt of court by a judge (opposer). In such a situation the lawyer often finds it expedient to apologize, beg for forgiveness, or assume a "country boy" naïveté to explain his wrongdoing. In order to negotiate successfully with the judge, he deliberately debases himself and works against his need for esteem.

Interorganizational. Speakers (negotiators) at Alcoholics Anonymous use this gambit to persuade other drinkers (opposers) to give up the habit. The speakers work against their own need for esteem, confess to their past misdeeds, and tell what positive benefits abstinence offers the alcoholic.

International. After World War II, West Germany (the negotiator) adopted a severe attitude in prosecuting its war criminals, to show the world that it repudiated its Nazi past. By giving up its need for esteem it hoped to rejoin the Free World (opposer) as an equal partner.

5. NEGOTIATOR WORKS AGAINST THE OPPOSER'S ESTEEM NEEDS

Interpersonal. By working against a person's need for esteem, you can cause that person to do many things. As an example, a father (negotiator) may teach his son (opposer) the family business and humility at the same time, by having him start at the bottom of the ladder. He is working against his son's need for esteem so that the son can acquire a full understanding of the business.

Interorganizational. When a fraternity (the negotiator) makes new pledges (the opposers) go through initiations that often degrade them and make them look ridiculous, they are negotiating against the esteem need of the prospective members. Similarly, the U.S. Army "negotiates" a man from civilian into a soldier by putting him through a stiff course of basic training that works against his esteem need. But once he becomes a private first class, he has worked to recover his esteem as a soldier, with interest.

International. When the United States (the negotiator) publicizes economic failures in the Soviet Union, in Communist China, or in Cuba, the United States is working against its opposers' need for esteem. An unfriendly power similarly worked against America's need for esteem early in the nineteenth century. When James Madison became president in 1809, David Erskine was the British minister to Washington. Erskine had an American wife and was conciliatory to the U.S. need for esteem in every way. He and Madison negotiated an agreement to withdraw the British Orders in Council against American trade with France, in return for a number of concessions. These concessions did not satisfy George Canning, the British foreign minister. Canning not only refused to recognize his minister's agreement but replaced Erskine with a stern ultra-Britisher, "Copenhagen" Jackson. "Copenhagen" had earned his nickname by presenting the ultimatum that preceded Britain's seizure of the Danish fleet in 1807. He was even more contemptuous of America's need for esteem than of Denmark's. He called Madison a "plain and rather mean-looking man." Madison's wife Dolly was "fat and forty, but not fair." Americans were "all alike" and "by many degrees more blackguard and ferocious than the mob in other countries." In line with Canning's intentions, Jackson proceeded to drive a hard bargain with the United States. He even accused the United States of acting in bad faith during the Erskine negotiations. But the British gambit boomeranged. Instead of knuckling under to Jackson's demands, U.S. Secretary of State Robert Smith refused to have any more dealings with the unpopular British minister.

6. NEGOTIATOR WORKS AGAINST THE OPPOSER'S AND HIS OWN ESTEEM NEEDS

Interpersonal. A boy and a girl, out on their first date, can get involved in a negotiating situation, as unromantic as that term may sound. Because it is her first date with the boy, the girl may act according to an accepted code. If the boy wants to go further than she does, she negotiates to have him drop the request on the ground that it is their first date. She (the negotiator) has worked against her own esteem need and also against the boy's (the opposer's). However, it is to be hoped that she has negotiated him into a second date.

Interorganizational. Labor-management disputes are often settled by both the negotiator and the opposer giving up their need for esteem. If management yields to labor, it loses esteem by having given in. If union negotiators yield to management, they have the same difficulty. Yet to reach a settlement it is often necessary for both opposers to compromise and yield to the demands of the other. There is a saying: "It is not a good settlement unless both parties are a little bloody."

International. Before India received its freedom from Britain it adopted a policy of nonviolence toward the British. The Indians (negotiators) gave up their need of esteem but at the same time they also forced the British (opposers) into giving up their need for esteem. In following their policy of nonviolence and noncooperation, the Indians were often put into degrading situations that meant the loss of esteem. On the other hand the British, in attempting to enforce the law, were driven to harsh measures against a nonresistant people. This naturally worked against *their* need for esteem.

V. NEEDS FOR SELF-ACTUALIZATION

I. NEGOTIATOR WORKS FOR THE OPPOSER'S SELF-ACTUALIZATION NEEDS

Interpersonal. This gambit is typified by the wife (negotiator) who tells her husband (opposer), "Okay, you can be boss." Whether she means it or not is beside the point. This is her negotiating technique. She may have strong convictions about what should be done, but she is not tipping her hand. She is playing on her husband's need for self-actualization, his inner need to develop his manly capacities. However, having granted her husband this privilege, she will expect concessions in return. There is the woman who brought harmony to her marriage by using the proven technique of permitting her husband to make all the big decisions: Should the United States stay out of foreign entanglements? Is a trip to the planets necessary for national security? She is content to make the small decisions: how the family income should be spent, or where they should spend their vacation.

In a confidence game in which the victim, or mark, is being set up to turn over a large sum of money to the con man, it is a rule of the game that the mark, not the con man, suggests handing over the money. The professional con man sets up the swindle so that the only logical result would be for the money to be turned over to him. However, the suggestion (motivation, self-actualization) must come from the victim.

Interorganizational. Large foundations (negotiators) often work for the self-actualization need of charitable and cultural organizations (opposers) by offering to match, dollar for dollar, any amount that is raised from other sources. This encourages the organizations to work harder at fund raising, of course doubles the impact of the foundation's program of creative giving, and enables the charity to develop to a fuller potential.

International. The "invention" of Panama, as it has been called, is an extreme example of the use of this gambit on the international level. In 1902, at about the time President Theodore Roosevelt (negotiator) had decided that the isthmus of Panama was the best place to dig a canal, Panama was a part of Colombia. But that country balked at giving the United States sovereignty over the necessary strip of land. Raging against "those contemptible little creatures in Bogotá," Roosevelt tacitly encouraged a revolution in Panama, and in November 1903 he sent three U.S. warships to prevent the landing of Colombian troops on the isthmus "if" revolution should break out.

The farce was over in a day. On November 3, the State Department wired the U.S. Consul in Panama: "Uprising on Isthmus reported. Keep Department promptly and fully informed." The consul replied that, alas, there had been no uprising yet but one was expected later that day. It happened on schedule and the Republic of Panama (opposer) was born. By working for the self-actualization need of the Panamanians (opposers), Roosevelt (negotiator) got exactly what he wanted: the most advantageous terms for building the Panama Canal.

2. NEGOTIATOR LETS THE OPPOSER WORK FOR HIS
SELF-ACTUALIZATION NEEDS

Interpersonal. By letting the opposer work for his need for self-actualization you will give him a great degree of satisfaction (assuming that he is successful). In some situations you will find that you can negotiate better by offering your opposer a tough job, one difficult to accomplish, rather than an easy assignment. Winston Churchill (negotiator), in his famous statement, "I have nothing to offer but blood, toil, tears and sweat," was offering the British people (opposers) a hard task whose accomplishment would fulfill, among other needs, their need for self-actualization.

If in this and other examples used in this book the term "opposer" seems excessive, consider Churchill's bitter account of his party's defeat in the 1945 elections: "At the outset of this mighty battle, I acquired the chief power in the State . . . all of my enemies having surrendered . . . I was immediately dismissed by the British electorate from all further conduct of their affairs." As any sucessful politician knows, the voters are his opposers; he must constantly negotiate with them if he is to stay in power.

Interorganizational. Industrial incentive plans and programs, where the employee has opportunities to perform in different capacities, work on the need of the employee (opposer) to feel that he can accomplish something worthwhile, that he can be important to the industry (negotiator)—in other words, they depend on his need for self-actualization. Many of the plans for redevelopment and slum clearance depend for their success on their ability to motivate the people in the depressed areas to join in the fight for neighborhood improvement. Here again we have the need for self-actualization.

International. Adolf Hitler (negotiator) made Great Britain and France (opposers) work for their self-actualization need in 1938 when he forced them to sign the Munich pact. The complacent democracies were willing to sacrifice their ally Czechoslovakia in exchange for "peace in our time," a peace that would ensure their complete freedom and domination over vast colonial empires. Only gradually did the democracies realize that they were exchanging the illusion of *self-actualization* for the more basic need of national survival.

3. NEGOTIATOR WORKS FOR THE OPPOSER'S AND HIS OWN
SELF-ACTUALIZATION NEEDS

Interpersonal. The success of the jury system is dependent on the constant use of this gambit. It is axiomatic that no two persons think alike, yet Anglo-Saxon law assumes that twelve persons can reach an agreement most of the time. A conscientious juror will attempt to make his opinion prevail in order to achieve self-actualization. However, he (negotiator) cannot force the other jurors (opposers) to agree with him. He must negotiate with them, treat their opinions with respect, and arrive at a verdict that each juror can claim as his own.

Interorganizational. We are apt to think that the interests of the employer and his employees are divergent and opposed. However, during the stress of World War II, these diverse interests were often brought into accord. United in the effort to step up production for the defense of the country, employer and employees worked together in defense plants. Each party (negotiator and opposer) subordinated its own interests to the accomplishments of a greater task: winning the war. Both parties worked for their joint needs. In negotiations both the employers and the unions called each other's attention to their greater purpose. Under the pressure of war, the need for self-actualization of both parties was changed from monetary gains to a fervent patriotism. Even in peacetime a proper identification of mutual goals in the economic world will also bring employee and employer together. Some European nations, Sweden for instance, have peaceful labor relations based on this very gambit.

International. There has probably never been a more eloquent plea for opponents to work for self-actualization than that of Abraham Lincoln's second inaugural address. The end of the Civil War was in sight when Lincoln addressed both North and South (negotiator and opposer): "With malice toward none, with charity for all; with firmness in the right, as God has given us to see the right, let us strive on to finish the work that we are in; to bind up the nation's wounds; to care for him who shall have borne the battle, and for his widow, and his orphan—to do all which may achieve and cherish a just, and a lasting peace, among ourselves, and with all nations."

4. NEGOTIATOR WORKS AGAINST HIS SELF-ACTUALIZATION NEEDS

Interpersonal. The great Negro educator Booker T. Washington (negotiator) used this gambit with success in his so-called Atlanta Compromise. In it he implied that he and his people would for the time being accept an inferior social and political status in return for economic opportunity. "In all things that are purely social," he told a white audience (opposers), "we can be as separate as the fingers, yet one as the hand in all things essential to mutual progress."

Washington sincerely believed that through education the black man could achieve economic advancement and, possibly, sometime in the future, integration into American life. His "bargain" with the white people did accomplish a great deal in the education and training of black people. Whether it was worth the price is another matter. Within a year of the speech, in 1869, the Supreme

Court endorsed the "separate but equal" doctrine for schools and soon afterward the Southern states began to pass the Jim Crow laws that were to plague the South for many years.

Interorganizational. In another compromise, this time between the Democratic and Republican parties, the Democrats worked against their need for self-actualization.

The presidential election of 1876 was close. Samuel J. Tilden, the Democratic candidate, was undoubtedly the winner, having a plurality of 250,000 votes, but there was a dispute over the electoral votes of three Southern states, where the returning boards dominated by Republicans certified electors that would vote for Rutherford B. Hayes. The confusion was compounded in Oregon, where one of the state's electoral votes was claimed by both the Democrats and the Republicans.

The Constitution has no provision for dealing with such a confused situation. Finally an Electoral Commission was set up, and with the tacit approval of Southern Democrats it had a pro-Hayes majority. The Democrats (negotiators) sacrificed their need for self-actualization—giving up the presidency, for which they had a valid claim—but obtained a high price from the Republicans (opposers). The last federal troops, which had occupied the South after the Civil War, were withdrawn. Promptly the remaining Republican state governments in the South were voted out of office. The South also got one of its own into Hayes's cabinet and received generous amounts of federal funds for internal improvements. All in all it was not a bad bargain for the side that had lost the war only eleven years before.

International. At one point in the Cuban missile crisis in 1962, the United States (negotiator) worked against its need for self-actualization by giving up its initiative. The United States was using every type of pressure to get the missiles out of Cuba. Finally President Kennedy ordered a blockade of the island, and our ships of war stood directly in the path of all approaching Russian vessels. We told Russia (opposer) that if its ships continued on course and met our line of blockade, we would proceed to board and inspect them to see if they carried military cargoes. We thus gave up the initiative and left it to the Russians to determine what the next step in the negotiations would be. Fortunately for world peace, several

Russian ships probably carrying contraband turned back. Russian ships with nonmilitary cargoes were allowed to proceed to Cuba unmolested.

5. NEGOTIATOR WORKS AGAINST THE OPPOSER'S SELF-ACTUALIZATION NEEDS

Interpersonal. Some companies (negotiators) have developed highly refined techniques for getting rid of an executive (opposer) without actually firing him. Their negotiations may run the gamut of his needs—from the safety need (cutting his pay) to the esthetic need (removing the carpet from his office). But the company's task is difficult because it is trying to get the man to give up his more basic homeostatic need—the salary he requires to support himself and his family (see Chapter 7).

One of the most effective ways of getting an executive to quit is to work against his self-actualization need. For a man accustomed to making important decisions and being the center of attention, nothing is more devastating than to be deprived of his decision-making power and then be simply ignored. He will usually rationalize that taking a risk on his more basic needs by quitting and looking for a new job is a lesser evil than being deprived of his need for self-actualization.

Interorganizational. Sometimes top executives (negotiators) who fear losing their positions try to eliminate all acts of self-actualization in their subordinates (opposers). They perpetuate an authoritarian rule by doing away with all intercommunication. They recognize that, without information, the subordinates must depend upon them entirely for all decisions. Further, they cannot be criticized for honest judgment when they are the only ones with the facts.

International. When a nation attempts to pursue a self-actualization need, another country often cries "aggression." Although wars in general, and wars of aggression in particular, are very much out of "fashion" these days, the nation that feels cheated will continue to fight the protector of a status quo. Pakistan's war with India over Kashmir was a typical example of an "aggressor," in this case Pakistan, trying to get what it considers its rightful territory. India, on the other hand, was willing to go to any lengths (except, apparently, negotiating the issue) to retain Kashmir; India (negotiators) thus worked against Pakistan's (opposers) need for self-actualization.

6. NEGOTIATOR WORKS AGAINST THE OPPOSER'S AND HIS OWN
SELF-ACTUALIZATION NEEDS

Interpersonal. When both parties to a dispute (negotiator and opposer) agree to place the matter in the hands of an arbitrator, then in a sense both sides are leaving the outcome to chance. By allowing an outsider to work out the solution, both sides have given up their need for self-actualization. One who feels strongly and capable of working to the fullness of his capacities will not usually turn the matter over to an independent arbitrator.

Interorganizational. The United States Constitution is an outstanding example of organizations, in this case states, giving up their self-actualization need. Under the Articles of Confederation the individual states were sovereign. This meant among other things that they could and did exact high tariffs for goods imported from neighboring states. This hampering of trade between the states was one of the main reasons for calling the Constitutional Convention. Fortunately the delegates went far beyond negotiations to ease trade restrictions and created a union of states in which each state (negotiator and opposer) gave up a degree of self-actualization for the more desirable goal of a strong central government.

International. The Washington Naval Agreement of 1922 was a well-intentioned but (for the United States) horrifying example of nations (negotiators and opposers) mutually working against their self-actualization needs. Great Britain had long depended on its navy to hold its far-flung empire together. The United States had tried to recapture the security that isolation from world affairs had once given it—meanwhile forgetting that twenty years before it had acquired a Pacific empire and was vitally concerned in Asian affairs. Yet both nations eagerly sought to limit the size of the navies of the major powers. In the agreement, the following ratios were decided on: Great Britain, 5; United States, 5; Japan, 3; France, 1.67; Italy, 1.67. Thus Japan, whose imperialist ambitions in Asia were becoming more and more apparent, was given a position of relative naval superiority in the Far East that it never could have obtained in a naval "arms race." In 1930 Japan's ratio was increased, but in 1935, when it was refused parity with Britain and the United States, it withdrew from the agreement. Despite this withdrawal and Japan's seizure of Manchuria, in the same year Britain, France, and the United States entered into a new agreement limiting the size of their navies!

VI. NEEDS TO KNOW AND UNDERSTAND

I. NEGOTIATOR WORKS FOR THE OPPOSER'S NEEDS TO KNOW AND UNDERSTAND

Interpersonal. Persuasion by using logic and reason is one of the most common and important negotiating techniques. Its most straightforward application, of course, is the clear, concise, accurate statement of facts. (In Chapters 4 and 5 we discuss ways of determining facts in a situation.)

Interorganizational. Organizations also frequently negotiate by appealing to logic and fact. For example, if an independent group such as the Citizens' Union or the League of Women Voters endorses a political candidate, his party is certain to cite such independent endorsement during his campaign against opposing candidates. Nonpartisan support lends credibility to the party's (negotiator's) claims and arguments. Such support appeals to the voters' (opposers') needs to know and understand. Advertisers also use this gambit when they quote the endorsement of independent investigators such as the Consumer's Union, *Good Housekeeping* magazine, or the American Dental Association. They seek through reason to persuade the consumer to buy their product, not their competitor's.

International. One of the most famous examples of working for an opposer's need to know and understand brought an end to the ten-year siege of Troy. The Greeks (the negotiators) pretended to abandon the siege but left behind a large wooden horse. The Trojans (the opposers) were "permitted" to learn that the horse was an offering to the gods. It had been made so large that it could not be brought through the gates of Troy. The Trojans, eager to make an offering to the goddess Athena, tore down part of their wall to bring the horse, and the Greek warriors it concealed, into the city.

2. NEGOTIATOR LETS THE OPPOSER WORK FOR HIS NEEDS TO KNOW AND UNDERSTAND

Interpersonal. When a girl (negotiator) tells her boy friend (opposer), "I know, but I won't tell you," she is making him work for his needs to know and understand. The story of the unscrupulous optometrist (negotiator) and the way he sold a pair of glasses is an example of exploiting the customer's (opposer's) need to understand. Just when the customer thinks he understands, he is hit again by more bad news. The customer asks, "How much?" The optometrist replies, "Ten dollars." If there is no violent reaction from the customer, he then adds, "For the frames." Then he follows this with, "The lenses are five dollars." If the customer still remains silent, the tricky optometrist adds the word "each." In the negotiation the poor customer is striving to understand, to satisfy his need to know, and in this way falls a victim to this gambit.

Interorganizational. Using this gambit once got me out of a very bad business venture. Indeed, the situation might have proved financially disastrous. I had been persuaded to become involved in a hotel in Buffalo, New York, in a venture with one of my associates. Since I knew absolutely nothing about the hotel business, it was agreed in advance with my colleague that I should have no responsibility for the management of the property. Unfortunately, my associate suffered a crippling heart attack shortly after we signed the final papers. I was then obliged to take over the complete management of the hotel, which was losing $15,000 a month. Within three days I was to be called upon as the "expert" from New York City to tell the 500 employees in Buffalo how to do their jobs. I studied what the Harvard Business School had to offer on running hotels, but it was not much help. I sat at my desk and concentrated. Everything seemed against me. Then suddenly I had an idea. Nobody in Buffalo knew that I was hopelessly ignorant about running a hotel. A person would have to be crazy to become involved in a venture losing $15,000 a month if he didn't know anything about the business. Everyone (opposers) would assume that I (negotiator) was an expert on running hotels, so I decided that my gambit was to act the expert.

Arriving at the hotel, I told the manager to arrange appointments for me every fifteen minutes throughout the day. One by one,

I interviewed every supervising employee as well as every person that sold the hotel food, supplies, or services. As each seller entered the room, I scowled and told him that I could no longer do business with him; I told each employee that he could no longer work for the hotel. Their jaws would drop, and then I would ask, "How can I continue with anyone who is incompetent? You seem like a nice fellow, but I cannot tolerate the ridiculous things that have been going on." At this point they would try to justify their previous actions.

I would then say, "Only if you can tell me that you're at least aware of how things should be done, and if you can prove to me that you know what you're doing wrong—then perhaps we can still do business."

Each and every person I interviewed during the next few days poured forth a flood of suggestions, new approaches, and new methods for improving the management of the hotel. Without evaluating a single suggestion, I put the whole lot into operation. Within one month the loss was reduced to $1000. The next month showed a profit of $3000. By the time my associate left the hospital I was able to turn over to him a hotel that was firmly in the black. To put it simply, I let the other people work for their need to know and understand. They thought they knew I was an expert. I let them continue to think that they knew. And they never discovered my total ignorance of the hotel business.

International. In 1797 Secretary of State Timothy Pickering announced that 316 ships sailing under the American flag had been captured by the French the previous year. To avert war, President John Adams sent a commission of three men to negotiate a settlement with France. The American envoys reached Paris only to find that no one on the Directory, the five-man body then ruling France, would receive them. At last the Americans were approached by three mysterious Frenchmen, obviously the agents of Talleyrand, the French minister of foreign relations and one of the most powerful men in the world. The agents reported that before French-American negotiations could begin, the Directory must receive an apology from President Adams, a bribe of 1.2 million livres, and a "loan" of 32 million florins. These terms seemed not only excessive but insulting to the Americans, and they left France in a huff. Many Americans demanded a declaration of war against France when President Adams announced the tactics of the mysterious agents he named X, Y, Z. In trying to make their opposer work for their need to know, arousing their curiosity, France (negotiator) had inadvertently worked against America's (opposer's) need for esteem—a disastrous maneuver in the case of the XYZ Affair.

3. NEGOTIATOR WORKS FOR THE OPPOSER'S AND HIS OWN NEEDS TO KNOW AND UNDERSTAND

Interpersonal. Longfellow immortalized a famous negotiation based on the need for both negotiator and opposer to know and understand. When Miles Standish commissioned John Alden to present his proposal of marriage to Priscilla Mullens, Standish was working for his need to know Priscilla's interest. Priscilla (negotiator), however, had her own negotiation in mind. "Speak for yourself, John," said she, thereby working for her need to know and for that of John (her opposer) as well. Priscilla's gambit defined the area of discussion—always a good idea in a negotiation.

Interorganizational. Organizations also profit from defining the areas of disagreement early in a negotiation. Early agreement on issues speeds their settlement later on. One of the top men in the Conciliation Service in Washington used a method which, in his opinion, helped to effect a speedy settlement. After a hearing he was to mediate, he would restate the case to the parties, but he would deliberately mix up the terms and positions that each party represented to him. At this, both sides would be so appalled that they would go into a huddle and settle without more ado for fear that worse might befall them. Each party (negotiator and opposer) in this instance was working for the need to know and to understand itself and the other. I feel, however, that the mediator caused both parties to lose faith in mediation as a means of reaching a settlement; and thus he performed a disservice to his function.

The following is a more positive way of working for a mutual need to know and understand.

Trade associations are faced with many problems, particularly in connection with the antitrust laws and price fixing. Price fixing by an association is illegal. There are, however, many things that trade associations can do legally in this field. For example, associations have initiated programs to educate their members in cost accounting procedures. The members are shown how to calculate the actual costs in their industry. They are then shown how to apply this data to their individual business by using uniform methods of accounting. After being thoroughly indoctrinated in this way, it is unlikely that any members will sell at prices below those that the association accountants suggest as the minimum. This is a form of negotiation in which each member works for his own and his competitor's (opponent's) joint need to know and understand.

International. One of the most successful gambits used by the United States (negotiator) to work for both its own and its opposer's need to know and understand is the Fulbright Act passed in 1946. By financing student exchanges, the United States promoted understanding of far greater scope than the specific study programs of the scholars. Foreign hosts learned to know and to understand Americans. Americans learned to know and to understand other countries. More than twenty-five nations participated in the program, including America's enemies in World War II, Japan, Italy, and Germany, although unfortunately East Germany, as well as other Iron Curtain countries, did not take part. In this case, the more basic needs prevented meaningful negotiations between nations.

4. NEGOTIATOR WORKS AGAINST HIS NEEDS TO KNOW AND UNDERSTAND

Interpersonal. We all have the need to know and understand, but sometimes in order to negotiate successfully, it is essential that we work against that need. For example, when a husband (the opposer) is unfaithful to his wife, the signs of his disaffection can be quite obvious. Rather than ask questions and provoke an unpleasant negotiation, his wife (the negotiator) may decide to remain quiet, to pretend to misunderstand what she sees. She gives up her need to know, tries to improve her marriage in more subtle ways, and leads her opposition toward a face-saving solution for them both.

Interorganizational. Sometimes in the course of a negotiation we may decide to stake the outcome on faith or to rely on luck. A religious organization might resort to such a negotiating gambit. And one of the most obvious examples in which a religious group consistently sacrifices the need to know, in the scientific sense, is when the Jehovah's Witnesses (negotiators) refuse a blood transfu sion, even when advised by physicians (opposers) that it may be a matter of life or death.

International. The U.S. ban on American reporters visiting Red China worked against America's (negotiator's) need to know and understand its opposer. Working against the need to know is not always to a nation's disadvantage, however. During the Cuban crisis between the United States and Russia in 1962, the following negotiation took place between President Kennedy and Chairman Khrushchev. President Kennedy had, for some unexplained reason, received two conflicting messages from Khrushchev. One message contained terms that were acceptable; the other did not. What should be done? In an August 4, 1964, article in the New York *World Telegram and Sun,* Roger Hilsman wrote: "It was Robert Kennedy who conceived a brilliant diplomatic maneuver. Later dubbed the 'Trollope ploy,' after the recurrent theme in Anthony Trollope's novels in which the girl interprets a squeeze of her hand as a proposal of marriage, Robert Kennedy's suggestion was to deal with . . . the acceptable message only, and to ignore the other message." Kennedy said that he would accept Khrushchev's offer and then went on to set forth his own ideas of what that offer was.

Khrushchev knew that he had sent two contradictory messages, but the president (opposer's) gambit allowed Khrushchev (the negotiator) to give up his need to know and understand, and to accept the Kennedy interpretation of the two messages.

5. NEGOTIATOR WORKS AGAINST THE OPPOSER'S NEEDS TO KNOW AND UNDERSTAND

Interpersonal. People (negotiators) often work against their opposer's need to know by omitting important facts in order to give a misleading impression. Mothers are wont to use this negotiating gambit with their children. How many times has "Drink your milk, dear" concealed the fact that Johnnie will drink his milk *plus* his medicine?

It is also possible to try to gain the advantage in a negotiation by creating misunderstandings and exploiting your opposer's need to know. The following example illustrates this gambit.

A Mr. J. Robert LeShufy (opposer) asked me to represent him in a purchase of land on Staten Island at the time of feverish activity preceding the building of the Verrazano Bridge from

Brooklyn. The seller (negotiator) with whom I was to negotiate was one of the largest landowners. I soon learned that he had a reputation as a shrewd bargainer, that he never closed a deal until he was convinced that he had obtained the best possible price. I also learned that he used a technique that I call "plateau" negotiation. An agent of this shrewd seller would meet with you, bargain about the price, and then shake hands on what you believed to be the agreed price and terms of the sale. But when you met the actual seller, you would find out that the terms were only those on which *you* had agreed to buy, but not those on which he had agreed to *sell*. He had worked on your need to know and understand and had subtly misled you. The seller himself then took up some item that had not been discussed previously and would use it as a wedge to get a raise in price or more favorable terms. He tried to raise you to a new plateau, to face you with the alternative of agreeing to the new terms or calling off the deal. He might use the strategy of demanding that title be taken within fifteen days instead of the customary forty-five to sixty days after the contract is signed. He would use this new demand to extract fresh concessions from the buyer. He had employed these devices so often that he could gauge the point where the buyer would rather withdraw than meet the new demand. With the "plateau" technique, it is not rare for the seller to take up his pen, ready to sign the final drafted contract, only to put it down again and continue to negotiate on one last condition. The great skill was in knowing when the opposer's patience had been stretched to its limit.

LeShufy could recognize this technique as soon as it was tried on him. He had come up with a countermove, which I call "exposure." After the first attempt to push him to a new plateau, LeShufy smiled and began to tell a story. It concerned a fictional character whom he called Mr. Dorf. LeShufy said that he could never buy land from Mr. Dorf because every time he thought he had a deal worked out, Mr. Dorf would keep pushing and pushing him. Dorf was never satisfied until the terms of the deal were past their absolute limits. "Exposure" proved to be a powerful countermove. Every time the seller tried to "plateau," LeShufy would look directly at the seller, smile, and say, "Now, now, you are acting just like Mr. Dorf." It never failed to halt the seller dead in his tracks and put a stop to his "plateau" maneuver. "Exposure" was a powerful countermove because it was based on the esteem need, which is more basic than the need to know and understand. This is an agreement with the principle that *the more effective gambit is the one that employs the more basic need.*

Interorganizational. You (negotiator) can occasionally work against your opposer's need to know and understand by giving out entirely too much information. You do this intentionally to confuse the opposition and make it difficult for him to follow the details of the negotiation. By presenting an overabundance of information, you manage to hide many of the vital facts. In government, budgets are often passed by using this negotiating gambit. It is also found useful in preventing stockholders from understanding too much when they read a corporation's annual report.

International. This gambit is used in intelligence and counterintelligence work. It involves all the spy techniques from propaganda to elaborate deceptions—such as the Allies (the negotiators) used to make Germany (the opposer) think the invasion of Europe would come at Calais instead of Normandy. Whenever misinformation is intentionally given out—and used—it works against an opposer's need to know and understand.

6. NEGOTIATOR WORKS AGAINST THE OPPOSER'S AND HIS OWN NEEDS TO KNOW AND UNDERSTAND

Interpersonal. If you (negotiator) and your opposer agree to leave the outcome of a negotiation to chance by abiding by a flip of a coin, or a roll of the dice, then you are working against your need to know and understand, and your opposer is working against his same need. You both have decided to leave the decision to the independent determination of an outside event.

Interorganizational. Rivalry can easily lead to silence, secrecy, and suspicion on the part of all parties. Certainly intraservice rivalry among the U.S. Army, Navy, and Air Force following World War II had this result. The trend toward a more centralized defense program threatened many servicemen whose loyalty to their own branch of the service outweighed other considerations. On too many occasions, the need for service esteem superseded not only the need to know but the needs of national security as well. Yet, whatever one may think of the results, all three services (negotiators) used this gambit in dealing with Congress (the opposer) regarding appropriations and with congressional efforts to have a deciding voice in the Defense Department. Each wanted Congress to give greater weight to its individual request—regardless of its relative importance and the facts presented.

International. The San Juan boundary dispute between the United States and Great Britain in the nineteenth century is a clear case of each party working against its need to know. The 1844 Democratic National Convention slogan "Fifty-four forty or fight" resulted in the Compromise Treaty of 1846. The Oregon Treaty of 1846 described the boundary between the British and American territory on the Northwest Pacific Coast as "the channel that separates the continent from Vancouver Island." In point of fact, the coastline was marked by several channels dividing the various San Juan islands from each other and from the mainland. The British naturally claimed that the channel referred to was the Rosario Strait, which would make most of the islands British. The United States claimed that it was the Haro Strait, which would make all the islands American.

Each nation tried to prove its point by force. In 1853 the Hudson's Bay Company started to farm sheep on one of the islands. The United States claimed the farm owed the United States taxes. When the Company refused to pay, the U.S. tax collector confiscated some sheep. Ensuing incidents became really serious when a pig belonging to the Company's agent, Charles Griffin, crawled under a fence and ate some potatoes belonging to an American settler, Lyman Cutler. Infuriated, Cutler shot the pig on its second foray. Griffin threatened to arrest Cutler and send him to England for trial. In response to a request for military protection, the United States sent in Captain George Pickett with sixty soldiers to guard American settlers. The governor of Vancouver retaliated by sending three warships to the area. Fortunately neither side fired a shot, and a joint patrol of the area was set up.

During the American Civil War, the "Pig War" quieted down to some degree, but still neither side could negotiate a solution. Finally, in 1871, both nations gave up their need to know and turned to an independent arbitrator, William I of Germany. He applied some reason and logic to the thorny problem, measured the various channels, and decided that the deepest was the correct boundary line. Because this was Haro Strait, the San Juan islands belonged to the United States.

VII. ESTHETIC NEEDS

1. NEGOTIATOR WORKS FOR THE OPPOSER'S ESTHETIC NEEDS

Interpersonal. To start a negotiation by making an excessive demand and then suddenly offering to split the difference is an all too frequent method of negotiating. When you (negotiator) do this, you are working on your opposer's need for balance and symmetry. However, it may be a dangerous tactic, because if the original demand is too unrealistic, it will discourage further bargaining and even bring matters to a dead stop. I have seen many insurance adjusters refuse to discuss a settlement when the opposing attorney has led off with a demand beyond all reason.

In line with this gambit one's position may become more balanced and acceptable if it is related to an unconnected external fact, precedent, pattern, or principle.

Interorganizational. In the world of fashion, the designer (negotiator) works for the need of the prospective buyer (opposer); he plays upon the buyer's esthetic need. The designer sets the fashions, displays the styles, and the buyer may simply look and thereby be persuaded. He climbs on the bandwagon so that he will be sure to buy goods that are "in style."

International. In negotiations between nations that do not share a common set of values, it is often advantageous to agree upon the formal rules that will govern the conference and the agenda for the meeting. With the negotiator working for the opposing nation's esthetic need for form and order, the meeting may be directed into constructive channels. In many negotiations with the Free World, Russia has used this gambit with such regularity that deciding on the rules and the agenda often consumes more time and effort than the negotiations themselves.

2. NEGOTIATOR LETS THE OPPOSER WORK FOR HIS
ESTHETIC NEEDS

Interpersonal. When a sales clerk (negotiator) faces the customer (opposer) across the counter of a retail store, he often uses this gambit. Large retail organizations have trained their sales personnel to make the customer work for his esthetic need. They try to lead the customer to the most balanced path, the line of least resistance, the most symmetrical view. Often a customer will buy when he sees other people buying. He is more apt to order a "large" orange drink if he is asked, "Do you want a large drink?" than if he is asked, "Do you want a large or small drink?"

Interorganizational. When a company provides an orderly atmosphere, with everything arranged and organized, it is offering the opposition an opportunity to work for its esthetic need. This is also true when the negotiator presents his opposer an almost completed job and allows him to finish it. Sales promotions that get the consumer interested in a product by offering prizes for completing jingles or finishing crossword puzzles are examples of this gambit.

International. Antonio López de Santa Anna, Mexican general and dictator, used this gambit very effectively during the Mexican-American War. President James K. Polk was determined to have California and all other Mexican lands between Texas and the Pacific Ocean. He hoped to get the land by purchase, but when this failed he resorted to war. Within a year American troops occupied all the land that Polk desired. However, he could not persuade the Mexican government to acknowledge the fact in a peace treaty.

Santa Anna (negotiator), who had been deposed in 1844, played on Polk's (opposer's) esthetic need for recognition of a de facto situation to get what he wanted: return to power. He offered Polk a peace treaty if the United States would engineer his return to Mexico. In August 1846 Santa Anna was passed through the U.S. naval blockade and landed at Veracruz. He rallied his supporters and quickly seized the government. However, in a typical example of honor among thieves, he announced that he would not accept a peace treaty and would recover Mexico's lost territory. It took the United States a year of hard fighting to depose Santa Anna and force a peace settlement on the new Mexican government.

3. NEGOTIATOR WORKS FOR THE OPPOSER'S AND HIS OWN ESTHETIC NEEDS

Interpersonal. A negotiator makes an appeal to the need for orderliness, the esthetic need, by reading the terms under negotiation over and over again and, temporarily ignoring the items not agreed to, listing all the points that *are* settled. This work of bringing order out of chaos feeds the opposer's sense of esthetics and often facilitates a solution.

Interorganizational. Sometimes, in negotiations, questions such as who should be chairman, or what items should be placed on the agenda, assume great importance and cause endless bickering. This problem has been successfully solved by the negotiating device of a rotating chairman as well as a rotating agenda. Such an approach works for the esthetic needs of all parties. Each day one of the parties to the negotiation has its representative in the chair and its most important item heads the agenda. The next day it changes. This idea of rotation may also be applied to reports on negotiation progress, each party's report heading the list in turn.

International. The cultural exchange program conducted by Russia (opposer) and the United States (negotiator) is an example of this gambit on the international level. The high value that each nation attaches to the program is indicated by the attention each gives to ensuring that it sends as many artists as the other does.

4. NEGOTIATOR WORKS AGAINST HIS ESTHETIC NEEDS

Interpersonal. Many times you (negotiator) are forced to accept the gambit of working against your esthetic need. People creating an artistic work, or writing a book, or decorating their house, often become impatient and sacrifice their esthetic need just to get the work finished. This also can be used when dealing with someone else. Therefore, when you (negotiator), after a long ordeal, say to the other side (opposer), "Let's get the thing over with," you may add new impetus to the negotiations.

Many religious customs and traditions, when viewed historically, can be considered negotiating gambits. In the late Middle Ages, among the Eastern European Jews, a married woman was required to shave off all the hair on her head. The Jewish woman (negotiator) gave up this esthetic need as protection (negotiation) against violation by mobs (opposers) in times of anti-Jewish excesses. Feminine vanity, however, brought about the introduction of the use of the *sheitel,* or wig, which was sometimes made from the hair clipped from the wearer's own head. These wigs were worn, however, at times when no danger threatened the ghetto.

Interorganizational. The city of New York applied a new method of real estate assessment in its taxation of the Seagram Building on Park Avenue. The city refused to give the building's owners any allowance for the beautiful construction of the ground-floor park, pool, and arcade. Indeed, the tax was raised about 200 percent. A *New York Times* article called the new approach a "tax on beauty." In this instance New York City (negotiator) was working against its need for esthetics in order to achieve a greater income. This negotiation might be shortsighted and cause the city to suffer because builders (opposers) will be even more inclined to put up the most prosaic low-tax structures.

International. When the United States (negotiator) sends displays of its latest new schools of art abroad, thus courting ridicule, it is, in a sense, giving up its esthetic need. However, what this does do is show the world (opposer) the freedom that exists in the United States. As a negotiating gambit this carries a larger message.

5. NEGOTIATOR WORKS AGAINST THE OPPOSER'S ESTHETIC NEEDS

Interpersonal. You (negotiator) can work against your opposer's need for esthetics by arguing the merits of conformity to tradition. When you are confronted with an advanced type of esthetic thinking, you may condemn it merely because it does not conform. This same tactic can be used to downgrade new ideas, new art, new styles, and new concepts. Many people will attempt to prove their position, not on facts or reason, but merely on the basis of conformity to the present acceptable taste—today's mother insisting on her son's getting a specific type of haircut.

Interorganizational. Whenever a beautiful building, a historic landmark, or some decorative relic of the past is torn down to make way for a luxury apartment or an office building, we may say that the builders (negotiators) are working against the public's (opposer's) esthetic need. The old and the beautiful are economically unsound because the new structures "pay better." This argument is advanced *ad nauseum* in the welter of new building programs that are destroying many lovely structures on Manhattan Island and elsewhere, replacing them with *only* tax-paying and economically utilized constructions.

International. Japan (negotiator) used this gambit in the nineteenth century when the United States (opposer) was attempting to open the country to Western trade. The Japanese tried to avoid dealing with the Western world and referred to them as esthetic "barbarians." Their motive was to conceal the essential weakness of the nation. Only a display of gunboat diplomacy brought an end to this very effective gambit.

6. NEGOTIATOR WORKS AGAINST THE OPPOSER'S AND HIS OWN ESTHETIC NEEDS

Interpersonal. You (negotiator) can work against the esthetic needs of both yourself and your opposer by the gambit of injecting humor into the negotiation. To laugh and joke is to distract, and is most helpful when a situation becomes tense. Humor has been defined as the playful, ridiculous, unbalanced attitude, and as such it might be considered as working against our need for balance and order.

Interorganizational. The huge billboards that so frequently mar the scenic beauty of our highways furnish an example of all parties working against their esthetic needs. The state (opposer) allows the signs because it collects taxes on them, and the sign company (negotiator) puts them up for profits. Recognizing the economic reasons for this defacement of natural beauty, the federal government has offered money incentives to states that prohibit billboards on major highways.

International. Thomas Jefferson's introduction of "pell mell" to the White House had international repercussions and is a wild example of this gambit. Although Jefferson (negotiator) was a Virginia aristocrat and a gracious host, he decided when he became president that his manners should reflect republican simplicity and informality. Therefore, when he received the British minister (opposer) and his wife, he was dressed in a worn-out suit and bedroom slippers. The couple, resplendently attired, was naturally shocked, but much worse was to come. Jefferson announced at White House dinners that "pell mell and next-the-door form the basis of etiquette in the societies of this country."

At the first dinner they attended, the British minister and his wife were almost trampled to death when dinner was announced. In the dining room they had to scramble for seats at the table. Their only consolation was that Jefferson had a superb French chef. The minister, consulting with other foreign diplomats, decided this was an insult to all their countries. But in spite of protests, pell mell remained the White House custom throughout Jefferson's presidency.

Although the custom sacrificed every esthetic principle of polite society, Jefferson was willing to give up his and the minister's esthetic needs to win over the American voters. He was not the first nor the last American politician to curry favor with the voters by twisting the British lion's tail.

APPLICATIONS

1. Life illustrations can be used in the following way:

   a. To stimulate your thoughts on alternative courses of action.

   b. To judge your course of action, your gambit of negotiating, on the basis of the possibilities of its being more forceful as a result of using a more basic need.

On the basis of difficulty of use in one to seven varieties of application, number 1 is less difficult to use than number 2, than number 3, etc. Number 6 involves the greatest possible difficulty to you. In the event that you must implement the negotiating gambit, it is much more difficult to implement that and it involves greater risk if it does not work.

2. Think of illustrations in your own life and apply the matrix and then check in the life illustration to see if these have been adequate for you and appropriate to your negotiating situation.

3. Use the illustrations to evaluate the strength of your opposer's gambit in your next negotiation.

BIBLIOGRAPHY

Allport, G. W., and P. Vernon. *Studies in Expressive Movement.*
New York: Hafner, 1967.

Bell, David. *The End of Ideology.* New York: Free Press, 1960.

Berelson, Bernard, and Gary A. Steiner. *Human Behavior: An Inventory of Scientific Findings.* New York: Harcourt Brace Jovanovich, 1964.

Berne, Eric. *Games People Play.* New York: Grove Press, 1964.

Birdwhistell, Ray L. *Kinesics and Context.* Philadelphia: University of Pennsylvania Press, 1970.

Boulding, Kenneth E. *The Meaning of the Twentieth Century.* New York: Harper & Row, 1965.

Buchler, Justus. *Nature and Judgment.* New York: Grosset & Dunlap, Universal Library, 1955.

Carr, Albert Z. *Business as a Game.* New York: New American Library, 1968.

Chapman, A. H. *Put Offs and Come Ons.* New York: Putnam, 1968.

Chase, Stuart. *The Most Probable World*. Baltimore: Penguin Books, 1969.

Darwin, Charles. *Expressions of Emotion in Man and Animal*. Chicago: University of Chicago Press, 1965.

Deutsch, Karl W. *The Nerves of Government: Models of Political Communication and Control*. New York: Free Press, 1966.

Discott, David S. *How to Make Winning Your Life Style*. New York: Peter H. Wyden, 1972.

Drucker, Peter F. *The Age of Discontinuity*. New York: Harper & Row, 1968.

———, *Managing for Results*. New York: Harper & Row, 1964.

Ellul, Jacques. *Propaganda: The Formation of Men's Attitudes*. New York: Knopf, 1966.

Epernay, Mark. *The McLandress Dimension*. Cambridge: Riverside Press, 1963.

Feldman, Sandor S. *Mannerisms of Speech and Gestures in Everyday Life*. New York: International Universities Press, 1959.

Fromm, Eric. *Forgotten Language*. New York: Grove Press, 1951.

Galbraith, John Kenneth. *The New Industrial States*. Boston: Houghton Mifflin, 1967.

Gardner, John W. *Self-Renewal: The Individual and the Innovative Society*. New York: Harper & Row, 1964.

Goffman, Erving. *Behavior in Public Places*. New York: Free Press, 1963.

Goldner, Bernard. *The Strategy of Creative Thinking*. Englewood Cliffs, N.J.: Prentice-Hall, 1963.

Gurr, Ted Robert. *Why Men Rebel*. Princeton: Princeton University Press, 1971.

Hall, Edward T. *Silent Language*. New York: Fawcett, Premier Books, 1959.

Herzberg, Frederick. *Work and the Nature of Man*. New York: World, 1966.

Hovland, Irving L., Carl I. Janis, and Harold Kelley. *Communication and Persuasion*. New Haven: Yale University Press, 1953.

Ikle, Fred C. *How Nations Negotiate*. New York: Harper & Row, 1964.

Jourard, Sidney M. *The Transparent Self*. New York: Van Nostrand Reinhold, 1964.

Journal of Conflict Resolution. Vol. 5, No. 3 (September 1961).

Kelley-Williams. *Make Conflict Work for You*. Harvard Business Review, July-August 1970.

Korzybski, Alfred. *Science and Sanity*. Lakeville, Conn.: International Non-Aristotelian Library Publishing Co., 1958.

Kostelanetz, Richard. *Human Alternatives*. New York: Morrow, 1971.

Lerner, Daniel, and Harold D. Lasswell. *The Policy Sciences*. Stanford, Calif.: Stanford University Press, 1951.

Maslow, Abraham. *Motivation and Personality*. New York: Harper & Row, 1954.

Michael, Donald N. *The Unprepared Society*. New York: Basic Books, 1968.

Nierenberg, Gerard I. *The Art of Negotiating*. New York: Hawthorn, 1968.

————, *Creative Business Negotiating*. New York: Hawthorn, 1971.

————, and Henry Calero. *How to Read a Person Like a Book*. New York: Hawthorn, 1971.

Nirenberg, Jesse S. *Getting Through to People*. Englewood Cliffs, N.J.: Prentice-Hall, 1963.

Overstreet, H. A., *Influencing Human Behavior*. New York: Norton, 1925.

Parnes, Sidney J., and Harold F. Harding (eds.). *Source Book for Creative Thinking*. New York: Scribner's, 1962.

Rapoport, Anatol. *Fights, Games and Debates*. Ann Arbor: University of Michigan Press, 1966.

Rogers, Everett M. *Diffusion of Innovations*. New York: Free Press, 1962.

Schelling, Thomas C. *Strategy of Conflict*. Cambridge: Harvard University Press, 1960.

Schwart, Robert J. *Perceiving, Sensing, Knowing*. New York: Doubleday, Anchor Books, 1965.

Shostrom, E. *Man—The Manipulator*. New York: Bantam, 1967.

Toffler, Alvin. *Future Shock*. New York: Random House, 1970.

INDEX

INDEX

Abel, I. W., 15
Accusations, issues and, 51
Acquisitions, *see* Mergers and acquisitions
Adams, John Quincy, 244–245, 276–277
Adler, Alfred, 33
Affection, need for, 82, 84
Affirmative statements, 113–116
Agency strategy, 171–174
   limited authority, 172
Agenda, negotiating, 54–55
Aggression, acts of, 32
Agreement, achieving, 21
Agua Caliente racetrack, 166
Albert Schweitzer complex, 104
Alcoholics Anonymous, 265
Alden, John, 277
Allen, Agnes, 218
American Dental Association, 274

American Indians, 145, 244, 266–267
American Labor Party, 155–156
American Revolution, 239, 240
American Tobacco Company, 163–164
Anschluss of 1938, 243
Apparent withdrawal, strategy of, 154–155, 179, 199–201
Arabs, 260
Aristotle, 42
Arnold, Matthew, 149
Art of Advocacy, The (Stryker), 67
Articles of Confederation, 273
Association, strategy of, 162–163, 179, 180, 200
Associationism, 32
Assumptions, 10, 70–81
   categories of, 76–81
      awareness, 78–81

295

Assumptions (*cont.*)
  extensional world, 76–77
  fact-finding session, 79–80
  intensional world, 77–78
  who is right, 78
  real estate, 16–19
  as source of misunderstandings, 71–76
Atlanta Compromise, 270
Austro-Hungarian Empire, 243

Bacon, Francis, 61–62, 143, 171–172
Barber of Seville, The (Beaumarchais), 239
Bass, B. M., 186
Bateson, Gregory, 58
Beatles (rock group), 168
Beaumarchais, Pierre de, 239–240
Beauregard, General, P. G. T., 252
Beer, William, 115–116
Behavior patterns, 31–46
  considering people's action, 37–44
  displacement, 38
  and habits, 33
  and objectives, 57–58
  predictions, 34–36
  projections, 37–38
  psychology of, 32–34
  rational, 40–44
  rationalization, 37
  reaction formation, 39
  repression, 38–39
  role playing, 39–40
  self-image, 39
  understanding what's happening, 44–46
Belonging needs, 249–261
Benchley, Robert, 22
Berelson, Bernard, 95
Better Business Bureau, 13
Bevin, Ernest, 143
Bicultural agents, 174
Biosocial psychology, 32
Black-market baby ring, 5
Blake, Robert R., 184

Bland withdrawal, strategy of, 153–154, 199
Blanketing strategy, 165–166, 200
Blinking, 142
Blocking a take-over, 220–221
Blushing, 141
Bontrager, Dr., 78–79
Boulware, Lemuel R., 225
Boulwarism, 224–225
Bracketing, strategy of, 170–171, 200–201, 205
Brainstorming, 66
Brandeis, Louis D., 40
Brandeis University, 82
Bretton Woods Conference, 249
British Orders in Council, 265–266
Brokers, real estate, 209–210, 231
Brothers Karamazov, The (Dostoevsky), 146
"Building," maneuver of, 166
Burgoyne, General John, 240
Buying/selling, components of, 201–202

Carnegie, Dale, 262
Causality, principle of, 44
Central Station Alarm Companies, 190
Chain-reaction theory, 162
Chase, Stuart, 145
Chicago, Burlington and Quincy, 255
China, 265, 279
  United Nations and, 260
Christian X, King of Denmark, 251
Christian Democratic Party (Italy), 249
Churchill, Sir Winston, 242, 252, 268–269
Citizen's Union, 274
Civil rights movement, 253
Civil War, 251–252, 270, 271, 282
Close-out questions, 126
Coalition bargaining, 161
Collective bargaining, 14–15
College administrators, 178

College students, 193
Committee for the Judiciary (U.S. Senate), 5–6
Common Market, 259
Commonwealth of Nations, 258
Communication, 4, 112, 114
  labor-management, 15
  nonverbal, 141–146
Communist Party (Italy), 249
Communist Party (U.S.), 250
Competition, 22
Compromise, 5–6
Con Edison (New York City), 157–158
Concessions, 52
Conciliation Service, 277
Conferences, 68
  pre-negotiation, 80
Congress of Racial Equality (CORE), 253
Constitutional Convention, 273
Consumer's Union, 274
Continental system, 245
Cool questions, 125
Cooperative approach, people and, 31–46
  considering action, 37–44
  displacement, 38
  predicting behavior, 34–36
  projection, 37–38
  psychology of, 32–34
  rational behavior, 40–44
  rationalization, 37
  reaction formation, 39
  repression, 38–39
  role playing, 39–40
  self-image, 39
  understanding what's happening, 44–46
Cooperative egotism, 22–25
Cooperative process, 20–29
  advantage of, 23–25
  compared to a game, 20–21
  competition, 22
  as an enterprise, 22–25
  newspaper business and, 21

reaching a life balance, 25–27
uncontrollable controls, 27–29
Corporate negotiation, 215–221
Coughing, 142
Counterlawsuit, 10
Counterproposals, 56, 61
Creative-alternative attitudes, 181–194
  labor relations and, 222–229
  meaning of, 182–183
  methods of, 223–225
  for mutual accommodation, 189–194
  win/lose stand, 184–189
Creative people, 107
Credit investigation, 63–64
Crossroads strategy, 164–165, 200
Cuba, 265
Cuban missile crisis, 271–272, 279
Culture shock, 104
Cutler, Lyman, 282

Da Vinci, Leonardo, 218
Daley, Richard, 192
Daniel Yankelovich, Inc., 87
Danish Jews, 251
Deal men, 211
Deals and negotiation, 211–214
  getting out of, 213
Declaration of Independence, 240
Democratic Socialist Party (Italy), 249
Denmark, invasion of (World War II), 251
Desa, Tavares, 68
Dicey, Albert V., 71
Dictionary of American Slang, 63
Direct needs, 10–12
Directive questions, 126
Disassociation strategy, 163–164, 200
Displacement, psychology of, 38
Disraeli, Benjamin, 36
Dr. Strangelove (motion picture), 253
Domino Theory, 162

Donneson, Baron Z., 25–26
Dostoevsky, Fëdor, 146

Einstein, Albert, 132, 222
Election of 1876, 271
Electoral Commission, 271
Elephant Child (Kipling), 131
Elizabeth II, Queen, 22
Embargo of 1807, 245–246
Emerson, Ralph Waldo, 48
Emotions, 106–107
"Empedocles on Etna" (Arnold),
    149
Empiricism, 43
Encyclopaedia Britannica, 148
Epstein, Brian, 168
Erskine, David, 265–266
Esteem needs, 83, 84–85, 262–267
Esthetic need, 83, 85, 283–288
Etc. (magazine), 133, 137
Existentialistic psychology, 32

Facial expressions, 142
Fait accompli, strategy of, 152–153,
    179, 199
Feedback, allowance for, 50
Feinting, strategy of, 159–160, 200,
    206
Feldman, Sandor S., 140, 141, 142
Fleishman, Alfred, 137
Florida, purchase of (1819), 244–
    245
Forbearance, strategy of, 150, 199
Fort Sumter, 251–252
Fortune (magazine), 87
Fortune 500 Directory, 87
Franco, Francisco, 250–251
Franklin, Benjamin, 196
French Revolutionary Wars, 245
Freud, Sigmund, 33, 38–39, 66, 139
Fulbright Act, 278
Functional psychology, 32
Functional questions, 118–130
    to bring to a conclusion, 121
    to cause attention, 119
    that can cause difficulty, 126

to get information, 120
to give information, 120–121
grammatical structure, 126–127
importance of, 129–130
that are manageable, 125–126
matrices, 121–124
how they operate, 128–129
process of construction, 127–128
to start thinking, 121
three or more, 124

Gallup, Dr. George, 116
Gauging questions, 126
Geis, Irving, 167
General Electric Company, 224
General semantics, 78–81
Gestalt psychology, 32, 33, 45, 73
Gestures, 141–146
    cultural differences, 144–145
    distinction between looking and
        seeing, 142
    importance of, 141
    meaning of, 141–142
    use of, 142–143
Getting Through to People (Niren-
    berg), 109
Gibb, Jack R., 186–187
Gilbert and Sullivan, 37
Glorious Revolution of 1688, 110
Goldberg, Arthur J., 14–15
Good Housekeeping (magazine),
    274
Great Northern Railroad, 255
Griffin, Charles, 282
Group drama (psychodrama and
    sociodrama), 65–68
Group psychotherapy, 66–67

Habits, behavior and, 33
Hamilton, Alexander, 103–104
Hamlet (Shakespeare), 39
Hanna, Mark, 115–116
Harriman, Edward H., 255
Harvard Business Review, 112–113
Harvard Business School, 275
Hayakawa, S. I., 75–76

Hayes, Rutherford B., 271
Heated questions, 126
Herodotus, 44–45
Hidden assumptions, 76–81
  awareness, 78–81
  extensional world, 76–77
  fact-finding session, 79–80
  intensional world, 77–78
  who is right, 78
Highway billboards, 287
Hill, James J., 255, 261
Hilsman, Roger, 279
Hitler, Adolf, 73, 243, 269
Holistic psychology, 32
Holmes, Oliver Wendell, 43
Holy Roman Empire, 258
Homeostatic, *see* Physiological needs
Hormic psychology, 32
House Un-American Activities Committee, 249–250
How to Lie with Statistics (Huff and Geis), 167
How Nations Negotiate (Ikle), 29
"How to Sabotage a Meeting" (Fleishman), 137
"How and Where" strategy, 160–178
How to Win Friends and Influence People (Carnegie), 262
Hudson's Bay Company, 282
Huerta, Victoriano, 263–264
Huff, Darrell, 167
Human behavior:
  knowledge of, 10, 12
  negotiation as, 4
  real estate negotiation, 16–19
Human Behavior: An Inventory of Scientific Findings (Berelson and Steiner), 95
Humanistic psychology, 32
Hume, David, 44
Humor, 193
Hungarian Communist Party, 169

Ikle, Fred Charles, 29
Impulse questions, 126

India, British Army in, 241
Indirect needs, 10–12
Individual vs. team negotiation, 48–50
Inductive Reasoning (Hume), 44
Institute of General Semantics, 78–79, 184
International Brigade (Spanish Civil War), 250–251
International Monetary Fund, 249
International negotiation, 90–91
Interorganizational negotiation, 90–91
Interpersonal negotiation, 90–91
Intuition, 144
Investigation, lawsuits and, 233–234
Iraq Petroleum Company, 248
Irrational behavior, 40–41
Israel, Arab boycott of, 260
Issues and positions, 50–52

Jackson, Andrew, 153, 244
Jackson, "Copenhagen," 266
Japan, occupation of, 257
Jefferson, Thomas, 245–246, 287–288
Jehovah's Witnesses, 278–279
Jim Crow laws, 271
Johnson, Lyndon B., 168, 247
Johnson, Samuel, 246
Jung, Carl Gustave, 33

Kashmir, Pakistan-India war over, 272–273
Kennedy, John F., 60, 73, 271–272, 279
Keynes, John Maynard, 44
Khrushchev, Nikita, 60, 279
Kipling, Rudyard, 131
Knowledge and understanding needs, 83, 85–86, 274–283

Labes, Leon M., 14
Labor-management negotiations, 14–15

Labor relations:
  communication and, 225–226
  creative alternatives, 222–229
    methods of, 223–225
  shifting levels strategy, 175–177,
    226–227
  stages in, 227–229
    development, 227–228
    formation, 227
    unifying, 228–229
Labor strikes, 21, 26
Lamb, Dr. Sydney, 75
Language, 76
Lawsuits, 230–237
  discussion of settlement, 230
  investigation, 233–234
  meaning and values involved in,
    231–232
  shifting levels in, 232–233
*Leadership and Interpersonal
    Behavior* (eds. Petrullo and
    Bass), 186
Leading questions, 125
League of Women Voters, 274
Lee, Irving L., 112–113
LeShufy, J. Robert, 279–280
Life Illustrations, 238–288
  esteem needs, 262–267
  esthetic needs, 283–288
  homeostatic needs, 239–246
  to know and understand, 274–
    283
  love and belonging needs, 254–
    261
  safety and security needs, 246–
    254
  self-actualization needs, 267–274
  use of, 288
Limits, strategy of, 158–159, 200
Lincoln, Abraham, 251–252, 270
Lindsay, John, 175
Listening, technique of, 139–141
Loaded questions, 126
Long, Baron, 166
Long, Huey, 193
Longfellow, Henry Wadsworth, 277

Long-range training, 58–59
Louisiana State University, 193
Love needs, 82, 84, 249–261
Luther, Martin, 259

McDonald, David J., 14–15
Machiavelli, Niccolò, 32, 114
McKinley, William, 115
Madero, Francisco, 263
Madison, Dolly, 266
Madison, James, 265
Mah-Jongg, 35
Malaysia, 261
Manchuria, Japanese seizure of
    (1930s), 274
Mannerisms (speech), 140–141
*Mannerisms of Speech and Gestures
    in Everyday Life* (Feldman),
    140, 141
Maritime Union, 160, 176
Marriage of Figaro, The (Beaumar-
    chais), 239
Marshall, John, 153
Marxism, 76
Maslow, Abraham H., 43, 82–83,
    95
Matrimony, 4
Maynard, Harry, 76–77
Meeting, the, 52–56
  agenda, 54–55
  difference between conference
    and, 68
  location, 52–53
  opening approach, 55
  in opposer's home territory, 53–
    54
  opposer's maximum position, 56
  physical arrangement of room, 53
  preparation and opening, 53–54
  revealing position, 56
  site, 52–53
Mergers and acquisitions, 215–221
  blocking a take over, 220–221
  degrees of success, 219–220
  dissenting groups and, 216

participation strategy, 162
projecting future plans, 216
sensitive areas in, 216–217
setting the price, 218–219
and not shooting the works, 217–218
Merton's principle, 185
Middle Ages, 250
Mikado, The (Gilbert and Sullivan), 37
Millay, Edna St. Vincent, 25
Miller, Arthur, 249–250
Misunderstandings, source of, 71–76
Monetary and Financial Conference (1944), 249
Monroe, James, 244
Moreno, J. L., 67
Morgan, J. P., 32, 115, 255–256, 261
Morris, C. W., 185–186
Motherhood, 103
Motivation, 82–88
    basic needs of, 82–86
    of creative people, 107
    individual's existence and, 86–88
    of salesmen, 85
Motivation and Personality (Maslow), 82–83
Mullens, Priscilla, 277
Munich pact (1938), 269
Murphy man (con man), 167
Murphy's Law, 57
Mutual accommodation, creative alternatives for, 189–194

Napoleon I, 245
Napoleonic Wars, 245
National Foundation for Infantile Paralysis, 241
National Heart Foundation, 248
National Labor Relations Board (N.L.R.B.), 161, 223, 224–225, 227
Nazi Party, 243, 265
Need abasement, 98
Need achievement, 99

Need acquisition, 97
Need affiliation, 97
Need aggression, 97
Need autonomy, 99
Need blame-avoidance, 98
Need cognizance, 99
Need conservance, 97
Need construction, 99
Need counter-action, 98
Need defendance, 98
Need deference, 97
Need disfavor-avoidance, 98
Need dominance, 98
Need exhibition, 98
Need exposition, 99
Need fulfillment, 10–12
    real estate negotiation, 16–19
Need inviolacy, 98
Need nurturance, 97
Need order, 99
Need play, 99
Need recognition, 98, 99
Need rejection, 97
Need retention, 97
Need similance, 97
Need succorance, 97
Need superiority, 98
Need theory, 89–108
    categories of application, 91–102
        basic to least basic needs, 96–99
        increasing risk and less control, 92–95
        levels of approach, 100
        structure and order of gambits, 101
    emotions and negotiations, 106–107
    fulfillment and deprivation, 104–106
    levels of negotiations, 90–91
    in motivating creative people, 107
    purpose of, 89–90
    reverse need-level order, 105–106
        esteem, 105–106
        esthetic, 105

Need theory (*cont.*)
  knowing and understanding, 105
  love and belonging, 106
  self-actualization, 105
  sublimation, 102–104
Needs:
  direct and indirect, 10–12
  how to recognize, 139–146
  gestures and, 141–146
  by listening, 139–141
  motivation and satisfaction, 82–88
Negrin, Juan, 251
New York City blackout (1965), 174
New York City newspaper strike (1960s), 239
New York Stock Exchange, 256–257
New York Supreme Court, 154–155
New York Times, The, 4, 160, 177, 239, 242, 286
New York *World Telegram and Sun,* 279
Newspaper business (New York City), 21, 239
1984 (Orwell), 140
Nirenberg, Jesse S., 109
Nonverbal communication, 141–146, 186
  evaluating, 144–145
  observing your opponent, 141, 144
North, John Ringling, 193–194
North Atlantic Treaty Organization (NATO), 160
Northern Pacific Railroad, 255
Northern Securities Company, 255, 261
Nuclear test ban treaty, 253–254
Nuremberg decrees, 59

Objectives:
  and behavior, 57–58
  establishing, 48

Ocean Hill-Brownsville School District (New York City), 175
Of Cunning (Bacon), 143
Of Negociating (Bacon), 61–62, 171–172
O'Hare Airport (Chicago), 192
Olympics (1964), 264
Open questions, 125
Open-end questions, 125
Opening the meeting, 55
Opinion, asking other person's, 206
Oregon treaty of 1846, 282
Orwell, George, 140

Panama Canal, 268
Participation, strategy of, 160–162, 200
Peace Corps, 104
People, 31–46
  cooperative approach and, 31–46
Petrullo, L., 186
Phenomenology, 32
Philosophies, 29–30
Physiological (homeostatic) needs, 82, 83–84, 239–246
Pickering, Timothy, 276
Pickett, Captain George, 282
Planned questions, 125
Plutarch, 26
Point Four Program, 256
Polk, James K., 284
Pope, Alexander, 31
Position:
  changing, 51
  opposer's maximum, 56
  revealing, 56
Powers, Bertram, 21
Predictability of mass behavior, 34–36
Preparation, 10, 47–69
  before asking questions, 111–112
  behavior and objectives, 57–58
  brainstorming, 66
  conference, 68
  establishing objectives, 48
  group drama, 65–66

individual vs. team negotiation, 48–50
issues and positions, 50–52
long-range training, 58–59
meeting, 52–56
  agenda, 54–55
  location, 52–53
  and opening, 53–54, 55
  in opposer's home territory, 53–54
  opposer's maximum position, 56
  physical arrangement of room, 53
  revealing position, 56
psychodrama, 67
real estate negotiation, 16–19
research, 60–65
Price fixing, 241
Price-cost negotiation, 202–203
Probability, importance of, 44–45
"Procedure for 'Coercing' Agreement" (Lee), 112–113
Projection, psychology of, 37–38
Protestant Reformation, 258–259
Psychoanalysis, 32
Psychodrama, 67
Public Service Commission, 157–158
Publishers Association, 239
Puerto Rican Consolidated Cigar Company, 222–223
Purchasing agent, function of, 197–199
Purchasing and selling, 196–207
  components of, 201–202
  price-cost negotiation, 202–203
  real estate, 208–210
  self-analysis (of the seller's), 203–207
  strategies for the seller, 199–201

Quakers, 150
Questions:
  affirmative statements, 113–116
  being concise, 112

controlling (no questions asked), 137–138
functions of, 118–130
  to bring to conclusion, 121
  to cause attention, 119
  classifications that can cause difficulty, 126
  classifications that are manageable, 125–126
  to get information, 120
  to give information, 120–121
  grammatically structuring, 126–127
  how they operate, 128–129
  importance of, 129–130
  matrices, 121–124
  process of construction, 127–128
  three-function, 124
how to answer (or not), 133–137
  with assumption other person has been answered, 133
  inaccurately, 135
  incompletely, 134–135
  leaving other person without desire to pursue further, 135–137
how to ask, 117–118
how to formulate, 116–118
for influencing negotiations, 112–113
knowing when to ask, 110
levels of, 132–133
phrasing, 110
preparing before asking, 111–112
proper use of, 111
self-, 131–132
statements as, 130–131
tone of voice, 112
use of, 109–137
what to ask, 117
when to ask, 118
wording of, 112

Rakosi, Matyas, 169
Rand Corporation, 177–178

Random sample, strategy of, 167–169, 200
Randomizing strategy, 166–167, 200
Rank, J. Arthur, 262
Rational behavior, characteristics of, 40–44
Rationalization, types of, 37
Reaction formation, psychology of, 39
Real Estate Board Form Leases, 73–74
Real estate negotiation, 6–10, 16–19, 208–210
Reflective or mirror questions, 126
Relation Between Law and Public Opinion in England During the 19th Century, The (Dicey), 71
Rent Commission of the City of New York, 154–155
Repression, psychology of, 38–39
Republicans (Italy), 249
Research, 60–65
 of adversary's witness, 62
 on business firms, 61
 credit investigation, 63–64
Research Institute of America, 85
Reuther, Walter, 175–176
Reversal strategy of, 10, 155–158, 200
Reverse need-level, 105–106
Reverse sour grapes, 37
Revolution of 1917, 262
Reynolds, Mrs., 103
Rockefeller, John D., 115
Rockefeller, John D., Jr., 115, 165
Role playing behavior, 39–40
Roman Catholic Church, 67, 72, 259
Rome (ancient), 189
Romeo and Juliet (Shakespeare), 260–261
Roosevelt, Franklin D., 22, 150, 241, 262–263
Roosevelt, Theodore, 256, 261, 268
Russian roulette, 253

Safety needs, 82, 84, 246–254
St. John, 17
Salami strategy, 169–170, 200
Sales negotiations, 12–14
Salesmen, motivation of, 85
San Juan boundary dispute, 282
Santa Anna, Antonio Lopez de, 284
Scapegoats, 38
Schuschnigg, Kurt von, 243
Scott, Douglas, 177
Seagram Building (New York City), 286
Security needs, 82, 84, 246–254
Seidenberg, Roderick, 34
Self-actualization needs, 83, 85, 267–274
Self-approval, 85
Self-image, psychology of, 39
Self-questioning, 131–132
Seller, the strategies for, 199–201
Selling, *see* Purchasing and selling
Seven Years War, 239
Shakespeare, William, 255, 260–261
Shaw, George Bernard, 38
Sheitel, 285
Shifting levels, strategy of, 175–178, 179, 180
Short-range preparation, 60–65
Sino–Japanese War, 103
Smith, Captain John, 247
Smith, Robert, 266
Social approval, 85
Social causality, 44
South Africa, 258
Spanish Civil War, 250–251
Stalin, Joseph, 263
Standish, Miles, 277
Stein, Gertrude, 155
Steiner, Gary A., 95
Stephen, Sir James, 110
Strategy in Handling People (Webb and Morgan), 115
Strategy and tactics, 10, 147–181
 creative-alternatives, 182–184
 for mutual accommodation, 189–194

operation example, 178–180
  win/lose stand, 184–189
 defined, 147–149
 how and where, 149–160
  agency, 171–174
  association, 162–163, 179, 180
  blanketing, 165–166
  bracketing, 170–171
  crossroads, 164–165
  disassociation, 163–164
  participation, 160–162
  random sample, 167–169
  randomizing, 166–167
  salami, 169–170
  shifting levels, 175–178, 179, 180
 real estate, 16–19
 for the seller, 199–201
 when strategy, 149–160
  apparent withdrawal, 154–155, 179
  bland withdrawal, 153–154
  fait accompli, 152–153, 179
  feinting, 159–160
  forbearance, 150
  limits, 158–159
  reversal, 155–158
  surprise, 150–152
Structural psychology, 32
Stryker, Lloyd Paul, 67
Sublimation, need theory and, 102–104
Success, 235–237
Suez crisis of 1956, 152
Surprise, 199

Team negotiation, 48–50
 specialization, 50
Techniques, 10, 147–181
 creative alternatives, 178–180
 how and where, 160–178
 when strategy, 149–160
Terry, Luther, 244
Thant, U, 247
Tilden, Samuel J., 271
Transactional psychology, 32

Treat questions, 125
Trick questions, 126
Trojan War, 274–275
Truman, Harry S, 256
Turner, John, 167

Understanding, *see* Knowledge and understanding needs
Union Carbide Corporation, 204
Union Pacific Railroad, 255
United Nations, 4, 68, 165, 247, 249, 260, 261
U.S. Constitution, 273
U.S. Customs Authority, 77
U.S. Department of Defense, 170, 282
U.S. Department of Justice, 4
U.S. Marines, 104–105
U.S. Supreme Court, 225, 261, 270–271
United Steel Workers of America, 14–15

Vanderbilt, Arthur T., 71
Verrazano Bridge, building of, 279–280
Versailles, Treaty of, 243
Vienna meeting, 60
Vietnam War, 48, 247

Warsaw Pact, 160
Washburne, Chandler, 133
Washington, Booker T., 270
Washington, George, 103–104
Washington Naval Agreement of 1922, 273–274
Watson, John B., 32–33
Wheeling and dealing, aspects of, 211–212
When to stop, learning, 27–29
"When" strategy, 149–160
William I, Emperor, 282–283
Wilson, Woodrow, 263
Window questions, 125
Win/lose attitude, creative alternatives to, 184–189

Woman's intuition, 144
World War I, 243
World War II, 7, 15, 45, 103, 155, 164, 169, 173, 174, 251, 252, 257, 269–270, 278

Xenophanes, 80

Xerox Corporation, 262
XYZ Affair, 277

Yale University, 75

Zambia, 151
Zeckendorf, William, 165